PUTTING FAITH IN HATE

While the right to freedom of speech is regarded as fundamental in democratic countries, most of these countries have also accepted that hate speech causes significant harm and ought to be regulated. Richard Moon examines the application of hate speech laws when religion is either the source or target of such speech. Moon describes the various legal restrictions on hate speech, religious insult, and blasphemy in Canada, Europe, and elsewhere and uses cases from different jurisdictions to illustrate the particular challenges raised by religious hate speech. The issues addressed are highly topical: speech that attacks religious communities, specifically anti-Muslim rhetoric, and hateful speech that is based on religious doctrine or scripture, such as anti-gay speech. The book draws on a rich understanding of freedom of expression, the harms caused by hate speech, and the role of religion in public life.

Richard Moon is Distinguished University Professor and Professor of Law at the University of Windsor, Ontario, Canada.

Putting Faith in Hate

WHEN RELIGION IS THE SOURCE OR TARGET OF HATE SPEECH

RICHARD MOON

University of Windsor

CAMBRIDGE
UNIVERSITY PRESS

CAMBRIDGE
UNIVERSITY PRESS

University Printing House, Cambridge CB2 8BS, United Kingdom

One Liberty Plaza, 20th Floor, New York, NY 10006, USA

477 Williamstown Road, Port Melbourne, VIC 3207, Australia

314–321, 3rd Floor, Plot 3, Splendor Forum, Jasola District Centre,
New Delhi - 110025, India

79 Anson Road, #06-04/06, Singapore 079906

Cambridge University Press is part of the University of Cambridge.

It furthers the University's mission by disseminating knowledge in the pursuit of
education, learning, and research at the highest international levels of excellence.

www.cambridge.org
Information on this title: www.cambridge.org/9781108425469
DOI: 10.1017/9781108348423

© Richard Moon 2018

First published 2018

Printed in the United Kingdom by Clays, St Ives plc

A catalogue record for this publication is available from the British Library

Library of Congress Cataloging-in-Publication data
Names: Moon, Richard, 1956– author.
Title: Putting faith in hate : when religion is the source or target of hate speech /
    Richard Moon, University of Windsor.
Description: Cambridge, United Kingdom ; New York, NY, USA : Cambridge University
    Press, 2018. | Includes bibliographical references and index.
Identifiers: LCCN 2017042217 | ISBN 9781108425469 (alk. paper)
Subjects: LCSH: Hate speech – Law and legislation. | Freedom of religion. | Freedom of
    speech in the church. | Offenses against religion – Law and legislation. | Religious
    institutions – Law and legislation.
Classification: LCC K5210 .M66 2018 | DDC 342.08/53 – DC23
LC record available at https://lccn.loc.gov/2017042217

ISBN 978-1-108-42546-9 Hardback

To Ellie

Contents

Contents

Acknowledgements

I began writing this book almost a decade ago. Had I been more single-minded, I might not have been so late to the debates addressed in the chapters that follow. However, during this time, I benefitted from the opportunity to present parts of the book to different audiences: Saint Thomas University in Fredericton (2008), King's College London (2010), the Centre for Ethics at the University of Toronto (2010), The University of Copenhagen (2011), Osgoode Hall Law School (2012), the University of Hull (2013), Erasmus University (2014), City, University of London (2015), and Ryerson University (2015). I am grateful for the comments of those who attended these talks. I am also grateful to Ron Krotoszynski and the anonymous reviewers for Cambridge University Press for their constructive criticisms of the manuscript.

Chapter 2 of the book draws on some of my earlier writing, and in particular *The Constitutional Protection of Freedom of Expression* (University of Toronto Press, 2000) and "Report to the Canadian Human Rights Commission Concerning Section 13 of the Canadian Human Rights Act and the Regulation of Hate Speech on the Internet" (Canadian Human Rights Commission, 2008). Elements of Chapters 3 and 4 of the book have been incorporated into a chapter I contributed to Andras Koltay and Jeroen Temperman, eds., *Blasphemy and Freedom of Expression after the Charlie Hebdo Massacre* (Cambridge University Press, 2017).

Finally, I want to thank Audrey, Sibyl, Ellie, Hopey, and Adina for more reasons than I can list or even recall.

1

Religion and Hate Speech

INTRODUCTION

Many recent hate speech cases in Canada and elsewhere involve religion either as the source of views that are alleged to be hateful or as the target of such views. The question this book will consider is what difference religion makes in the application of hate speech law, when it is either the source or target of speech that is alleged to be hateful.

"Religious" hate speech cases are difficult or contentious for the same reason that all hate speech cases are difficult. There is significant disagreement in the community about whether or to what extent the restriction of hate speech can be reconciled with the public commitment to freedom of expression. There is, however, another reason that hate speech cases involving religion are so difficult, which has to do with our complex conception of religious adherence or membership. Religion is viewed by the courts and other public institutions as a personal commitment to a set of claims about truth and right, but also as a cultural identity involving a shared and rooted commitment to a set of beliefs and practices.

If religious adherence is viewed as a personal commitment to a set of set of truth claims, then the individual's religious beliefs and practices must be open to criticism, including criticism that is harsh in tone. This seems even more obvious when we recognize that religious beliefs often have public implications – that they often say something about how we should act towards others and about the kind of community we should work to create. But if religious membership is instead viewed as a cultural identity, then it can be argued that attacks on religious belief should sometimes be restricted, because they undermine the religious group's standing in the community or strike at the individual member's sense of self. As well, if religious membership is viewed as a cultural identity, then censorship of religiously based speech (that is alleged to be hateful) may be experienced by the speaker as a repudiation of her defining values and beliefs, as a denial of her equal worth, and as the marginalization of her community.

Most countries have laws restricting speech that expresses or encourages hatred against the members of religious and other groups, although these laws take very different forms.[1] Anti-hate or anti-vilification laws prohibit speech that seeks to intimidate the members of a religious or other identifiable group or to stir up hatred against the group's members. The Dutch penal code, for example, prohibits the incitement of hatred, discrimination, or violence against community members because of their race, their religion, or their life philosophy, among other grounds.[2] Other jurisdictions have enacted hate speech prohibitions that are concerned specifically with the protection of religious individuals or groups. In the United Kingdom, s. 29B of the *Racial and Religious Hatred Act, 2006* provides that "A person who uses threatening words or behaviour, or displays any written material which is threatening, is guilty of an offence if he intended thereby to stir up religious hatred."[3] Some jurisdictions also ban more specific forms of racial or religious hatred such as Holocaust denial. Article 130 of the amended Criminal Code of Germany provides that an individual who publicly denies, diminishes, or approves an act committed under the regime of National Socialism in a way likely to disturb the peace shall be punished.[4] In a number of European jurisdictions there are laws that restrict the ridicule or disparagement of religious beliefs, symbols, or practices. The Austrian Penal Code makes it an offence to disparage religious doctrines and the Swiss Penal Code includes the offence of maliciously offending or ridiculing the religious convictions of others or to disparage a person's convictions, objects of veneration, places of worship, or religious articles.[5]

---

[1] The European Commission for Democracy through Law (the "Venice Commission"), which is the Council of Europe's advisory body on constitutional matters, in a 2008 report, distinguished three types of regulation of anti-religious speech: (1) the restriction of blasphemy, (2) the restriction of religious insults, and (3) the restriction of religious hate speech. The first and second types – restrictions on blasphemy and religious insult – may now be indistinguishable, or nearly so, in practice. For a discussion of the report see I. Leigh, "Damned if they do, damned if they don't: The European Court of Human Rights and the protection of religion from attack", 17 *Res Publica* 55 (2011) at 57.

[2] Art. 137d *Wetboek van Strafrecht (Sr.)* (Dutch Penal Code). In Germany, *Volksverhetzung* (incitement of popular hatred) is prohibited under s. 130 of the Criminal Code (*Strafgesetzbuch, StGB*).

[3] The *Racial and Religious Hatred Act, 2006 (UK) s. 29B c.* 1, amending *The Public Order Act* 1986 (UK) c. 64. See also the State of Victoria (Australia) *Racial and Religious Tolerance Act 2001*, which makes religious vilification unlawful. Section 8(1) of the Act provides, "A person must not, on the ground of the religious belief or activity of another person or class of persons, engage in conduct that incites hatred against, serious contempt for, or revulsion or severe ridicule of, that other person or class of persons."

[4] German Criminal Code (*Strafgesetzbuch, StGB*). In Austria, Art. 3h of the *Prohibition Act* prohibits persons from "publicly denying the National Socialist genocide, or other National Socialist crimes." Art. 3h, *Verbotsgesetz (VerbotsG)* (Prohibition Act, 1947).

[5] The Austrian Penal Code, Art. 188, *Strafgesetzbuch* (StGB). The Swiss Penal Code, Art. 261, *Strafgesetzbuch* (StGB). The Dutch Penal Code also prohibits insulting a group because of their religion or their life philosophy, as well as on other grounds (Art. 137c). The German Criminal Code, Art. 166 (n. 2), makes it an offence to insult a religious worldview (*Weltanschauung*) publicly. In this regard, it is also worth noting that the UN Human Rights Council in 2007 adopted a non-binding resolution condemning the "defamation of religion", although in a 2011 resolution the Council modified

Hate speech in Canada is currently restricted by both federal and provincial laws. The *Criminal Code* of Canada prohibits the advocacy or promotion of genocide, the incitement of hatred against an identifiable group "where such incitement is likely to lead to a breach of the peace", and the "wilful promotion of hatred" against such a group.[6] Under the *Criminal Code* an "identifiable group" "means any section of the public identified by colour, race, religion, ethnic origin, age, sex, sexual orientation, gender identity or expression, or mental or physical disability."[7] Anyone who is found by a court to have wilfully promoted hatred may be imprisoned for up to two years. However, relatively few prosecutions have been brought under this provision.[8]

Hate speech is also restricted by human rights laws. Until its repeal in 2014, Section 13 of the *Canada Human Rights Act* [*CHRA*] prohibited Internet communication that is "likely to expose the members of an identifiable group to hatred or contempt".[9] The human rights codes of British Columbia, Alberta, Saskatchewan, and the Northwest Territories continue to include a provision similar to Section 13 of the *CHRA* that prohibits hate speech on signs or in publications.[10] In contrast to the criminal ban on hate speech, individuals may be found to have breached the human rights code ban even though they did not *intend* to expose others to hatred or realize that their communication might have this effect. The ban focuses on the effect of words and not the intention behind them. The ordinary remedy against an individual who is found to have breached the ban is an order that he or she cease his or her discriminatory practice. Once again there have been very few cases in which a tribunal or court has found a breach of these code provisions.[11]

---

its position, removing any reference to religious defamation and focusing instead on religious hatred. Human Rights Council, *General Comment 34*, July 2011: "Prohibitions of displays of lack of respect for a religion or other belief system, including blasphemy laws, are incompatible with the Covenant, except in the specific circumstances envisaged in article 20, paragraph 2, of the Covenant."

[6] *Criminal Code*, R.S. 1985, c. C-46, s. 318–319.

[7] *Criminal Code* (n. 6), s. 318(4). An individual will not be found to have promoted hatred "if, in good faith, he expressed or attempted to establish by argument an opinion on a religious subject" (s. 319(3)(b)).

[8] Between 1994 and 2004, there were 93 prosecutions under s. 319. Thirty-two convictions were entered, and of these, 27 resulted in prison sentences and 5 in conditional sentences (CERD, Consideration of Reports, Comments and Information Submitted by State Parties under Article 9 of the Convention, Seventeenth and Eighteenth Periodic Reports of Canada, 2008). Prosecution under the provision cannot be initiated without the consent of the provincial Attorney-General.

[9] *Canadian Human Rights Act*, R.S., 1985, c. H-6. 3. (1) The prohibited grounds of discrimination include race, national or ethnic origin, colour, religion, age, sex, sexual orientation, gender identity or expression, marital status, and family status.

[10] *Saskatchewan Human Rights Code*, R.S.S., 1979, c. S-24.1, s. 14; *Human Rights, Citizenship and Multiculturalism Act*, R.S.A., 2000, c. H-14, s. 2 (Alberta); *Human Rights Code*, R.S.B.C., 1996, c. 210, s. 7 (British Columbia); *Consolidation of Human Rights Act*, R.S.N.W.T., 2002, c. 18, s. 13 (Northwest Territories).

[11] Richard Moon, *Report to the CHRC Concerning Section 13 of the CHRA and the Regulation of Hate Speech on the Internet*, October 2008 at 12: Between January 2001 and September 2008, the CHRC received seventy-three s. 13 complaints (about 2% of the total number of complaints received by the

The *Criminal Code* of Canada also includes a prohibition on the publication of "blasphemous libel", although the prohibition does not extend to expression of "an opinion on a religious subject" that is made "in good faith and in decent language".[12] There have been no prosecutions under this provision for almost seventy years and most commentators assume that the ban would not survive a constitutional challenge.

I RELIGION AS THE TARGET OF HATE SPEECH

A Anti-Semitic Speech

The leading Canadian hate speech cases involve anti-Semitic speech. *R. v. Keegstra* involved a high school teacher in the small town of Eckville, Alberta, who for more than a decade told his classes about an all-encompassing conspiracy by Jews to undermine Christianity and control the world.[13] The teacher, James Keegstra, taught his students that Jews were "treacherous", "subversive", "sadistic", "power-hungry", and "child killers". He was charged, and ultimately convicted, under s. 319(2) of the *Criminal Code* with "wilfully promoting hatred" against the members of an identifiable group. As part of his defence Keegstra challenged the constitutionality of the *Criminal Code* ban on hate speech. The Supreme Court of Canada held that section 319(2) breached the freedom of expression right (s. 2(b)) under the *Canadian Charter of Rights and Freedoms* (the *Charter*), but that the restriction was justified under section 1, the *Charter's* limitation provision.[14]

The issue in *Canada v. Taylor* was whether a telephone hate line operated by the Western Guard Party, and its leader, John Ross Taylor, breached the human rights code ban on hate speech.[15] Members of the public who dialled a telephone number that had been publicized by Taylor and his party would hear a short pre-recorded

---

CHRC). Of these, thirty-two were closed or dismissed by the CHRC and thirty-four were sent to the CHRT for adjudication. (When these numbers were compiled in September 2008, two of the seventy-three complaints were under investigation by the CHRC and five were awaiting decision by the CHRC.) Of the thirty-four complaints that were sent to the CHRT, ten were resolved prior to adjudication. In September 2008, eight of the complaints forwarded to the CHRT were awaiting conciliation/adjudication. In the remaining sixteen cases, the CHRT found that s. 13 had been breached and imposed a cease and desist order.

[12] *Criminal Code* (n. 6), s. 296.   [13] *R. v. Keegstra* [1990] 3 SCR 697.

[14] In the Court's view, the restriction was justified because its purpose – to prevent the spread of hatred in the community – was "substantial and compelling" and because it limited only a narrow category of extreme speech that "strays some distance from the spirit of section 2(b)" (*Keegstra* (n. 13), paras. 85, 99).

[15] *Canada v. Taylor* [1990] 3 SCR 892. The UN Human Rights Committee dismissed a complaint brought by Taylor under the *International Covenant on Civil and Political Rights* [ICCPR] (adopted 16 December 1966, entered into force March 23, 1976) 999 UNTS 1717: *Taylor v. Canada* (1983) Communication No. 104/1981: Canada (6 April 1983) CCPR/C/18/D/104/1981 (UN Human Rights Committee).

message that made a variety of false claims about Jews. Taylor and the Western Guard were found by the Canadian Human Rights Tribunal to have engaged in telephonic communication "that is likely to expose a person or persons to hatred or contempt" because of his or her membership in an identifiable group, contrary to s. 13 of the *Canadian Human Rights Act*. As part of his defence, Mr. Taylor argued that the human rights code ban on hate speech was unconstitutional. The Supreme Court of Canada, drawing on its decision in *Keegstra*, held that the ban did not breach the *Charter of Rights*.[16]

In *R. v. Zundel*, the author and publisher of numerous Holocaust denial tracts was charged under s. 181 of the *Criminal Code* with publishing news that he knew was false and was likely to cause injury or mischief to the public interest.[17] Zundel was convicted at trial of spreading "false news". However, the Supreme Court of Canada, on appeal, held that s. 181 was too vague to be considered a reasonable limit on freedom of expression (s.2(b) of the *Charter*), and set aside Zundel's conviction. Zundel was later found to have breached s. 13 of the *CHRC*. The Human Rights Tribunal determined that a Holocaust denial website, which was operated under Zundel's direction, was likely to expose Jews to hatred and contempt.[18] The Tribunal found that in challenging "[v]irtually every aspect of the holocaust", Zundel "branded [Jews] as liars, swindlers, racketeers and extortionists . . . criminals and parasites" "who wield[]extraordinary power and control."[19]

In *Ross v. New Brunswick School District No. 15* (1996), the Supreme Court of Canada held that a public school teacher who expressed racist and anti-Semitic views in public settings away from the school was properly dismissed from his teaching position.[20] The Court upheld the decision of an adjudicator, appointed under the New Brunswick *Human Rights Code*, that ordered the school board to remove Mr. Ross from the classroom. The Court found that Mr. Ross's expression of anti-Semitic views at public meetings and in the local media had "poisoned" the learning environment in the school.

Anti-Semitism has played a similarly central role in European hate speech jurisprudence. In *X v. Germany*, for example, the European Court of Human Rights (ECtHR) held that a ban on the display of Holocaust denial material was a justified restriction of freedom of expression under the *European Convention on Human Rights (ECHR)*.[21] Similarly, in *Garaudy v. France*, the ECtHR upheld a restriction

---

[16] In the more recent decision of *Whatcott v. Saskatchewan Human Rights Commission* [2013] 1 SCR 467, the Supreme Court similarly found that the hate speech ban in the *Saskatchewan Human Rights Code* was compatible with the *Charter*.

[17] *R. v. Zundel* [1992] 2 S.C.R. 731. The case was commenced as a private prosecution under s. 181 after the Attorney-General of Ontario refused to consent to prosecution under s. 319(2).

[18] *Citron v. Zundel*, TD 1/02 (2002).   [19] *Citron* (n. 18) at paras. 137–39.

[20] *Ross v. New Brunswick School District No. 15* [1996] 1 SCR 285. In *Ross v. Canada*, the UN Human Rights Committee dismissed the complaint brought by Ross under the Optional Protocol, ICCPR.

[21] *European Convention on Human Rights* (Nov 4, 1950). *X v. Germany* (1982) Appl. no. 9235/81, Decision of 16 July 1982. See also *Kühnen v. Federal Republic of Germany*, Appl. no. 12194/86, Decision of

on speech denying the Holocaust.[22] The ECtHR also sustained a hate speech conviction in *The Jewish Community of Oslo v. Norway*.[23] In that case a public speech that honoured Nazi Rudolph Hess and asserted that Jews continued to plunder and degrade the country was found to breach the Norwegian penal code. The UN Human Rights Committee in *Faurisson v. France* found that the conviction of an individual under French law for publishing a book denying the Holocaust did not breach the *International Covenant on Civil and Political Rights* (ICCPR).[24]

B Anti-Christian Speech

In countries in which Christians are an ethnic minority, anti-Christian speech may sometimes include claims about the rooted characteristics of group members. However, in Canada and other countries in which Christianity is the dominant faith, anti-Christian speech seldom involves claims about the inferior or dangerous character of Christians – the ordinary form of hate speech. Instead, anti-Christian speech most often involves criticism or ridicule of the beliefs of Christians. The harm that may stem from this speech is not the marginalization of the group or the risk of violent action against its members, but instead the hurt or humiliation experienced by the group's members when what they regard as sacred is denigrated.

While Christians in Canada have sometimes been subjected to harsh criticism, there are no significant modern cases in Canada dealing with attacks on Christians or Christianity. In the late nineteenth and early twentieth centuries, there was a series of blasphemy prosecutions in Canada against individuals who criticized the doctrine and clergy of the Protestant and Roman Catholic churches; however, there have been no reported blasphemy cases in Canada since the early 1900s.[25]

There are, however, a number of decisions in Europe and elsewhere, under blasphemy or religious insult laws, that deal with anti-Christian expression, and more particularly expression that denigrates the sacred symbols of the Christian faith.

In *Whitehouse v. Lemon*, a gay publication in England was found to have breached the now-repealed English blasphemy law when it published a poem

---

12 May 1988; *W.P. and Others v. Poland*, Appl. no. 42264/98, Decision of 2 September 2004; *Hosnik v. Austria*, Appl. no. 25062/94; *Marais v. France*, Appl. no. 31159/96; *M'Bala M'Bala v. France*, Appl. no. 25239/13 (Oct 20, 2015).

22 *Garaudy v. France*, Appl. No 65831/01 (24 June 2003).

23 *The Jewish Community of Oslo v. Norway*, Comm No. 30/2003 (15 Aug. 2005).

24 *Faurisson v. France*, Communication No. 550/1993.

25 In the middle of the last century, Christian sects such as the Jehovah's Witnesses experienced persecution by both state and private actors – most notably in Quebec during the 1950s. In response to what many in the predominantly Roman Catholic province of Quebec regarded as blasphemy or insult against the Catholic Church, the provincial government enacted a variety of measures designed to suppress the proselytizing activities of the Jehovah's Witness community. In *Saumur v. City of Quebec* [1953] 2 S.C.R. 299, the Supreme Court of Canada struck down a by-law that forbade the distribution of literature in the streets of Quebec City without the prior consent of the Chief of Police – a by-law that was understood by all as directed at the Jehovah's Witness community.

depicting a same-sex encounter involving Jesus, as well as sexual acts performed on his crucified body.[26] A jury decided that the poem would "shock and outrage the feelings of ordinary Christians".[27] The publisher argued before the European Commission on Human Rights that its conviction under UK law breached Article 10 (1) (freedom of expression) of the *ECHR*. The application was dismissed by the Commission, which held that the offence of blasphemy could be viewed as "necessary" in a "democratic society": "If it is accepted that the religious feelings of the citizen may deserve protection against indecent attacks on the matters held sacred by him, then it can also be considered as necessary in a democratic society to stipulate that such attacks, if they attain a certain level of severity, shall constitute a criminal offence".[28]

In the *Otto-Preminger-Institute* case, a film society in Austria announced that it would be showing as part of its season a film entitled *Das Liebeskonzil* [Council of Heaven].[29] The film depicted Mary, the mother of Jesus, as a "loose woman", God as "senile", and Jesus as "cretinous". The Austrian authorities seized the film prior to its screening and commenced an action against the institute under a provision of the penal code that prohibited the disparagement of religious doctrine. Even though the action was dropped, the government refused to return the film. After exhausting all domestic remedies, the institute claimed before the ECtHR that the seizure of the film breached the freedom of expression provision of the *ECHR*. The ECtHR, however, dismissed the claim, maintaining that the state had a legitimate role in protecting religious believers from insult to their religious feelings. In the Court's view, even though offensive speech fell within the scope of freedom of expression under the *ECHR*, speech that was "gratuitously" insulting could legitimately be restricted by the state.

In subsequent cases, the ECtHR has been more willing to overturn convictions for blasphemy or religious insult. In *Giniewski v. France*, a French journalist who

---

[26] *Whitehouse v. Gay News Ltd* [1979] AC 617 (HL).

[27] *Whitehouse* (n. 26) at 657. Lord Russell of Killowen in the House of Lords decision indicated that "as an ordinary Christian" he found the publication "quite appallingly shocking and outrageous".

[28] *Gay News Ltd. and Lemon v. U.K.*, Application No. 8710/79 (7 May 1982), para. 12. In another English case, the British Board of Film Classification (and the Video Appeals Committee) refused to issue a classification certificate for a video that it judged to be blasphemous: *Wingrove v. The United Kingdom* (19/1995/525/611) 25 November 1996; *Wingrove v. UK* (application no. 17419/90), Nov 25, 1996 at para. 57. The video, entitled *Visions of Ecstasy*, depicted St Teresa of Avila experiencing sexual raptures, stimulated by an image of the crucified Christ. The object of the film, according to its makers, was to "explore the relationship between mysticism and repressed sexuality" (Leonard W. Levy, *Blasphemy*, University of North Carolina Press, 1955, at 567). The film board, though, could see "no attempt to explore the meaning of the imagery beyond engaging the viewer in an erotic experience" (Levy at 567). The decision of the British board was upheld by the ECtHR, which accepted that the "refusal to grant 'Visions of Ecstasy' a distribution certificate was intended to protect 'the rights of others', and more specifically to provide protection against seriously offensive attacks on matters regarded as sacred by Christians" and so did not breach the *ECHR*.

[29] *Otto-Preminger-Institut v. Austria*, No. 13470/87, [1994] ECHR 26.

argued that the Roman Catholic Church (and a particular papal encyclical) had promoted a doctrine that contributed to anti-Semitism and the Holocaust was convicted in the French courts of defaming Christian belief.[30] The ECtHR, however, held that the conviction breached freedom of expression under the Convention, noting that the journalist's argument could be viewed as addressing an issue of public concern, and so was not "gratuitously offensive".[31]

C Anti-Muslim/Islam Speech

In the last several years, there have been a number of high-profile cases in Canada involving anti-Muslim speech or speech that attacks or ridicules Islam. The best known of these cases is the human rights code complaint against *Maclean's* magazine and columnist Mark Steyn. *Maclean's* published an excerpt from Steyn's book, *America Alone*, in which he argues that Muslims will soon become the majority community in many European countries (through higher birth rates and immigration), that their goal is to impose Sharia law on these countries, and that many Muslims are prepared to use violence to achieve this goal.[32] As noted below, a similar view has been advanced in one form or another by a number of European authors, raising alarm about what is sometimes referred to as the "Muslim Tide" or the rise of "Eurabia".

Complaints about Steyn's piece in *Maclean's* were made under the *Canada Human Rights Act* and the British Columbia *Human Rights Code*.[33] The complaint against *Maclean's* was dismissed by the Canadian Human Rights Commission and did not go to the Canadian Human Rights Tribunal for adjudication. In British

---

[30] *Giniewski* v. *France*, App. No. 64016/00 (Eur. Ct. H.R. Jan. 31, 2006).

[31] See also *Klein* v. *Slovakia*, Application no. 72208/01 (31 Oct 2006), and *Aydin Tatlav* v. *Turkey*, App. No. 50692/99 (2 May 2006) (ECtHR). In the Australian case of *Pell* v. *NSW Gallery*, an Anglican bishop brought a private prosecution under the blasphemy prohibition in the New South Wales criminal code against a public art gallery that displayed the "Piss Christ" – a photograph by the artist Serrano of a plastic crucifix immersed in a jar of his own urine. The Court held that the offence had not been established, since there was no evidence that the publication was intended to outrage the feelings of Christian believers or was likely to lead to a breach of the peace (*Pell* v. *Council of Trustees of the National Art Gallery of Victoria* (Unreported), Supreme Court of Victoria, Harper J., Oct 9, 1997). In many parts of the world blasphemy laws are still vigorously applied. For a survey see Paul Marshall and Nina Shea, *Silenced: How Apostasy and Blasphemy Codes Are Choking Freedom Worldwide* (Oxford University Press, 2011).

[32] Mark Steyn, "The future belongs to Islam", *Maclean's Magazine*, Oct 23, 2006; Mark Steyn, *America Alone: The End of the World as We Know It* (Regnery Publishing, 2006).

[33] A complaint was also made under the *Ontario Human Rights Code*, R.S.O. 1990, C. H. 19 (OHRC), but the Commission found that it did not have jurisdiction to hear the complaint, because unlike the Canada and BC Codes, the Ontario Code does not include a ban on hate speech. The Commission, however, did issue a statement expressing concern that Steyn's article contributed to Islamophobia and was inconsistent with the spirit of the OHRC. See Ontario Human Rights Commission, Press Release, "Commission statement concerning issues raised by complaints against *Maclean's* Magazine" (Apr 9, 2008), www.ohrc.on.ca/en/news_centre/commission-statement-concerning-issues-raised-complaints-against-macleans-magazine.

Columbia, there is no commission that receives and filters complaints and so all complaints go directly to a tribunal for adjudication. The tribunal, in this case, dismissed the complaint following a hearing.[34] In the tribunal's view Steyn's claims were not sufficiently extreme or intemperate to count as hate speech and were offered as a contribution to an ongoing public discussion about immigration and terrorism.

Another well-publicized Canadian case was the complaint made to the Alberta Human Rights Commission against a right-wing publication, the *Western Standard*, following its publication of the "Danish Cartoons" depicting the Prophet Moham- mad. This complaint was also dismissed prior to adjudication. The Commission investigated the complaint, as required by the human rights code, but decided that even though the cartoons were "stereotypical, negative, and offensive" they were relevant to "timely news" and "not simply gratuitous[]".[35]

While neither of these complaints succeeded, in *R. v. Harding* a more vitriolic attack on Muslims resulted in conviction under the *Criminal Code* hate speech provision.[36] Mr. Harding, a Christian pastor, published and distributed several pam- phlets in which he asserted that Muslims are violent and hateful towards Chris- tians, Jews, and other "non-believers", are conspiring to take over Canada, and are "wolves in sheep's clothing" who will use violence to achieve their goals.[37] Mus- lims, he wrote, "are full of hate, violence and murder" and are incapable of living peacefully among non-Muslims.[38] The court saw the pamphlets as an invitation to readers "to take defensive action against the threat of violence posed by Muslims as a group" leading to "the inevitable conclusion . . . that Muslims are deserving of ill- treatment".[39] The court concluded that the claims made by Mr. Harding amounted to the wilful promotion of hatred, contrary to s. 319(2) of the *Criminal Code*.

In the last decade, European Muslims have increasingly become the focus of speech that is, or is alleged to be, hateful. In most cases, the focus of attack is directly on Muslims – on those who identify with the Islamic tradition. The speech attributes to the members of the group certain undesirable traits or entrenched beliefs and practices, and so is similar in character to anti-Semitic speech. While the followers of Islam may come from a variety of ethnic/cultural backgrounds, they are presented in this speech as culturally homogeneous. A number of books and blogs assert that Muslims will soon form a majority in Europe, as a consequence of continuing immi- gration from Muslim-majority countries and high birth rates among those who have settled in Europe, and that they are willing to employ a variety of means, includ- ing violence, to impose the Islamic faith on "native" Europeans. It is claimed that Muslim "culture" includes a variety of barbaric practices that are incompatible with

---

[34] *Elmasry and Habib v. Rogers' Publishing and MacQueen (No. 4)*, 2008 BCHRT 378.

[35] Joseph Brean, "Magazine publisher Levant wins Danish cartoon dispute", *National Post*, Aug 8, 2008.

[36] *R. v. Harding* (1998), O.J. No. 2603, affirmed in Ontario Court of Appeal, 160 CCC (3d) 225; 48 C.R. (5th) 1.

[37] *Harding* (n. 36), para. 5.　　[38] *Harding* (n. 36), para. 5.　　[39] *Harding* (n. 36), para. 10.

the (Christian-inspired) liberal democratic culture of Europe, and that Muslims are so steeped in their religious culture that they simply cannot be assimilated into Western society.[40]

One of the more prominent European hate speech cases involved the anti-Islam film *Fitna*, produced by the Dutch MP Geert Wilders, and released via the Internet in 2008. The short film portrayed Islam as a violent religion that requires its followers to impose its beliefs and practices on non-believers. *Fitna* is described by Caspar Melville as "not so much a film as a cut-and-paste web montage" that "intercuts verses from the *Quran* calling for violence against non-believers with images culled from news footage of terrorist attacks".[41] The film then invokes the past struggles and victories in Europe against Nazism and Communism and declares that Islamization must be stopped. The film ends abruptly with the explosion of a bomb – represented as Mohammad's turban – an image that is "superimposed on a *Quran*".[42] Wilders was acquitted of the charge of hate speech in 2011, because, in the court's judgment, the film's attacks were directed at Islamic belief and not at Muslim believers, and because it contributed to an ongoing public debate.[43] However, in December 2016, Wilders was found guilty by a court in the Netherlands of inciting discrimination against Dutch Moroccans.[44] Wilders had made derogatory remarks about Moroccans to a public gathering and said that if elected he would ensure their exclusion from the Netherlands.[45]

In *Norwood* v. *DPP*, the English courts held that Mr. Norwood breached s. 5 of the *Public Order Act, 1986*, which prohibits the display of a sign or other writing that "is threatening, abusive or insulting within hearing or sight of a person likely to be caused harassment, alarm or distress thereby".[46] Mr. Norwood had displayed in the window of his home a poster with an image of the twin towers in flames, accompanied by the words "Islam out of Britain – Protect the British People" and the crescent and star symbol marked as prohibited (within a circle with a diagonal line through it). A judge of the Queen's Bench upheld Mr. Norwood's conviction in the lower court, noting that "The poster was a public expression of attack on all Muslims in this country, urging all who might read it that followers of the Islamic religion here should be removed . . . and warning that their presence here was a threat or a danger to the British people".[47] Following his conviction in the British courts, Norwood

---

[40] Some notable examples include Christopher Caldwell, *Reflections on the Revolution in Europe* (Anchor Books, 2010); Bruce Bawer, *While Europe Slept: How Radical Islam Is Destroying the West from Within* (Anchor Books, 2007); Bat Ye'or, *Eurabia: The Euro-Arab Axis* (Farleigh Dickinson University Press, 2005).

[41] Caspar Melville, *Taking Offence* (Seagull Books, 2009) at 4.

[42] Melville (n. 41) at 6.   [43] www.bbc.co.uk/news/world-europe-13883331.

[44] Wilders, though, was acquitted of inciting hatred against this group.

[45] www.theguardian.com/world/2016/dec/09/geert-wilders-found-guilty-in-hate-speech-trial-but-no-sentence-imposed.

[46] *Norwood* v. *DPP* [2003] EWHC 1564 (Admin).

[47] *Norwood* (n. 46) at para. 13. In the judge's view, the poster could not reasonably "be dismissed as merely an intemperate criticism or protest against the tenets of the Muslim religion, as distinct from an unpleasant and insulting attack on its followers generally" (para. 33).

brought his case before the ECtHR, arguing that the restriction of his expression breached the *ECHR*.[48] In dismissing Mr. Norwood's claim, the ECtHR said that "the words and images on the poster amounted to a public expression of attack on all Muslims in the United Kingdom" and that "[s]uch a general, vehement attack against a religious group, linking the group as a whole with a grave act of terrorism, is incompatible with the values proclaimed and guaranteed by the Convention, notably tolerance, social peace and non-discrimination."[49]

In *Feret v. Belgium*, the ECtHR upheld a conviction under Belgian law of a politician for inciting hatred against Muslims.[50] Mr. Feret, an elected member of the Belgian Parliament, had produced and distributed leaflets which claimed that recent Muslim immigrants were inclined to engage in criminal activities. The ECtHR accepted that such a claim might encourage (particularly among the less sophisticated members of the community) distrust and hatred towards the targeted group. In *Soulas and Others v. France*, the ECtHR also upheld the conviction of the authors of a book entitled *The Colonization of Europe* for inciting hatred and violence against Muslim immigrants from North Africa.[51]

In other cases, however, the complaint was not, or not simply, that Muslims were being defamed or vilified, but was instead that Islamic beliefs and practices were being ridiculed, causing offence or upset to the group's members. This form of anti-Muslim speech is similar then to the anti-Christian speech in the European blasphemy cases described earlier, except of course that the impact of religious insult may be different when directed at a religious minority. Religious insult or ridicule often occurs alongside more familiar forms of hate speech that attribute undesirable traits to the members of a marginalized community. But even when it is not joined with hate speech, harsh criticism or ridicule of the beliefs and practices of a religious minority may contribute to the group's sense of exclusion or marginalization within the larger community, particularly when the speech is seen by the group's members as misrepresenting their faith to an audience composed primarily of members of the dominant or majority religious/secular community. In practice, then, these two harms (the spread of hatred against the group and insult to the group's beliefs) may sometimes be difficult to separate, at least when the target of attack is a religious minority.

The publication of Salman Rushdie's novel *The Satanic Verses* in 1988 led to protests initially in England and eventually around the world.[52] Many Muslims thought that the book defamed the Prophet Mohammad and presented a distorted picture of Islam. In R. v. *Chief Metropolitan Stipendiary Magistrate, Ex parte Choudhry*, the English courts dismissed a charge of blasphemy against Rushdie

[48] *Norwood v. UK* (ECtHR) (Application No. 23131/03) Nov 16, 2004.
[49] *Norwood* (n. 46) 47. The Court found that the poster was intended to be insulting and was likely to cause "significant mental upset" (para. 3).
[50] *Feret v. Belgium*, No. 15615/07.
[51] *Soulas and Others v. France*, No. 15948/03. See also *Le Pen v. France* (Application No. 18788/09).
[52] Salman Rushdie, *The Satanic Verses* (Viking, 1997).

and the publisher of his book, on the grounds that the protection from blasphemy (intemperate criticism of religion) under English law extended only to the established faith – the Church of England, or more generally the Christian church.[53] According to the court, the ban did not protect Islam and other non-Christian faiths from ridicule or intemperate criticism.[54]

A series of cartoons depicting the Prophet Mohammad were published by the Danish Newspaper *Jyllands Posten* in 2005. The "Danish Cartoons" were viewed by many in the Muslim community as ridiculing or insulting the Prophet, which led to protests and demonstrations, principally in Muslim majority countries. The cartoons were reprinted by several other publications in Europe. Legal complaints were considered but dismissed in a number of European countries. In Denmark, for example, a complaint was made under s. 140 of the Danish Penal Code, which prohibits disturbing the public order by publicly ridiculing or insulting the dogmas of worship of any lawfully existing religious community in Denmark.[55] Following investigation, the prosecutor decided not to proceed with the complaint.[56]

II RELIGION AS THE SOURCE OF HATE SPEECH

A *Religious Anti-religious Speech*

Speech that attacks a particular religious community or belief system is often grounded in another, competing, religious belief system. Anti-Semitic speech in Europe was long rooted in Christian doctrine, and in particular the scriptural

---

[53] R. v. *Chief Metropolitan Stipendiary Magistrate, Ex parte Choudhry* [1991] 1QB 429. Lord Scarman, in his dissent in *Lemon* (n. 26), argued for a reading of the blasphemy law that extended protection to other religious belief systems. The Canadian law may be broader in the scope of its protection: See Jeremy Patrick, "Not Dead, Just Sleeping: Canada's Prohibition on Blasphemous Libel as a Case Study in Obsolete Legislation", 41 UBC Law Review 193 (2008).

[54] See Chapter 4 for a discussion of the repeal of the English blasphemy ban.

[55] See Art. 140, *Straffeloven (Strfl)* (Danish Penal Code). For a thorough and thoughtful account of the "Danish Cartoons" controversy, see Jytte Klausen, *The Cartoons That Shook the World* (Yale University Press, 2009).

[56] The decision of the Regional Public Prosecutor was upheld by the Director of Public Prosecution. See "Decision on Possible Criminal Proceedings in the Case of Jyllands-Posten's Article 'The Face of Muhammed'", the Director of Public Prosecutions, File No. RA-2006–41–0151 15, March 2006. In France, a complaint brought against the magazine *Charlie Hebdo*, which had republished the cartoons, was also dismissed. In *I.A.* v. *Turkey*, the publisher of a book entitled *God, the Religion, the Prophet and the Holy Book* was convicted under Turkish blasphemy law: *I.A.* v. *Turkey*, No. 42571/98 (13 Sept. 2005). The ECtHR held that the application of blasphemy law in this case did not breach the ECHR. The Court distinguished between provocative opinions and abusive attacks on religion and held that in this case the author had engaged in an abusive attack on the Prophet Mohammad, including claims that some of his revelations were "inspired in a surge of exultation, in Aisha's arms". The Court accepted that Muslims might reasonably experience this and other passages in the book as a gratuitous attack on their faith.

attribution to Jews of responsibility for the death of Jesus.[57] However, sometime in the nineteenth century, anti-Semitic speech began to focus more directly on the "racial" characteristics of Jews, which were said to include greed and dishonesty. This racial view of Jews was advanced by Keegstra, Zundel, Taylor, and Ross in the cases described earlier. Yet even with this shift in the focus of anti-Semitism from the undesirable beliefs and practices of Jews to their undesirable racial character-istics, the practical concern remained the same – the defence of Christian society and its values. Those who believe that Jews, through deceit and manipulation, are endeavouring to control the major institutions of society see this as a plot to under-mine Christian society, which is characterized by an adherence to certain moral principles.

In *R. v. Harding* (described earlier), false and demeaning claims about Muslims were made by a Christian clergyman. While Mr. Harding's claims were not explic-itly rooted in Christian doctrine, he presented Islam or Muslims as a threat to Chris-tian society and its values. In *Islamic Council of Victoria v. Catch the Fire Ministries*, the Civil and Administrative Tribunal in the Australian state of Victoria held that two Christian ministers had breached s. 8(1) of the *Racial and Religious Tolerance Act, 2001*, which provides that "A person must not, on the ground of the religious belief or activity of another person or class of persons, engage in conduct that incites hatred against, serious contempt for, or revulsion or severe ridicule of, that other person or class of persons".[58] The Tribunal found that the ministers had asserted at a public meeting that the Quran supported the use of violence and deception to advance the Islamic faith. The Tribunal's decision, however, was overturned by the state Court of Appeal, which determined that the Tribunal had misdescribed many of the statements made by the ministers – making them appear more extreme than they were.[59]

B *Religious Racism*

Racism, particularly against individuals of African descent, was once justified on religious grounds. At an earlier time, when Christianity was widely practiced in the West, the contest between those who regarded blacks as the subject of property (and later segregation) and those who pressed for the end of slavery (or the legal pro-tection of racial equality) took place on religious terrain and concerned the proper reading of scripture. However, racial inequality is today rarely justified on religious

---

[57] According to the Gospel of Matthew, when the Roman Governor Pontius Pilate asked whether Jesus, an innocent man, should be punished, the Jews present at the court demanded his punishment, and replied, "His blood be on us, and on our children": Matt. 27:25 (AV).

[58] See *Islamic Council of Victoria v. Catch the Fire Ministries Inc (Final)* [2004] VCAT 2510 (22 Dec 2004).

[59] See *Catch the Fire Ministries Inc & Ors v. Islamic Council of Victoria Inc* [2006] VSCA 284 (14 Dec 2006) (SCCA, Victoria).

grounds. And even when racist views are rooted in religion (based on claims that some races are not made in God's image or have been cursed by God), they are generally dismissed by legal authorities as too odious or baseless to be considered part of a legitimate belief system. The assumption seems to be that no sincere or coherent religion could include such views, which therefore have no reasonable claim to respect or accommodation.

C *Religious Anti-gay Speech*

Religious doctrine and scripture are often the basis for anti-gay (LGBTQ) speech. Indeed, it is increasingly difficult to imagine grounds for opposition to same-sex relationships, other than scriptural proscription. Most religious anti-gay speech simply asserts that homosexual practice is sinful (citing the Bible) and so is not sufficiently extreme to count as hate speech. In contrast to religiously grounded racist speech, anti-gay views are still held by a significant number of Christians, Muslims, and others (even if that number is rapidly diminishing), and so such views are not easily dismissed or ignored as "bad" religion. Anti-gay speech may amount to hate speech, though, when it calls for the punishment (and, in its most extreme form, the death) of those who breach the Biblical prohibition on homosexuality or when it links homosexuality to paedophilia (a connection that has no explicit religious basis), presenting gays as a menace, or, in religious terms, a source of evil and corruption.

In *Owens v. Saskatchewan Human Rights Commission*, Mr. Owens placed an advertisement in the Saskatoon newspaper, in which he expressed his opposition to same-sex relationships. The advertisement included citations of several Biblical passages condemning homosexuality, including Lev. 20:13.[60] Just beneath these citations was an equals sign followed by an image of two stickmen holding hands within a circle with a diagonal line running through it – the "not permitted" symbol. The complainants argued that the advertisement, and in particular its citation of biblical passages that call for the death of any man who "lies with another man"[61] would have the effect of encouraging or stirring up hatred against gays. The provincial human rights tribunal agreed with the complainants that the advertisement breached the *Code*.[62] The Saskatchewan Court of Appeal, though, overturned the Tribunal's decision.[63] The Court of Appeal thought that the references in the advertisement to passages such as Lev. 20:13 should not be read literally – as calling for

[60] The advertisement in smaller print referred the reader to the New International version of the Bible.

[61] Lev. 20:13: "If a man lies with a man as one lies with a woman, both of them have done what is detestable. They must be put to death; their blood will be on their own heads". Another cited passage was Lev. 18:22: "Do not lie with a man as one lies with a woman; that is detestable."

[62] *Hellquist v. Owens* (2001), 40 CHRR D/197 (Sask. Bd. Inquiry). On appeal a judge of the Court of Queen's Bench agreed with the Tribunal that the advertisement breached the Code provision. See *Owens v. Saskatchewan (Human Rights Commission)*, 2002 SKQB 506 (CanLII).

[63] *Owens v. Saskatchewan (HRC)* [2006] S.J. No. 221.

the death of gays – and so did not amount to hate speech, or in the language of the *Code*, did not "expose" gays to hatred.

In *Lund* v. *Boissoin*, a Christian pastor wrote a letter to the Red Deer newspaper in which he sought to warn others in the community about the danger of homosexuality. Pastor Boissoin's letter described gays as a source of corruption in society.[64] He claimed that children were being "targeted" and "psychologically abused" by homosexuals. Homosexuals, he said, were "recruiting our young into their camps" and were "just as immoral as pedophiles". Boissoin was found by an Alberta Human Rights Panel to have breached the provincial code's ban on hate speech.[65] However, the Alberta Court of Appeal disagreed and held that the letter was not sufficiently extreme to breach the hate speech ban.[66] In the Court's view, the letter could be seen as a contribution to an ongoing public debate on matters of public interest.[67]

In *Whatcott* v. *Sask HRC*, the issue was whether anti-gay flyers that were left in home letter boxes in Saskatoon breached the hate speech ban in the Saskatchewan *Human Rights Code*. The Saskatchewan Human Rights Tribunal decided that the four flyers distributed by Mr. Whatcott were likely to expose gay and lesbians to hatred and so breached the Code.[68] The Supreme Court of Canada, on appeal, determined that only two of the flyers contained text that breached the Code's hate speech ban.[69] In the Court's view, these flyers "portrayed the targeted group as a menace that could threaten the safety and well-being of others", drew on authoritative sources, such as the Bible, "to lend credibility to the negative

---

[64] The text of the letter can be found at *Lund* v. *Boissoin*, 2012 ABCA 300 para. 4.

[65] Section 3 (1) of the *Human Rights, Citizenship and Multiculturalism Act* (n. 10). *Lund* v. *Boissoin and the Concerned Christian Coalition*, Nov 30, 2007 (Alta. Human Rights Panel).

[66] *Lund* v. *Boissoin*, 2012 ABCA 300. In *Boissoin* v. *Lund*, 2009 ABQB 592, the QB judge, in reversing the tribunal decision, held that the purpose of the hate speech ban is not "simply to restrain hateful or contemptuous speech *per se*" but rather to restrict speech that encourages acts of discrimination in employment and other contexts covered by the Act. The Alberta Court of Appeal agreed with the conclusion reached by the Court of Queen's Bench but disagreed with its narrow reading of the statutory ban.

[67] The Court recognized that Mr. Boissoin's views were "expressed in strong, insensitive, and some might say bigoted terms" but accepted that "the aim of the letter was to stir apathetic people, who agreed with him, to his cause": *Boissoin* (CA) (n. 66) at para. 71.

[68] The Tribunal's decision was upheld by the Sask. Court of Queen's Bench (2002 SKQB 399) but overturned on appeal to the Saskatchewan Court of Appeal (*Whatcott* v. *Saskatchewan (Human Rights Tribunal)*, 2010 SKCA 26).

[69] *Whatcott* v. *Saskatchewan HRC*, 2013 SCC 11. The Court, though, concluded that the other two flyers distributed by Whatcott did not breach the Code (*Whatcott*, n. 68, at para. 195). Both flyers reprinted classified ads from "Saskatchewan's largest gay magazine". The flyers described these as ads in which men were "seeking boys" – although the Court expressed some doubt about this reading of the ads. Alongside the reproduced ads, Mr. Whatcott wrote the following words borrowed from the Bible: "'If you cause one of these little ones to stumble it would be better that a millstone was tied around your neck and you were cast into the sea' Jesus Christ". He also wrote that "[t]he ads with men advertising as bottoms are men who want to get sodomized. This shouldn't be legal in Saskatchewan!" (para. 195). These flyers may be offensive, said the Court, but they did not clearly "manifest hatred".

generalizations", and created "a tone of hatred" through the use of "vilifying and derogatory representations".[70]

Cases involving religiously based anti-gay speech have also come before the courts in various European jurisdictions. Among the more prominent of these cases was that of Ake Green, a Swedish pastor who gave a sermon in his church in which he described homosexuality as a "cancerous growth on the body of society".[71] While "emphasiz[ing] that not all homosexuals are pedophiles", Green suggested there was a link between them: "The pedophiles of today do not start out as pedophiles, but begin by changing their social intercourse. That is how it starts."[72] Pastor Green was convicted at trial of breaching Sweden's hate speech law, but was later acquitted on appeal. The Supreme Court of Sweden held that the conviction of Pastor Green for hate speech was inconsistent with the freedom of expression and freedom of religion provisions in the *ECHR*, which had been incorporated into Swedish law.

In *Hammond* v. *DPP*, an English court found that an Evangelical Christian pastor who delivered an anti-gay speech in the town centre in Bournemouth had breached s. 5 of the *Public Order Act 1986*, which prohibited the display of a sign or writing that was "threatening, abusive or insulting within the hearing or sight of a person likely to be caused harassment, alarm or distress".[73] Mr. Hammond had expressed his views about homosexuality to passers-by, while holding a sign that read "Stop Immorality", "Stop Homosexuality", and "Stop Lesbianism". Members of the audience who objected to his views sought to prevent him from speaking. The police then intervened and charged Mr. Hammond with the public order offence. He was convicted at trial and the conviction was upheld on appeal by the Divisional Court, which accepted the trial's judge's finding that Mr. Hammond's sign was insulting, even though its language was not intemperate, because it described homosexuality as sinful or immoral.[74]

Vejdeland and Others v. *Sweden* concerned four members of the National Youth organization, who distributed anti-gay leaflets in a high school.[75] The leaflets described homosexuality as a deviant tendency that has "a morally destructive effect

---

[70] *Whatcott* (n. 68) at para. 187. The Court also pointed to references in the flyers (e.g., "Our children will pay the price in disease, death, abuse") that seemed to portray gays as child abusers or predators (para. 189).

[71] *Prosecutor General* v. *Ake Green*, the Supreme Court of Sweden, Case No. B 1050–05, 29 November 2005 at 3.

[72] *Ake Green* (n. 71) at 3.   [73] *Public Order Act* (n. 3).

[74] *Hammond* v. *DPP* [2004] EWHC 69 (Admin). The statutory provision under which Mr. Hammond was convicted was subsequently amended to exclude the term "insulting", and so the result in a case such as this might now be different. In *Snyder* v. *Phelps*, 562 US 443 (2011), the U.S. Supreme Court held that an anti-gay protest by a church group was protected by the First Amendment, even though the protest was directed at those attending the funeral of a deceased American soldier. The harm at issue in that case was not the potential spread of hateful views about gays or even the hurtful impact of the speech on gays, but rather the distress inflicted on those who were attending the funeral to grieve the loss of their family member or friend.

[75] *Vejdeland and Others* v. *Sweden*, No. 1813/07.

on the substance of society".[76] The courts in Sweden held that the leaflets "agitat[ed] against a national or ethnic group", contrary to Swedish law. According to the Swedish Supreme Court, even if the purpose behind the leaflets was to start a debate about a matter of public interest, and specifically about "the objectivity of the education in Swedish schools", this purpose "could have been achieved without statements that were offensive to homosexuals as a group".[77] In the Court's view, the arguments offered "were formulated in a way that was offensive and disparaging for homosexuals as a group" and constituted "an assault on their rights ... without contributing to any form of public debate which could help to further mutual understanding".[78] The individuals involved took their case to the ECtHR, arguing that their conviction under Swedish law violated Article 10 of the *ECHR*. The ECtHR, though, rejected this claim, finding that any interference with the claimants' freedom of expression could reasonably be viewed as necessary to protect the rights and reputation of others in the community.[79]

III WHY RELIGION PLAYS SUCH A ROLE

Religious groups have been the target of hate speech for obvious reasons. Religious membership or commitment is deep-rooted and shapes the believer's worldview. It is for many individuals an identity that is marked by adherence to certain beliefs and practices. It connects the individual to a group of believers and separates him or her from others or "outsiders".

Because religious belief involves claims about what is true and right, some of which have public implications, it may generate social and political conflict that sometimes seems intractable. In a multi-cultural/multi-faith society such as Canada, in which there is interaction between different religious groups, there is plenty of opportunity for such conflict. Some of this conflict may be an extension of conflicts that are occurring elsewhere in the world.

Non-believers may be concerned that a particular religious group is seeking to impose an objectionable spiritual/moral system on the larger community. The New Atheist movement, for example, has expressed concern that conservative Christians and Muslims are seeking to impose their regressive moral values on non-believers. The Eurabia writing, discussed in Chapter 3, imagines that Muslims form a homogenous group that is united in its desire to impose its faith, and its anti-democratic values, on the populations of Western democracies. At the same time, the withdrawal of a religious group from public life and its unwillingness to accept certain civic duties, such as military service, may generate resentment in the larger community. Religious communities that are withdrawn or insular may appear mysterious and irrational to outsiders. And so even if a religious group does not seek to

---

[76] *Vejdeland* (n. 75) at para. 8.   [77] *Vejdeland* (n. 75) at para. 15.
[78] *Vejdeland* (n. 75) at para. 15.   [79] *Vejdeland* (n. 75) at para. 59.

impose its views on others, its presence may give rise to fear and suspicion in the larger community.[80]

The cultural or rooted character of religious belief also lies behind its significance as a source or basis for hateful views. Religious belief sometimes provides support for positions that seem to lack any rational foundation and are otherwise difficult to defend. Literalist readings of scripture may be used to support ancient prejudices. For example, the claim that homosexuality is immoral is difficult to grasp outside the doctrine or scripture of a particular religious tradition and often seems insulated from reasonable challenge. Furthermore, the tendency of some religious traditions to see the world as divided between goodness/purity and evil/corruption may encourage fear of outsiders and the projection of evil intentions onto others.

IV HATE SPEECH AND FREE SPEECH

Freedom of expression protects the individual's right to express his or her views and to hear the views of others – even when those views are regarded by many as wrong or offensive. Respect for the autonomy of the individual, as either the speaker or listener in a communicative relationship, means that speech is not ordinarily regarded as a "cause" of subsequent action. A speaker does not "cause" harm (or is not legally responsible for harm) simply because he or she persuades the audience of a particular view and the audience acts on that view in a harmful way. The listener must be allowed to hear and assess the merits of competing claims. The listener alone is responsible for actions he or she takes in response to speech, whether he or she acts in agreement with, or in opposition to, what is said.

The protection of freedom of expression rests on several assumptions. The most important of these is that humans are substantially rational beings capable of evaluating factual and other claims. The freedom of expression right rests also on the assumption that individuals have a meaningful opportunity to participate in public discourse and/or that public discourse is open to a wide range of views. The familiar free expression position that bad or erroneous speech should be answered and not censored depends on public discourse being open to different perspectives that may be assessed by individual audience members. The courts, though, have recognized that these assumptions about independent judgment do not always hold. Freedom of expression doctrine has generally permitted the restriction of expression that incites or manipulates – that occurs in a form and/or context that limits independent

---

[80] Charles A. McDaniel Jr., "Violent yearnings for the Kingdom of God: Munster's militant Anabaptism", in James K. Wellman, Jr. (ed.), *Belief and Bloodshed* (Rowman Littlefield, 2007) at 73: "A separatist religious community's existence apart from mainstream civilization often is perceived as a challenge to the social order." Such was the reaction to the Hutterite community in Alberta in the mid-twentieth century. The Hutterites are an Anabaptist community that is committed to an agrarian lifestyle and the collective ownership of property. In 1942, the government of Alberta placed restrictions on the purchase of land by Hutterites. At the time, the principal complaint about the Hutterites was that they were were "aloof from the surrounding community". See "The Hutterite Brethren", www.ualberta.ca/~german/AlbertaHistory/Hutterites.htm.

and informed judgment by the audience or that inhibits the audience's ability to rationally assess the claims made and the implications of acting on those claims.

Hate speech is said to cause injury to others, either directly by intimidating or harassing the members of a racial or other identifiable group, or indirectly by persuading a more general audience that the members of such a group are dangerous or undesirable and should be treated accordingly. The restriction of speech that intimidates or harasses the members of a target group can in principle be reconciled with the commitment to freedom of expression, even if there is dispute about where the line should be drawn between threats and harsh criticism or between harassment and uncivil speech. The larger question in such cases is whether the speech can be seen as engaging the audience – as contributing to public discourse – or whether instead it should be viewed as an attempt to intimidate or harass its audience.

In contrast, the regulation of speech that aims to convince its audience of the dangerousness or undesirability of the members of a particular group represents a more basic challenge to the public commitment to freedom of expression – the freedom of the audience to make its own judgment about the truth or worth of the claims made to it. The argument for the restriction of this form of hate speech must go something like this: Despite our commitment to freedom of expression, we know that individuals are not always in a position to assess the claims made to them carefully or rationally. The failure to ban the extreme or radical edge of prejudiced speech – speech that is hateful in its content and visceral or irrational in its impact – carries too many risks, particularly when it circulates within a racist subculture that operates at the margins of public discourse. When the speaker makes false claims about the members of a group that are so extreme that they may be understood as justifying violent action against them, we ought not to take the risk that these claims will influence the audience's thought and action. Hate speech may create a significant risk of harm (a risk that may be viewed as the speaker's responsibility) when it is directed at a sympathetic audience in a context that limits the opportunity or likelihood of independent judgment – more particularly, when it plays to fears and resentments, builds on existing prejudices, and occurs away from critical scrutiny. The concern is not, or at least not principally, that hate speech will contribute to the spread of hateful or discriminatory attitudes across the general community, leading to more widespread discrimination against minority groups. Instead, the concern is that individuals, or small groups, who are already inclined to bigoted or racist thinking may be encouraged or emboldened to take extreme action against the target group's members.

V RELIGION AS A TARGET OF HATE SPEECH

In hate speech regulation, a distinction is generally made between an attack on a group or group member, which if sufficiently extreme may amount to hate speech, and an attack on the individual's or group's beliefs, which must be protected, even when it is harsh and intemperate in character. However, our complex conception of religious membership – as both personal judgment and cultural identity – complicates this distinction in two ways.

The first complication has to do with the attribution of belief to a religious group, whose members may adhere to different versions of the faith and may identify with the group in various ways. Hate speech directed at a religious group often falsely attributes dangerous or undesirable *beliefs* (rather than traits) to all of the group's members. While it is true that the beliefs that an individual holds may tell us something about his or her character and likely behaviour, the beliefs or practices that are attributed to the group in these cases are often held by few, if any, of its members (those who identify with the tradition). The falsely attributed beliefs, though, are described as an essential part of the group's belief system or tradition.[81] The belief serves the same role as a falsely attributed racial characteristic: To be a member of the group is to think and act in a way that is deeply undesirable or anti-social. What is presented as an attack on belief then may sometimes amount to an attack on the group. If the attack (the false attribution of belief) is sufficiently extreme, it may breach the hate speech ban.

Most contemporary anti-Muslim speech takes this form, presenting Islam as a regressive and violent belief system that is incompatible with liberal democratic values. The implication is that those who identify as Muslims – those who hold such beliefs – are dangerous and should be treated accordingly. Beliefs that may be held by a fringe element in the tradition are falsely attributed to all Muslims. This form of hate speech ignores the diversity of belief in the group and elides the space or distinction between the individual and the religious group or tradition with which he or she identifies. Belief becomes an attribute shared by the members of the group and the attack on belief becomes an attack on those who associate with – or may be associated with – the religious tradition.

The second difficulty with this distinction between belief (which must remain open to challenge) and believer (who should be protected from hate speech) is that, because religious beliefs are deeply held, an attack on the individual's beliefs (on the beliefs he or she actually holds) may be experienced by the believer personally and profoundly. It is, for this reason, sometimes argued that religious beliefs should be insulated from ridicule or "gratuitous" insult. A ban on ridicule or insult may be seen as a middle position that recognizes that religious adherence is not only a personal commitment to certain truths that must be open to debate and criticism, but also an aspect of the individual's identity (or cultural membership) that should be treated with respect. This middle ground, however, is unworkable for several related reasons. First, it is difficult to define enforceable standards of civility in public discourse, and nearly impossible to do so when religion is the subject of debate.

---

[81] Because the beliefs of a religious tradition or group are not fixed and remain the subject of debate and disagreement among those who identify with the tradition, it may not be apparent to the audience that the attribution of belief is unfounded.

Second, if a restriction on intemperate criticism of religious belief rests on the idea that religion is deeply rooted, a matter of identity, then why would we imagine that temperate criticism might sometimes lead the religious believer to rethink her views? We might, instead, see a greater role for ridicule or intemperate criticism in disrupting entrenched views. Third, religious beliefs often have public implications and so must be subject to criticism that is deeply felt and sometimes very harsh.[82]

VI RELIGION AS A SOURCE OF HATE SPEECH

There are at least two ways in which the religious basis for speech that is alleged to be hateful may complicate the application of hate speech law. These two complications roughly mirror the complications that arise when religion is the target of hate speech. The first is the difficulty in determining the individual's meaning or purpose when he or she invokes religious text or tradition to justify his or her opposition to a particular group and its practices. Just as it is difficult to determine whether an attack on religious belief amounts to an attack on a religious community (because the beliefs within any religious community or tradition are subject to debate and disagreement), it may also be difficult to determine an individual's meaning or intention when he or she invokes scripture or doctrine in support of the condemnation of a group such as gays. When an individual expresses opposition to gay marriage, by invoking Lev. 20:13, which declares that when a man lies with another man he should be put to death, should this be understood as calling for the death of gays? Within every religious tradition there are different approaches to scriptural interpretation and different readings of particular passages of scripture, making it difficult sometimes to determine the meaning of such references – as intended by the speaker or understood by the audience.

The second complication stems from the judicial (and public) commitment to state neutrality in religious matters (the idea that the state should take no position on the question of spiritual truth) and the underlying conception of religion as a cultural identity. The courts may hesitate to find that religiously based speech promotes hatred and breaches the ban on hate speech (i.e., that it is intended by the speaker to carry a hateful message or to stir up hatred). Because religious beliefs are often deep-rooted, a matter of identity rather than simply judgment, individual adherents may regard state restrictions on the expression of their beliefs as an insult to their dignity and a denigration of their spiritual community.[83] In a sense this is the mirror of the claim, described above, that an individual believer is harmed when his or her beliefs or practices are ridiculed or harshly criticized by others. But just

---

[82] Indeed, it is often the public or civic elements of the belief system, rather than the personal or communal rituals, that generate social criticism and conflict.

[83] This may explain the exemption in s. 319(2)(c) of the Canadian *Criminal Code* from the ban on hate speech: "If, in good faith, the person expressed or attempted to establish by an argument an opinion on a religious subject or an opinion based on a belief in a religious text".

as the individual's (actual) religious beliefs and practices should not be protected from critique, even that which is harsh and intemperate, so too the expression of hateful views should not be protected from state regulation simply because they are grounded in a religious belief system. When religion addresses civic issues, such as the rights and interests of others in the community (rather than personal and communal spiritual practices), it should be treated as a moral or political position that may be either accepted or rejected by democratic law-makers.[84] And when religion provides the basis for hateful views about other groups in the community, it should not be insulated from legal restriction.

At the same time, the conception of religion as an identity may cut in the other direction and strengthen the argument for the restriction of religiously based speech that is alleged to be hateful. The restriction of hate speech rests on a recognition that some members of the community may be unduly influenced by such speech when it occurs in a form or context that discourages independent judgment. When hateful views are expressed by an individual who claims to speak with religious authority (a minister or imam, for example), bases his or her speech on the word of God, and directs this appeal to other believers, we might wonder about the potential of "more speech" to correct such views. As well, the hateful character and irrational appeal of such speech will be greater in religious communities (or sub-groups) that imagine good and evil to be in constant struggle in the world and think that the integrity or purity of the spiritual community is threatened by "outsiders", who must be resisted through either violence or martyrdom.

VII THE REMAINDER OF THE BOOK

Chapter 2 will offer a general review of contemporary hate speech regulation and the challenges involved in reconciling a ban on hate speech with the public commitment to freedom of expression.

Chapter 3 will discuss the legal regulation of speech that attacks a religious community – that falsely attributes dangerous or undesirable beliefs to its members. The focus of this discussion will be anti-Muslim speech, which now seems to be the most significant form of such speech.

Chapter 4 will consider the restriction of speech that ridicules or "gratuitously" insults religious beliefs or sacred objects.

Finally, Chapter 5 will look at the role of religion when it is the source rather than the target of hate speech – when views that are alleged to be hateful are grounded in a religious belief system. The focus in this chapter will be on anti-gay speech. The chapter, though, will also say something about the promotion of terrorist activity, when based on religious claims.

---

[84] Richard Moon, *Freedom of Conscience and Religion* (Irwin Law, 2014) at xiii.

2

Freedom of Expression and the Regulation of Hate Speech

I HATE SPEECH REGULATION

One of the lessons of World War II (WWII) and the Holocaust was that in the right circumstances a campaign of racist propaganda could result in systematic violence against a targeted group such as Jews.[1] In the post-war period, the international community recognized, in a series of treaties and conventions, the need for legal restrictions on hate speech. The *International Convention on the Elimination of All Forms of Racial Discrimination*, which was adopted by the United Nations General Assembly in 1965, required states to prohibit by law the "dissemination of ideas based on racial superiority or hatred, incitement to racial discrimination, as well as all acts of violence or incitement to such acts against any race or group of persons of another colour or ethnic origin".[2] The *International Covenant on Civil and Political Rights* [*ICCPR*], a multilateral treaty adopted by the UN a year later in 1966, recognized (in Article 19) the right to freedom of expression, but provided that expression could be restricted for certain reasons including respect for the "rights or reputations of others" and "the protection of national security or of public order (*ordre public*)".[3] Article 20 of the *ICCPR* went further and obligated states to prohibit "advocacy of national, racial or religious hatred that constitutes incitement to discrimination, hostility or violence".[4]

---

[1] *R. v. Keegstra* [1990] 3 SCR 697 at para. 66.

[2] *International Convention on the Elimination of All Forms of Racial Discrimination*, 21 Dec 1965, 660 UNTS 195 (entered into force Jan. 4, 1969). Article 4 provides as follows: "States Parties condemn all propaganda and all organizations which are based on ideas or theories of superiority of one race or group of persons of one colour or ethnic origin, or which attempt to justify or promote racial hatred and discrimination in any form, and undertake to adopt immediate and positive measures designed to eradicate all incitement to, or acts of, such discrimination".

[3] *International Covenant on Civil and Political Rights* (adopted 16 Dec 1966, entered into force March 23, 1976) 999 UNTS 171 (ICCPR), Art. 19.

[4] Article 20.2 of the ICCPR provides that any advocacy of national, racial, or religious hatred that constitutes incitement to discrimination, hostility, or violence shall be prohibited by law. According to

Also, during the post-WWII period, various European states enacted bans on hate speech.[5] The Dutch penal code prohibits the incitement of hatred, discrimination, or violence against the members of racial, religious, and other groups.[6] In Germany, incitement of popular hatred is prohibited by the Criminal Code.[7] The German code also prohibits the public denial, diminution, or approval of "an act committed under the regime of National Socialism . . . in a way likely to disturb the peace".[8] The Austrian *Prohibition Act* similarly prohibits the public denial of "the National Socialist genocide, or other National Socialist crimes".[9] Incitement to racial or religious hatred is banned in the UK by the *Racial and Religious Hatred Act, 2006 (UK) c.1*.[10]

In 1970, the Canadian government enacted criminal restrictions on the advocacy of genocide, the incitement to hatred likely to lead to a breach of the peace, and the wilful promotion of hatred against a group identified on the basis of race, religion, or ethnicity.[11] These additions to the *Criminal Code* were made on the advice of the Cohen Commission, which had reported to Parliament five years earlier. It could no longer be assumed, said the Commission, that hate speech – the vilification of a particular racial group – would fall on deaf ears:

The triumphs of Fascism in Italy, and National Socialism in Germany through audaciously false propaganda have shown how fragile tolerant liberal societies can

the United Nations Human Rights Committee (General Comment 11), there is no conflict between Articles 19 and 20 of the ICCPR: "In the opinion of the Committee, these required prohibitions are fully compatible with the right of freedom of expression as contained in article 19, the exercise of which carries with it special duties and responsibilities. . . . For article 20 to become fully effective there ought to be a law making it clear that propaganda and advocacy as described therein are contrary to public policy and providing for an appropriate sanction in case of violation. The Committee, therefore, believes that States parties which have not yet done so should take the measures necessary to fulfil the obligations contained in article 20, and should themselves refrain from any such propaganda or advocacy." Article 20 is the only provision in the Covenant that imposes a duty on states to prohibit an activity. For a discussion see Jeroen Temperman, *Religious Hatred and International Law: The Prohibition of Incitement to Violence or Discrimination* (Cambridge University Press, 2015).

5 In France the *Press Law, 1881* (Loi du 29 juillet 1881 sur la liberté de la presse), was amended in 1938 to include a prohibition on the incitement to hatred on grounds of race and religion: For a discussion see Julie C. Suk, "Denying experience: Holocaust denial and the free-speech theory of the state", in Michael Herz and Peter Molnar (eds.), *The Content and Context of Hate Speech* (Cambridge, 2012) at 155. Also, the French Gayssot Law, 13 July 1990 (Loi Gayssot), prohibits denial of the Holocaust and other crimes of the Nazi era.

6 Art. 137d *Wetboek van Strafrecht* (Sr.) (Dutch Penal Code).

7 Section 130, *Strafgesetzbuch*, StGB (German Criminal Code).

8 German Criminal Code (n. 7), Art 3h, *Verbotsgesetz* (VerbotsG), (Prohibition Act, 1947).

9 Article 3h Art 3h, *Verbotsgesetz* (VerbotsG) (Prohibition Act, 1947) (Austria).

10 *The Racial and Religious Hatred Act, 2006* (UK) c. 1. This Act amended the *Public Order Act, 1986* (UK) c. 64.

11 Sections 318–19 of the *Criminal Code*, RSC 1985, c. C-46. In Canada, the enlargement of anti-discrimination laws and the introduction of the ban on hate speech were tied to the growth of diversity and more importantly to the re-conception of Canada as a multi-cultural society.

be in certain circumstances. They have also shown us the large element of irrationality in human nature, which makes people vulnerable to propaganda in times of stress and strain.[12]

The Commission thought that the community was morally required to respond not only to acts of discrimination and violence against racial and religious groups but also to the expression of hateful views that might lead to such acts.

A prosecution under s. 319(2), the Canadian *Criminal Code* ban on the wilful promotion of hatred, may be commenced only with the consent of the Attorney-General in the particular province. To be convicted of promoting hate, the accused must be shown to have engaged in speech that either stirred up hatred in its audience or created a risk that such hatred would be generated, and to have done this either intentionally or with knowledge that the speech was likely to have this effect.[13] The *Code* includes several defences to the charge of hate speech, including that a person shall not be convicted under the section "if, in good faith, he expressed or attempted to establish by argument an opinion on a religious subject or on an opinion based on a belief in a religious text" (s. 319(3)(b)), or if the claims were true (s. 319(3)(a)), or if the statements were relevant to any subject of public interest, the discussion of which was for the public benefit, and if on reasonable grounds the speaker believed them to be true (s. 319(3)(c)). If found by a court to have committed the offence, an individual may be sentenced to a fine or a term of imprisonment. The *Criminal Code* also includes a section that enables a court to order the seizure or erasure of material that it determines to be "hate propaganda".[14] The *Criminal Code* ban on the wilful promotion of hatred has not been widely enforced.[15] In some provinces the Attorney-General has been reluctant to give consent to prosecution – either because he or she is concerned that prosecution may give hate promoters increased publicity for their hateful views or more frequently because he or she is conscious that conviction is difficult to achieve.

Even in cases in which the Attorney-General has given his or her consent to prosecute, the rate of conviction has been low. In *R. v. Ahenekew*, for example,

[12] *Report of the Special Committee on Hate Propaganda in Canada* (Queen's Printer, 1966) [Cohen Commission].

[13] *Mugesera v. Canada* (Minister of Citizenship and Immigration) [2005] 2 SCR 100; 2005 SCR 40 at para. 102.

[14] *Criminal Code* (n. 11), s. 320.

[15] See R. Moon, *Report to the CHRC Concerning Section 13 of the CHRA and the Regulation of Hate Speech on the Internet*, October 2008 at 15. Between 1994 and 2004, there were 93 prosecutions under s. 319. Thirty-two convictions were entered and of these 27 resulted in prison sentences and 5 in conditional sentences (*CERD*, Consideration of Reports, Comments and Information Submitted by State Parties under Article 9 of the Convention, Seventeenth and Eighteenth Periodic Reports of Canada, 2008). It is not clear whether the number of prosecutions is small because the police do not pursue hate promotion claims or because provincial Attorneys-General are reluctant to give consent to prosecution. There is certainly a perception in some provinces that the consent requirement is a barrier to prosecution – and has the effect of discouraging police investigations of hate speech on the Internet and elsewhere.

a high-profile aboriginal leader was acquitted on the charge of hate speech, even though his anti-Semitic remarks were, according to the judge, "revolting, disgusting, and untrue". He was acquitted because the judge found that he did not intend to promote hatred.[16] Following a public speech in which Mr. Ahenekew had made some brief, but disturbing, references to Jews, he was approached by a reporter who pressed him to explain these references.[17] Among the more odious comments made by Mr. Ahenekew to the reporter were the following:

[REPORTER] Q: *Okay. D'you think it was a good thing that he [Hitler], that he killed six million Jews? Isn't that a horrible thing?*
[AHENEKEW] A: Well, Jews owned the goddam world and look at what they're doing. They're killing people in the Arab countries. I was there, I was there.
Q: *I know but how can you justify the Holocaust? Six million?*
A: You know how, how, how do you get rid of a, a, a, you know a disease like that that's gonna take over, that's gonna dominate, that's gonna everything, and the poor people, they . . . [18]

The exchange between Ahenekew and the reporter was described by the Saskatchewan Court of Appeal as "heated". However, the Court thought that although Mr. Ahenekew intended to express hateful views, it was less certain in the circumstances that he intended to *promote* hatred – to stir up hatred in the community.

In 1977, the federal government amended the *Canadian Human Rights Act* [*CHRA*] to include a ban on "telephonic" communication that is likely to expose the members of an identifiable group to hatred or contempt.[19] The scope of the s. 13 ban was later extended to include hate speech on the Internet.[20] The immediate impetus for the enactment of section 13 was a telephone hate line operated in Toronto by the Western Guard and its leader, John Ross Taylor.[21] Members of the public who dialed a telephone number that had been publicized by the Western Guard would hear a short pre-recorded hate message. Because the hate line operated as a series of one-on-one "private" communications (individuals calling and receiving privately the recorded hate messages), there was concern that it might not be caught by 319(2) of the *Criminal Code*, which by its terms does not apply to

---

[16] *R. v. Ahenekew*, 2008 SKCA 4 at para. 51.
[17] In his speech, Ahenekew made a variety of claims about Jews, including that they had "created" WWII – *Ahenekew* (n. 16) at para. 6.
[18] *Ahenekew* (n. 16) at para. 7.
[19] *Canadian Human Rights Act*, R.S., 1985, c. H-6. Section 3(1): "For all purposes of this Act, the prohibited grounds of discrimination are race, national or ethnic origin, colour, religion, age, sex, sexual orientation, gender identity and expression, marital status, family status, genetic characteristics, disability and conviction for which a pardon has been granted."
[20] Section 13(2) was added to the *CHRA* (n. 19) in 2001.
[21] Moon, *Report to the CHRC* (n. 15) at 5.

private conversations. The Western Guard phone line was the subject of the first s. 13 complaint heard by the Canadian Human Rights Tribunal [CHRT].[22]

Section 13 of the *CHRA* was repealed by the federal government in 2012.[23] However, the human rights codes of British Columbia, Alberta, Saskatchewan, and the Northwest Territories continue to include provisions similar to section 13 that are applicable to signs and publications.[24]

The human rights code ban on hate speech is complaint driven. An individual or organization makes a complaint, which (under most of the codes) is investigated by a human rights commission. The commission must decide whether the complaint has substance and should be referred to a tribunal for adjudication. The process has been altered in a few provinces. In British Columbia, a commission no longer performs this filtering role and all complaints go directly to a tribunal for adjudication,[25] while in Saskatchewan, a commission still receives and investigates complaints, but now refers complaints to the courts for adjudication rather than to a specialized tribunal.[26]

The purpose of the human rights code ban on hate speech is not to condemn and punish the person who committed the discriminatory act, but rather to prevent or rectify discriminatory practices or to compensate the victims of discrimination for the harm they have suffered. In contrast to the criminal ban on hate speech, an individual may be found to have breached the human rights code ban even though he or she did not *intend* to expose others to hatred or realize that his or her communication might have this effect. The focus is on the effect of the act and not the intent with which it was performed. The ordinary remedy against an individual who is found to have breached the human rights code ban is an order that he or she cease his or her discriminatory practices.

The *Criminal Code* prohibits the wilful promotion of hatred against an "identifiable" group – a group identified by colour, race, religion, ethnic origin, age, sex,

---

[22] *Canada (HRC) v. Taylor* [1990] 3 S.C.R. 892. This case is discussed later in this chapter.

[23] *An Act to Amend the Canadian Human Rights Act (Protecting Freedom)*, SC 2013, c. 37, s. 2, repealing *Canadian Human Rights Act*, RSC 1985, c. H-6, s. 13. As I will argue later in this chapter, there are a number of ways in which the human rights process is not well suited to the regulation of hate speech. However, the repeal of s. 13 occurred following a much-publicized disinformation campaign directed at the CHRC and human rights codes and commissions more generally. For a discussion of this campaign, see R. Moon, "The attack on human rights commissions and the decline of public discourse", 73 *Saskatchewan Law Journal* 93–129 (2010).

[24] For example, the *BC Human Rights Code*, RSBC 1996, c. 210, s. 7, prohibits the display or publication of any sign, publication, or notice that either discriminates against a person or a group of persons or is likely to expose them to hatred. See also *Saskatchewan Human Rights Code*, R.S.S., 1979, c. S-24.1, s. 14; *Human Rights, Citizenship and Multiculturalism Act*, R.S.A., 2000, c. H-14, s. 2 (Alberta); *Consolidation of Human Rights Act*, R.S.N.W.T., 2002, c. 18, s. 13 (Northwest Territories).

[25] *BC Human Rights Code* (n. 24). This is also the process now in Ontario – although the Ontario code does not include a hate speech ban: *Ontario Human Rights Code*, RSO 1990, cH19.

[26] *Saskatchewan Human Rights Code* (n. 24). Complaints are adjudicated by the Saskatchewan Court of Queen's Bench.

sexual orientation, gender identity or expression, or mental or physical disability.[27] The human rights code restrictions on hate speech protect an even wider range of groups, including groups defined on the basis of marital status and income source. Hate speech laws were introduced as a response to racist and anti-Semitic speech, and these remain in the public mind the central cases of such speech.

It has become increasingly apparent that laws prohibiting discrimination or hate speech apply differently, and sometimes very awkwardly, to groups that are defined on grounds other than race – and in particular on grounds such as religion that involve a shared belief system or a common set of cultural practices, or marital status or citizenship that involve an element of choice in membership. The question addressed in subsequent chapters is how well the ground of religion fits within the framework of hate speech law (either criminal or human rights) or, put another way, what difference does it make in the application of hate speech law when the (hateful) attack is directed at a religious group. If religious adherence or membership is not simply a matter of biology or even cultural practice, but involves also, or instead, a commitment to a set of beliefs about truth and right, it may not fit easily into the standard model of hate speech regulation.

However, before considering the difference religion makes to the application of hate speech law, when it is either the source or the target of hate speech, something needs to be said about the general structure of hate speech regulation and the tension between this regulation and the public commitment to freedom of expression. The discussion that follows will refer to cases from a variety of jurisdictions, but will focus on a few Canadian decisions – in particular, *R. v. Keegstra* and *Whatcott* v. *Saskatchewan Human Rights Commission* – in which the courts have held that the legal restriction of hate speech is a justified limit on the right to freedom of expression in the Canadian *Charter of Rights and Freedoms*.[28]

Many domestic and regional human rights charters, following the model of the *ICCPR*, provide that freedom of expression is subject to limits designed to prevent the spread of hatred. For example, s. 16 of the *Constitution of South Africa, 1996*, states that freedom of expression "does not extend to ... (c) advocacy of hatred that is based on race, ethnicity, gender, or religion and that constitutes incitement to cause harm."[29] More often, though, rights charters, such as the *European Convention on Human Rights* [ECHR], provide that freedom of expression may be restricted by laws protecting "the rights of others" or public order or safety – which according to the ECtHR includes laws prohibiting hate speech.[30] But even if it is accepted that a ban on hate speech is a necessary or justified limit on expression, the courts, when applying these charters, must still make judgments about the scope of the ban,

---

[27] *Criminal Code* (n. 11), ss. 319(2), (7), and 318(4).

[28] *Charter of Rights and Freedoms*, Part 1 of the *Constitution Act*, 1982, being schedule B to the Canada Act 1982 (UK), 1928, c. 11 [Charter].

[29] *Constitution of the Republic of South Africa*, 1996.

[30] *European Convention on Human Rights* (Nov 4, 1950).

taking account of the competing claims of freedom of expression and equality (or dignity).[31]

II FREEDOM OF EXPRESSION

A *A Social Right*

Freedom of expression does not simply protect individual liberty from state interference. It protects the individual's freedom to communicate with others.[32] The right of the individual is to engage in an activity that is deeply social in character and that involves socially created languages and the use of collective resources.

There are many arguments for protecting freedom of expression, but all seem to focus on one or a combination of three values: truth, democracy, and individual autonomy/self-realization. Freedom of expression must be protected because it contributes to the public's recognition of truth or the growth of public knowledge,[33] or because it is necessary to the operation of a democratic form of government,[34] or because it is important to individual self-realization or autonomy.[35] But whether the emphasis is on truth, democracy, or autonomy, each of the established accounts of the freedom's value rests on a recognition that human autonomy or agency is deeply social in its realization. Each account represents a particular perspective on, or dimension of, the constitution of human agency in community life. We become individuals capable of thought and judgment, we flourish as rational and feeling persons, when we join in conversation with others and participate in collective life. In communicating with others an individual gives shape to his or her ideas and aspirations, becomes capable of reflection and evaluation, and gains greater understanding of himself or herself and the world. It is through communicative interaction that an individual develops and emerges as an autonomous agent in the positive sense of being able to direct his or her life and to participate in the direction of the

---

[31] It is noteworthy that in *Islamic Unity Convention v. Independent Broadcasting Authority*, the Constitutional Court of South Africa relied on Canadian hate speech cases, and in particular the decision in R. v. *Keegstra*, when defining the scope of the hate speech exception to freedom of expression. Canadian jurisprudence has also been a resource for international guideline documents such as the *Rabat Plan of Action* (which was produced by the Office of the UN High Commissioner for Human Rights and discusses the obligation of states to restrict the incitement to hatred) and the *Camden Principles on Freedom of Expression and Equality*. For a discussion see Jeroen Temperman, *Religious Hatred and International Law* (n. 4), where it is observed that the drafters of these documents drew on Canadian cases.

[32] For a fuller account see R. Moon, *The Constitutional Protection of Freedom of Expression* (University of Toronto Press, 2000).

[33] J.S. Mill, *On Liberty* (Penguin, 1982 [1859]).

[34] Alexander Meiklejohn, *Political Freedom* (Oxford University Press, 1965); Robert Post, *Constitutional Domains* (Harvard University Press, 1995) at 312.

[35] M. Redish, "The Value of Free Speech", 13 *Univ. of Pa. L.R.* 591 (1982); Ronald Dworkin, *A Matter of Principle* (Harvard University Press, 1985).

community. Through communication, an individual creates different kinds of relationships with others and participates in different collective activities, such as self-
government and the pursuit of knowledge.

The relationship of communication is valuable because individual agency and
identity develop in the joint activity of creating meaning. Our ideas and feelings
take shape in the social process of expression.[36] When we give our ideas and feelings
linguistic form we "bring them to fuller and clearer consciousness".[37] We reflect on
them by placing them before others as part of an ongoing discourse. We understand
our articulated ideas and feelings in light of the reactions of others. At the same time,
our views are reshaped in the process of hearing, understanding, and reacting to the
words of others. Understanding is an active, creative process in which the listener
locates and evaluates the speaker's words (or other symbolic forms) within the framework of his or her own knowledge and memory.[38] Listeners use these symbolic forms
"as a vehicle for reflection and self-reflection, as a basis for thinking about themselves, about others and about the world to which they belong."[39] In this way, our
knowledge of self and the world emerges in the public articulation/interpretation
of experience.[40] As Mikhail Bakhtin observes, the individual's thought is "born and
shaped in the process of articulation and the process of interaction and struggle with
others' thought".[41]

The established accounts of the value of freedom of expression are often
described as either instrumental or intrinsic (or as concerned with the realization of
a social goal or with the protection of an individual right).[42] Some accounts see freedom of expression as valuable in itself. The freedom is intrinsically valuable because
it enables free and rational beings to express their ideas and feelings. Or the freedom
must be protected out of respect for the autonomy of individuals. Other accounts
see freedom of expression as important because it contributes to a valued state of
affairs: freedom of expression is instrumental to the realization of social goods such
as public knowledge or democratic government.

---

[36] "[W]e becomes individuals", Clifford Geertz observes, "under the guidance of cultural patterns, historically created systems of meaning in terms of which we give form, order, point, and direction to
our lives". Clifford Geertz, *The Interpretation of Cultures* (Basic Books, 1973) at 52.

[37] Charles Taylor, *Human Agency and Language* (Cambridge University Press, 1985) at 257. The general
account of expression in this section draws heavily on Taylor's writing. When we speak, we bring to
"explicit awareness" – to consciousness – that of which before we had only an "implicit sense". (Taylor,
256).

[38] J.B. Thompson, *The Media and Modernity* (Stanford University Press, 1995) at 39.

[39] Thompson, *Media and Modernity* (n. 38).

[40] At the same time, individuals adapt the symbolic forms of language to their needs in particular communicative contexts and is so doing recreate, extend, alter, and reshape the language (Taylor, *Human
Agency*, n. 37 at 97).

[41] M. M. Bakhtin, *Speech Genres and Other Late Essays*, trans. V. McGee (University of Texas Press,
1986) at 92.

[42] McLachlin J. in *R. v. Keegstra* (n. 1) at para. 194. See also Kent Greenawalt, *Fighting Words* (Princeton
University Press, 1993) at 3.

Intrinsic accounts assume that freedom of expression, like other rights, is an aspect of the individual's fundamental liberty or autonomy that should be insulated from the demands of collective welfare. Yet any account that regards freedom of expression as a liberty (as a right of the individual to be free from external interference) seems unable to explain the other-regarding or community-oriented character of the protected activity of expression – of individuals speaking and listening to others.[43] Instrumental accounts, on the other hand, recognize that the freedom protects an other-regarding or social activity and so accept that it must be concerned with something more than respect for individual autonomy, something more than individual venting or the exercise of individual reason. They assume that the freedom must be concerned with social goals (such as truth and democracy) that are in some way separate from, or beyond, the individual and his or her communicative actions. Yet if freedom of expression is an instrumental right, its fundamental character seems less obvious. Its value is contingent on its contribution to the goals of truth and democracy. And there is no shortage of arguments that freedom of expression does not (always) advance these goals.

The value of free expression will remain unclear as long as the discussion is locked into this intrinsic/instrumental dichotomy, in which the freedom is concerned with either the good of the community or the right of the individual.[44] However, once we recognize that individual agency and identity emerge in the social relationship of communication, the traditional split between intrinsic and instrumental accounts (or social and individual accounts) of the value of freedom of expression dissolves. Expression connects the individual (as speaker or listener) with others and in doing so contributes to his or her capacity for understanding and judgment, to his or her engagement in community life, and to his or her participation in a shared culture and collective governance. The arguments described as instrumental focus on the contribution of speech to the collective goals of truth and democracy. However, as Mill recognized, we value truth not as an abstract social achievement but rather as something that is consciously realized by members of the community, individually and collectively, in the process of public discussion.[45] Similarly, freedom of expression is not simply a tool or instrument that contributes to democratic government. We value freedom of expression not simply because it provides individuals with useful political information, but more fundamentally because it is the way in which citizens participate in collective self-governance and become democratic citizens.[46]

---

[43] Why the activity of expression should be specially protected remains a central issue in debates about the justification of freedom of expression. For a discussion see Moon, *The Constitutional Protection of Freedom of Expression* (n. 32) at 19–21.

[44] For a more extensive discussion see Moon, *The Constitutional Protection of Freedom of Expression* (n. 32) at 24.

[45] Mill, *On Liberty* (n. 33) at 97.

[46] Post, *Constitutional Domains* (n. 34), at 312, argues that public discourse is essential to democratic governance because it fosters in the citizen a sense of participation and identification: "Public discourse

There is no way to separate the goal from the process or the individual good from the public good. Attaching the label "intrinsic" to autonomy or self-realization accounts of the freedom seems also to misconstrue the value at stake. Communication is a joint or public process (which takes place between individuals and within a community) in which individual participants realize their human capacities. The individual does not simply gain satisfaction from expressing his or her pre-existing views on things. An individual's views, and more broadly his or her judgment and identity, take shape in the communicative process.

B *The Value and Harm of Expression*

Recognition that individual agency and identity emerge in communicative interaction is crucial to understanding not only the value of expression but also its potential for harm. Our dependence on expression means that words can sometimes harass, intimidate, deceive, manipulate, or denigrate the individual. Expression is valuable because individual agency and identity are shaped by what we say and by what other say to us and about us; but expression can also contribute to a distorted public image of the individual (or group) or undermine his or her standing or sense of security in the community, particularly when conditions of unequal communicative power prevent him or her from playing a meaningful role in the definition of his or her public identity. Similarly, while expression is important as a source of knowledge and insight, it can also serve to mislead or manipulate its audience. Speech is not simply a "cause" of audience thought and action; but neither is it ever entirely rational and transparent in its meaning or influence.

At issue in many of the debates about free speech protection is whether a particular form of expression engages the audience and encourages independent judgment or whether instead it intimidates, harasses, or manipulates the audience.[47] The judgment that expression is valuable and worthy of protection, or is instead harmful and appropriately subject to restriction (that it is not simply uncivil or confrontational but is instead harassing or intimidating or manipulating), is a relative one that will depend on a number of factors, including the form of the expression and the context in which it occurs.[48] When speech seems intended to harass, deceive, or intimidate

---

merits unique constitutional protection because it is the process through which the democratic 'self', the agent of self-government, is itself constituted through the reconciliation of individual and collective autonomy." See also Cass Sunstein, *Democracy and the Problem of Free Speech* (The Free Press, 1993): Through participation in public discourse, the individual becomes a citizen capable of understanding, and identifying with, the concerns and opinions of others.

[47] R. Moon, "Justified Limits on Expression: The Collapse of the General Approach to Limits on Charter Rights", 40 *Osgoode Hall LJ* 337 (2002). Manipulation involves "speech" that leads audience members to think and/or act in a particular way, without realizing the intent behind the speech or the implications of acting on its claims.

[48] I have elsewhere argued that this determination does not involve the balancing or trading off of competing interests. See R. Moon, "Limits on Expression" (n. 47) and R. Moon, "Limits on Constitutional Rights: The Marginal Role of Proportionality Analysis", 30 *Israel Law Rev.* 1 (2017).

its audience, it may no longer be viewed as communicative engagement – as part of a discourse that is entitled to constitutional protection.

C *The Premises of Freedom of Expression*

A commitment to freedom of expression means that an individual must be free to speak to others and to hear what others may say, without interference from the state. It is said that the answer to bad or erroneous speech is not censorship, but rather more and better speech.[49] Importantly the listener, and not the speaker, is seen as responsible (as an independent agent) for his or her actions, including harmful actions, whether these actions occur because he or she agrees or disagrees with the speaker's message. In other words, respect for the autonomy of the individual – whether as speaker or listener – means that speech is not ordinarily regarded as a "cause" of harmful action. A speaker does not "cause" harm simply because he or she persuades the audience of a particular view and the audience acts on that view in a harmful way.

The commitment to freedom of expression (and the refusal to treat speech as a cause) rests on a belief that humans are substantially rational beings capable of evaluating factual and other claims and an assumption that public discourse is open to a wide range of competing views that may be assessed by the audience. The claim that "bad" speech should not be censored, but instead answered by "better" speech, depends on both of these assumptions – the reasonableness of human judgment and the availability of competing perspectives. A third, but less obvious, assumption underpinning the protection of freedom of expression is that the state has the effective power to either prevent or punish harmful action by the audience. Individuals will sometimes make poor judgments. The community's willingness to bear the risk of such errors in judgment may depend on the state's ability to prevent the harmful actions of audience members or at least to hold audience members to account for their actions.

D *Incitement and Manipulation*

Expression cannot be restricted by the state simply because it might persuade its audience to act in a harmful way or because it might negatively affect an individual's or group's self-understanding or self-esteem. The courts, though, recognize that the assumptions about the audience's agency or judgment that underlie the protection of speech may not always hold (and indeed never hold perfectly). Prohibitions on false or misleading product claims have been supported because advertisers have overwhelming power in the "marketplace of ideas" and information (so that others

---

[49] Brandeis J. in *Whitney v. California*, 247 US 357 (1927) at 37: "the remedy to be applied is more speech".

have limited opportunities to correct misleading ads) and because so much commercial advertising is non-rational or visceral in its appeal. Similarly, the restriction of defamatory speech rests on a recognition that false claims made about an individual are not easily corrected through "more speech". The harm of defamatory speech may persist, because the audience is not always in a position to assess the false and damaging claims and, people being as they are, the correcting speech may not spread as effectively as the original defamation.

Freedom of expression doctrine has always permitted the restriction of expression that occurs in a form and/or context that discourages independent judgment by the audience or that impedes the audience's ability to assess the claims made. When speech incites or manipulates the audience to take violent action, the speaker may be seen as responsible for, and perhaps even as a participant in, any violence that follows. For example, in *On Liberty*, J.S. Mill thought that the authorities would be justified in preventing a fiery speech given near the home of a corn merchant to a crowd of farmers angry about crop prices. A heated speech delivered to a "mob" appeals to passion and prejudice and might lead to impulsive and harmful actions.[50] Speech is described as incitement when the time and (reflective) space between the speech and the (called-for) action is so limited that the speaker may be viewed as leading the audience into action and not simply as trying to persuade them to take action.

In American free speech jurisprudence, the classic example of a failure in the conditions of ordinary discourse comes from a judgment of Justice Holmes, who said that "The most stringent protection of free speech would not protect a man in falsely shouting fire in a theatre and causing a panic".[51] The false yell of fire in a crowded theatre represents a clear deviation from the conditions of ordinary speech. The theatre audience in such a case would not have time to stop and think before acting on the communicated message. The panic that would follow the yell of fire in these circumstances would almost certainly result in injury.

The examples given by Mill and Holmes involve circumstances that limit the audience's ability to carefully or dispassionately assess the communicated message. The assumption is that ordinarily, when an individual communicates with others, he or she appeals to their independent and reasoned judgment. In exceptional circumstances, however, an individual's words may appeal to passions and fears and may encourage unreflective action. In these circumstances, the state may be justified in restricting the expression. Speech may be treated as a cause of audience action

---

[50] Mill, *On Liberty* (n. 33) at 119.

[51] *Schenck v. United States*, 249 US 47 (1919) at 52. But note that in that case Holmes J. thought that the distribution of literature encouraging draft resistance during WWI was the equivalent of the "yell of fire" and so could be restricted.

when the time and space for independent judgment are compressed, or when emotions are running so high that audience members are unable or unlikely to stop and reflect on the claims being made. While the line between rational appeal or conscious argument, on the one hand, and on the other, manipulation or incitement, may not be easy to draw (and indeed is a relative matter), it is at least possible to identify some of the circumstances in which reasoned judgment is significantly constrained.

Criminal restrictions on *incitement* to violence apply only to speech that is closely tied by both time and place to ensuing violence. For example, section 319(1) of the Canadian *Criminal Code*, which prohibits incitement of hatred against an identifiable group, is breached only when "the incitement is likely to lead to a breach of the peace."[52] The judgment that speech is likely to have such an effect (the recognition of a "causal" link between the speech and the action) rests in part on the character of the expression, but more significantly on the context in which it occurs, and in particular the absence of space for the audience to make a careful or independent judgment before taking action. A speaker who calls on a group (whose emotions are running high) to take immediate action may be seen as leading the audience into that action – as causing, or contributing to, the harm that follows.[53] According to the courts in the United States, only when such speech is likely to lead to imminent lawlessness ("fighting words" or "incitement") will its restriction be constitutionally acceptable.[54]

The courts in Canada and other jurisdictions, in contrast to the U.S. courts, have upheld restrictions on hate speech (in various forms) even when violence is not the certain and imminent consequence of the speech. These courts have determined that the public interest in freedom of expression is outweighed by the harm (or risk of harm) caused by hate speech – harm to the members of targeted minority groups in the form of discrimination, intimidation, harassment, and violence. Hate speech laws, though, do not address discrete failures in public discourse (of the sort described by Mill and Holmes), but instead rest on more general concerns about the character and scope of communicative engagement, and so they raise a significant challenge to the public commitment to free expression.

---

[52] Criminal Code (n. 11), ss. 319(1).

[53] In most such cases, the relevant expression will be oral in form – speech. In contrast to the written word, oral communication often involves a more direct and immediate expression of the speaker's thoughts and feelings. The spoken word is performance-oriented, "embedded in the human life world, connected with action and struggle" (Walter Ong, *Orality and Literacy* (Methuen, 1982) at 101). Oral communication is more likely to be spontaneous, impulsive, and emotional because it is more closely connected with the immediate context.

[54] The United States Supreme Court in *Brandenburg v. Ohio*, 395 US 444 (1969) at 447 held that the First Amendment precluded the government from restricting the advocacy of violence "except where such advocacy is directed to inciting or producing imminent lawless action and is likely to incite or produce such action."

III HATE SPEECH REGULATION

While it might not be quite right to say that there are two kinds of hate speech, there are perhaps two general kinds of harm that hate speech can cause.[55] The first harm is that suffered *directly* by the members of a racial or other target group – the group that is both the subject and audience of the hate speech. This form of harm may include fear, humiliation, and emotional trauma resulting from speech that is threating or insulting. The second kind of harm is the spread of hateful views in the larger community that may lead to acts of violence and discrimination against target group members and contribute more generally to the group's sense of vulnerability in the community. The type of harm caused by a particular instance of hate speech will depend on the content and the audience of the speech – on what is said and to whom it is said.

The issue for the courts and other government actors in various jurisdictions is whether the regulation of speech that "causes" or contributes to these harms can be reconciled with a commitment to freedom of expression. The answer may be different depending on the type of harm the law seeks to prevent or the form of speech that it restricts.

A *Intimidation and Harassment*

Because individual agency and identity take shape in public discourse – are formed inter-subjectively – speech is valuable but also potentially injurious. Speech can sometimes undermine the individual's sense of self and place in the world and his or her sense of security – particularly when the attacks on the individual or the group with which he or she identifies are systematic and difficult to avoid. The U.S. courts have held that "true threats" of violence and "fighting words" fall outside the scope of the constitutional right – that the harms of fear, insecurity, and trauma generated by such threats or provocations are significant and justify the restriction of this speech.[56] The question, though, is just how serious the threat must be, or how

---

[55] Richard Moon, "Hate Speech Regulation in Canada", 36 *Florida State LR* 79 (2008). Alexander Brown, *Hate Speech Law: A Philosophical Examination* (Routledge, 2015) describes 10 clusters of laws/regulations/codes that constrain hate speech.

[56] *Watts v. United States*, 394 U.S. 705 (1969) (threats); *Chaplinsky v. New Hampshire*, 315 U.S. 568 (1942) (fighting words). It could, of course, be argued that even "true" threats ought to be protected under the First Amendment – that while the state should prohibit and punish the threatened act of violence (if actually carried out), it should not be permitted to ban the threat itself, which is simply an act of expression. But no one seems willing to argue this. As noted in Eric Heinze, "Review essay: Hate speech and the normative foundations of regulation", 9 *Int. J of Law in Conflict* 590 (2016) at 595, even the "most serious opponents of bans" do not question restrictions on "stalking, 'fighting words', or workplace discrimination". Another argument in support of restricting threats may be that by simply uttering a threat the idea of violence may be made more real – imaginable (and more likely to occur) – for the person who has said the words. But this concern would apply to both real and general threats.

imminent or likely the threatened violence, before state restriction is justified.[57] Robert Post describes the U.S. courts' approach in this way: "[I]f incivilities occurring in public discourse threaten to undermine the very idea of a democratic community, if they threaten to undermine the norms of civility that allow public discourse to serve its function, the [U.S. Supreme] Court will permit regulation. But what is permissible will be a very thin form of regulation at the margins, and we will characterize unprotected speech with labels like 'fighting words' or 'true threats'".[58] The U.S. courts' insistence that the category of restricted threats and provocations be very narrowly defined, so that it does not include general racist threats or insults, exemplifies American free speech exceptionalism.[59]

In *Collin v. Smith*, the U.S. Court of Appeals held that municipal regulations introduced to prevent a neo-Nazi march in a predominantly Jewish neighbourhood (a section of Chicago in which a large number of Holocaust survivors resided) breached the First Amendment right to free speech.[60] The Court acknowledged that many of the community's residents would experience emotional distress due to the march. However, in the Court's view, the march did not represent a true threat to these residents, since they would be protected by state authorities from any violence.

Similarly, in *RAV v. City of St. Paul*, a case involving two young men who erected a burning cross in front of the home of a black family that had moved into an historically white neighbourhood, the U.S. Supreme Court struck down a city ordinance that prohibited the erection of racist symbols, such as burning crosses and swastikas, on public property.[61] The state courts had determined that the ordinance applied only to "fighting words" (speech that is likely to provoke a breach of the public peace), which fell outside the protection of the First Amendment.[62]

---

57 The requirement that the threat be true or real – that it be serious – refers not simply to the intention of the person making the threat (does he or she actually intend to carry out the threatened action) but also to the likelihood that the threat will be carried out, which depends on whether that person has the means to carry out the threat and on whether the state is in a position to prevent the threatened action.

58 "Interview with Robert Post", in Michael Herz and Peter Molnar, *The Content and Context of Hate Speech* (Cambridge, 2012) at 2. Jeremy Waldron, *The Harm in Hate Speech* (Harvard, 2012), advocates a broader exception. Waldron at 151 recognizes both the need to draw a line separating injurious from protected speech and the difficulty in locating such a line, when he refers to the "adverbial" element in distinguishing proscribable hate speech from merely offensive speech: "No doubt the adverbial element is important: we want to catch only hate speech that is expressed in an abusive, insulting, or threatening way. But usually... that adverbial element will be indicated by the content of the words or written material itself, rather than by non-content based elements such as tone, volume, shrillness".

59 The other free speech cases that seem to distinguish the United States from the rest of the world are the decisions striking down limits on election spending. See, for example, *Citizens United v. Federal Election Commission*, 558 US 310 (2010).

60 *Collin v. Smith*, 578 F. 2d 1197 (7th Circ. 1978).   61 *RAV v. City of St. Paul*, 505 US 377 (1992).

62 The U.S. Supreme Court in *Chaplinsky v. New Hampshire* (n. 56), held that "fighting words" (words uttered to inflict injury or tending to incite an immediate breach of the peace) were not protected. For a discussion see Kent Greenawalt, *Fighting Words* (Princeton University Press, 1993), at 48.

The U.S. Supreme Court, however, held that the ban, even if limited to "fighting words", violated the First Amendment because it was not "content neutral". The ordinance prohibited racist speech (symbols) but not anti-racist speech and, according to Justice Scalia, the municipality "has no such authority to licence one side of a debate to fight free style, while requiring the other to follow Marquis of Queensberry rules".[63] Yet the Court's insistence on the need for fairness and balance in a "discourse" involving threats and degrading insults seems misplaced. Racist speech is not simply a position in a debate on a public issue. The neo-Nazi marchers and the cross burners are not seeking to persuade their immediate audience, Jews and African-Americans, to reconsider their position – something that Justice Scalia's boxing metaphor serves to obscure by conflating discursive and physical engagement. Nor are anti-racism and racism simply two sides – two perspectives – on the issue, each the mirror of the other. Anti-racist words and symbols are not imbued with the same violent history as the burning cross or the swastika. They are not part of a systemic practice of exclusion and oppression. Their meaning and impact are entirely different.[64]

In the later case of *Virginia* v. *Black*, the U.S. Supreme Court seemed to be more open to a ban on cross burning when it was performed to intimidate others.[65] A majority of the Court recognized that this activity has long been used by white supremacists to intimidate African-Americans and has often been a prelude to violence. Justice O'Connor, writing for the majority of the Court, thought that the First Amendment did not prevent the state from banning "this subset of intimidating messages" because cross burning is a "particularly virulent form of intimidation" that has a "long and pernicious history as a signal of impending violence".[66] However, the Court found that the challenged Virginia law was overbroad in its scope, because it provided that the burning of a cross "shall be prima facie evidence" of an intent to intimidate. The Court was concerned that this presumption might result in the conviction of an individual who burned a cross not to intimidate others, but simply to affirm "a statement of ideology" or "group solidarity".[67] This, of course, ignores the way in which cross-burning may contribute to the other harm of hate speech – discussed below – by reinforcing the ideology of violent racism within the white-supremacist group and encouraging its members to take action.[68]

[63] *RAV* (n. 61) at 392.

[64] It is difficult to think of many examples of anti-racist symbols, other than peace signs or rainbows. These symbols do not seem to signal a violent purpose.

[65] *Virginia* v. *Black*, 538 US 343 (2010), at 356: When directed at an individual or group, cross-burning may serve as a "message of intimidation designed to inspire in the victim a fear of bodily harm". O'Connor J. claimed that the Court's judgment in this case was consistent with its earlier decision in *RAV* (n. 61).

[66] *Virginia* v. *Black* (n. 65) at 363.   [67] *Virginia* v. *Black* (n. 65) at 365–366.

[68] Michael Rosenfeld, "Hate speech in constitutional jurisprudence: A comparative analysis", in Herz and Molnar (n. 58) at 259: "As Klan members are predisposed by their ideology to contemplate perpetrating violence motivated by racial hatred, the ritualistic convenings involving cross burning seem

Those who argue that racist threats should be protected from state restriction often seek to discount the injury caused by such threats, describing it as simply personal offence – a subjective experience. But the harm is more tangible than that. Even if the speaker does not intend to act on his or her threatening words, or is not in a position to carry out the threat immediately, these words are intended to intimidate or upset his audience. Even if the threatened action is not imminent, and even if there is little prospect that it will ever occur, the threat will create fear and insecurity.[69] Even if the threats (neo-Nazi marches and burning crosses) do not seem realistic to an outside observer, they should be viewed from the perspective of the target group member, who experiences them as part of a continuing practice of intimidation and violence against that group.[70] The history and context of violence gives rise to genuine and understandable insecurity. The members of the target group may know that the particular threat cannot be carried out (although it is not clear why they would feel confident about this), but, because the threat is so closely linked to a larger practice of violent oppression, it will cause, or contribute to, significant anxiety and upset.

A burning cross, planted on the front lawn of the home of the first black family to move into a previously all-white neighbourhood, is experienced as threatening because it evokes the history of Klan violence against blacks. Similarly, a march with swastikas and SS uniforms in a Jewish neighbourhood is experienced as threatening because it evokes the history of Nazi persecution of Jews. Those who march wearing Nazi uniforms or who burn crosses say to their audience, "we want to do you harm, to murder you". The broader context of racist violence provides a basis for distinguishing unacceptable threats – such as a burning cross – from the "rough and tumble" of public debate, which is sometimes unpleasant and impolite – such as the harsh anti-racist speech imagined by Justice Scalia in *RAV*. This background makes the threat real or tangible to the audience. If a racist threat were truly an isolated act, and not part of a practice of racist abuse and violence, then it might be thought to cause nothing more than hurt feelings – or personal offence – and might be protected as part of the rough and tumble of discourse. But such threats are not isolated acts.

Even if we accept that the Neo-Nazi march, for example, manifests some kind of political solidarity among its participants or amounts to a political statement to other members of the community, who witness it or hear about it, the march is,

---

particularly apt to whip up emotions, to exacerbate the hatred, and to dispel any lingering inhibitions to turn the shared hatred to violence."

[69] Section 264.1(a) of the *Criminal Code* of Canada, (n. 11) provides that it is unlawful to knowingly utter, convey, or cause any person to receive a threat of death or bodily harm. The test is whether a "reasonable person" with knowledge of the circumstances, would understand the utterance to be a threat. In R. v. *Upson*, 2001 NSCA 89 at para. 42, an utterance against "members of the black race" was held to be a threat under this provision.

[70] Moon, *The Constitutional Protection of Freedom of Expression* (n. 32), at 129.

in the first instance, a threat against the Jewish residents of the neighbourhood. The political meaning or significance of the march stems from its threatening character – from its primary message to the target group. Under some accounts of freedom of expression, threats of violence may have some value, inasmuch as they express personal feelings or convey a crude viewpoint. However, the limited value of these words must be weighed against the intended injury to others. Speech may confront and challenge its audience. It may express anger and outrage to them. But when it seeks to intimidate the members of a racial group, its primary or initial audience, the speech should be viewed as part of a practice of racist oppression, rather than an attempt to engage with the audience.

The background of racist violence and oppression may also contribute to the justification for the restriction of racist insults, at least in particular contexts. This background adds significantly to the emotional impact of such insults. Indeed, insults are often a prelude to violent action. The frequent expression of racist insults (from different sources) means that they cannot easily be avoided by individual target group members. Each insult is experienced as part of a practice of harassment that gives rise to a general injury of humiliation and insecurity and contributes to the marginalization of the targeted group's members.[71] When individuals are subjected to repeated racist insults (along with threats of racist violence), so that they have little effective opportunity to respond, they will feel harassed, intimidated, and silenced – as having little power to define their place in the larger community.[72] In such a context "more speech" is a hollow remedy.

Yet, at the same time, the censorship of all such insults, whenever or wherever they occur, would involve extraordinary intervention by the state into public discourse and so may not be a practical option. Any ban on racist insults raises questions about the accountability (and punishment) of an individual who utters a racist insult for a harm or injury that is systemic in character. Such a ban also raises a variety of line-drawing issues, such as the distinction between a racist insult and a claim or argument about race or the distinction between the use of a term to demean a group's members and the use of the same term – a term such as "queer" – by the members of the historically targeted group in order to neutralize its negative force.

---

[71] Concerns about the silencing effect of hate speech have been expressed in several Canadian hate speech cases, for example, *Whatcott v. Saskatchewan HRC*, 2013 SCC 11 at para. 27, where the Supreme Court of Canada noted that hate speech prevents target group members from "interacting and participating in free expression and public debate". For an early academic discussion of the harm of silencing see Mari J. Matsuda, Charles R. Lawrence III, Richard Delgado, and Kimberle Williams Crenshaw, *Words That Wound: Critical Race Theory, Assaultive Speech, and the First Amendment* (Westview, 1993). Insults directed at a particular group may be experienced by the group's members as intimidating or humiliating and may undermine their sense of security and belonging. According to Waldron, *The Harm in Hate Speech* (n. 58), at 4, speech that is intentionally abusive or insulting undermines "the public good of inclusiveness" and interferes with group members' "sense of security in the space we all inhabit".

[72] Matsuda et al., *Words That Wound* (n. 71).

This practice is, as Judith Butler observes, "a reminder of the hope and possibility that the link between 'word and wound' might be broken".[73] However, it is now widely accepted that racist insults should be banned in the workplace, in schools, and in other similar environments – where they are difficult to avoid. The workplace environment is both closed and hierarchical and so a higher standard of civility may reasonably be expected.[74]

B *The Spread of Hate*

The leading hate speech cases in Canada and elsewhere involve the restriction of racist claims that are meant to persuade members of the general community about the dangerous or undesirable character of the members of a particular group – the second harm described earlier. The concern is that those who hear racist claims may come to view the target group differently and act towards its members in a discriminatory or even violent way.

In several decisions, the Canadian courts have sought to reconcile the regulation of hate speech with the constitutional commitment to freedom of expression by limiting the scope of the restriction to a narrow category of extreme or hateful speech that is intended and likely to stir up hatred in the community. However, there are at least two difficulties with the way in which the courts have justified hate speech laws. First, if hate speech causes harm by persuading its audience of the truth of certain ideas, then its restriction may be incompatible with a commitment to freedom of expression. As earlier noted, a commitment to free speech means that the speaker cannot be held responsible for any unlawful or anti-social action the audience may take in response to her speech – that speech cannot ordinarily be treated as a cause of audience behaviour. Second, if hate speech does cause or lead to hatred in the community, it can only do so as part of a systemic practice. No one instance of hateful speech will lead to hatred. The spread of hateful attitudes can only occur through the repetition of extreme racist claims and perhaps, also, less extreme forms of racial stereotyping. It may be difficult then to isolate a narrow category of extreme speech (speech that causes harm) for restriction.

---

[73] Judith Butler, *Excitable Speech* (Routledge, 1997) at 100. And at 80, "racist speech could not act as racist speech if it were not a citation of itself; only because we already know its force from prior instances do we know it to be so offensive now, and we brace ourselves against its future invocations".

[74] *Turley v. ISG Lackawanna Inc.*, No. 1:2006-cv-00794, Doc. 251 (WDNY), in which an African-American employee was awarded damages after experiencing years of racist harassment at the workplace. Regarding schools and universities, see Richard Moon, "Demonstrations on campus and the case of Israeli Apartheid Week", in James L. Turk (ed.), *Academic Freedom in Conflict: The Struggle over Free Speech Rights in the University* (James Lorimer, 2014). There is also an argument, although one contested by many, that insults should be restricted in general discourse when they are extreme – when they are vitriolic in tone. An extreme insult might also be viewed as a threat – or at least as an assertion that group members should be treated in a harsh or violent way.

1 The Constitutionality of the Criminal Ban on Hate Speech: *R.* v. *Keegstra*

In *R.* v. *Keegstra*, the leading Canadian hate speech case, the Supreme Court of Canada held that the *Criminal Code* ban on the "wilful promotion of hatred" was a justified limit on the freedom of expression right in the *Charter of Rights*.[75] In 1968, James Keegstra was hired to teach at the public high school in the town of Eckville, Alberta. Initially he taught auto mechanics – the subject area in which he was qualified to teach – but a few years later he was invited to teach a social studies course in the school.[76] He continued to teach this course for more than a decade. During this time, he taught his students about a conspiracy by the Jews to under-mine Christian civilization. He taught them that the banking system, the media, Hollywood, the universities, most publishers, most of the churches, and almost all political leaders were agents of this conspiracy. He told his students that Jews were "treacherous", "subversive", "sadistic", "money-loving", "power hungry", and "child killers".[77] In his teaching, he made use of a variety of anti-Semitic tracts, including *The Protocols of the Elders of Zion*.[78] He used the teacher's punishment and reward powers to ensure that his students parroted his ideas. Students who did not adopt, or acquiesce in, his views did poorly in his class.

When his teaching finally became a public issue, Keegstra was dismissed from his position at the school. A year later he was charged under section 319(2) of the *Criminal Code* with wilfully promoting hatred. At his trial, Keegstra challenged the constitutionality of section 319(2), arguing that it violated his freedom of expression under s. 2(b) of the *Charter of Rights*. Chief Justice Dickson, writing for the major-ity of the Supreme Court of Canada, held that section 319(2) restricted expression and so breached s. 2(b). However, he found that the restriction was justified under section 1, the *Charter's* limitation provision, because its purpose – to prevent the spread of hatred in the community – was "substantial and compelling" and because it limited only a narrow category of extreme speech that "strays some distance from the spirit of section 2(b)".[79] Justice McLachlin, in her dissenting judgment, agreed that preventing the spread of hateful ideas was an important public purpose but did not accept that the criminal prohibition advanced this purpose effectively or at minimal cost to freedom of expression.

---

75 *R.* v. *Keegstra* (n. 1).

76 David Bercuson and Douglas Wertheimer, *A Trust Betrayed: The Keegstra Affair* (Doubleday, 1985) at 17.

77 Bercuson and Wertheimer (n. 76) at 19: "James Keegstra is a true believer. There is no evidence that he was, or is, at all cynical about the message of hate he taught in the classroom. He lives in an imaginary world run by Jewish conspirators who exist behind the scenes in a variety of guises controlling and manipulating the events which determine the course of human history."

78 *The Protocols of the Elders of Zion* (1903). For a discussion, see Stephen Eric Bronner, *A Rumor about the Jews: Reflections on Antisemitism and the Protocols of the Learned Elders of Zion* (St. Martin's Press, 2000).

79 *Keegstra* (n. 1) at para. 99.

At the outset of his section 1 (limitations) analysis, Chief Justice Dickson identified two "very real harms" caused by hate speech.[80] He noted first the emotional or psychological injury experienced by the members of the target group. According to Dickson CJ, the "derision, hostility and abuse encouraged by hate propaganda" negatively affect the members of the group because their "sense of human dignity and belonging to the community at large is closely linked to the concern and respect accorded to the groups" with which they identify.[81] Because an individual's identity is partly constituted by association and interaction with others, he or she experiences attacks on the group(s) to which he or she belongs personally and sometimes very deeply. The second injury or harm identified by Dickson CJ is the harm that hate speech does to "society at large."[82] If members of the larger community are persuaded by the message of hate speech, they may engage in acts of violence and discrimination, causing "serious discord" in the community.[83]

Chief Justice Dickson was prepared to say that hate speech causes or contributes to the spread of hatred in the community because he was sceptical about the role of reason in the communicative process, at least in certain circumstances. He repeated the Cohen Commission's observation that "individuals can be persuaded to believe almost anything if the information or ideas are communicated using the right technique and in the proper circumstances."[84] The Chief Justice also found that the restriction was narrowly drawn in scope and therefore limited in its impact on freedom of expression. He emphasized that the restriction applies only when an individual wilfully *promotes* hatred.[85] To promote hatred, the *actus reus* of the offence, involves more than simple encouragement: It is to actively support or instigate hateful views. Dickson CJ accepted that the causal link between a particular act of expression and the generation of hatred in the community may be difficult to establish.[86] To require "direct proof" of a causal link "between a specific statement and hatred of an identifiable group" would, in the Chief Justice's view, severely limit the effectiveness of the ban. Instead the issue for the court is whether the speech creates a "risk of harm" – and, more particularly, whether it is the kind of speech that might lead to the spread of hatred.[87]

As well, the speaker must *wilfully* promote hatred ("subjectively desire the promotion of hatred"), or he must recognize that the promotion of hatred is the likely consequence of his expression – that it is "certain or substantially certain" to result

---

[80] *Keegstra* (n. 1) at para. 64.   [81] *Keegstra* (n. 1) at para. 65.   [82] *Keegstra* (n. 1) at para. 66.

[83] *Keegstra* (n. 1) at para. 66.   [84] *Keegstra* (n. 1) at para. 66.

[85] *Keegstra* (n. 1) at para. 117: "It is clear that the word 'wilfully' imports a difficult burden for the Crown to meet and in so doing serves to minimize the impairment of freedom of expression".

[86] See also *Mugesera* (n. 14) at para. 102: "The intention of Parliament was to prevent the risk of serious harm and not merely to target actual harm caused. The risk of hatred caused by hate propaganda is very real."

[87] *Keegstra* (n. 1) at para. 119.

from the speech.[88] As the Court noted in the later judgment of *Mugesera* v. *Canada*, "[a]lthough the causal connection need not be proven, the speaker must desire that the message stir up hatred".[89] The Chief Justice accepted that, when deciding if the accused intended to promote hatred, "the trier will usually make an inference as to the necessary *mens rea* based upon the statements made."[90] In other words, the court will generally look to the content and tone of the speech, as well as its intended audience, when determining whether the speaker intended to stir up hatred.[91] But if, as Chief Justice Dickson acknowledged (when discussing the *actus reus* of the offence), it is difficult to establish a link between speech and the promotion of hatred (the inculcation or reinforcement of racist attitudes among the audience), how can it ever be said that the speaker foresaw that hatred was substantially certain to result from his or her speech? A speaker may sometimes intend to spread hatred, but can he or she ever be certain about the impact of his or her speech?

Finally, Chief Justice Dickson thought that s. 319(2) did not interfere with freedom of expression in a significant way because the provision restricts only a narrow category of "extreme" expression (that causes or is likely to cause hatred) and does not catch expression that is merely unpopular or unconventional.[92] According to Dickson C.J., the term "hatred" connotes "emotion of an intense and extreme nature that is clearly associated with vilification and detestation" and so "[o]nly the most intense forms of dislike fall within the ambit of this offence."[93] Hatred "belies reason" and when directed against the members of an identifiable group, it signals that they are to be "despised, scorned, denied respect, and made subject to ill-treatment" because of their group membership.[94]

The Court's focus on the character of the speech (is it hateful in content or tone?), rather than on its demonstrable impact (does it stir up hatred and encourage extreme action?), rests on an assumption that extreme speech causes extreme beliefs and actions. The Court avoids the question of whether less extreme forms of bigoted speech might contribute in some way to the spread of hatred in the community.

2 The Constitutionality of Human Rights Code Regulation – *CHRC* v. *Taylor* and *Whatcott* v. *Sask HRC*

John Ross Taylor and his organization, the Western Guard, operated a telephone hate line for several years. Members of the public who dialed a telephone number

---

[88] *Keegstra* (n. 1) at para. 120. It is sufficient, according to Dickson CJ., if the speaker intends or foresees "as substantially certain, a direct and active stimulation of hatred against an identifiable group." In R. v. *Buzzanga and Durocher* (1979), 49 CCC (2d) 369, the Ontario Court of Appeal said that an individual will be found to have breached s. 319(2) only if he or she has, as a conscious purpose, the promotion of hatred against the identifiable group, or foresees that the promotion of hatred against that group is certain to result from the communication.

[89] *Mugesera* (n. 13) at para. 104.   [90] *Keegstra* (n. 1) at para. 122.

[91] The Supreme Court of Canada in *Mugesera* (n. 13), at para. 103, described the elements of the s. 319(2) offence of wilfully promoting hatred, noting that the analysis must look at the speech in "its social and historical context".

[92] *Keegstra* (n. 1), at para. 121.   [93] *Keegstra* (n. 1), at para. 121.   [94] *Keegstra* (n. 1), at para. 121.

that was publicized by Mr. Taylor's organization would hear a short pre-recorded anti-Semitic message. In 1979 a complaint was made against Taylor under s. 13 of the *CHRA*.[95] The CHRT decided that Taylor's messages breached the section, and issued a cease and desist order against him. Mr. Taylor nevertheless continued to operate the hate line and, as a result, was found in contempt of court and sentenced to one year in prison.[96] Following his release from prison, he re-established the phone line and the CHRC again commenced contempt proceedings against him. However, in 1982, shortly before the second contempt proceeding, the *Canadian Charter of Rights and Freedoms* came into force. Mr. Taylor argued at that proceeding that section 13 was now unconstitutional, because it violated section 2(b) of the *Charter* and could not be justified under section 1.

In upholding section 13 of the *CHRA* as a justified limit on freedom of expression, Chief Justice Dickson followed a line of reasoning similar to that he adopted in the *Keegstra* decision. He noted the "substantial psychological distress" caused by hate speech and the "damaging consequences" that such speech can have for the target group members, including "loss of self-esteem, feelings of anger and outrage and strong pressure to renounce cultural differences that mark them as distinct."[97] He further noted that hate speech may "convince listeners, even if subtlely, that members of certain racial or religious groups are inferior", resulting in acts of discrimination and even violence.[98] As in *Keegstra*, he interpreted the scope of the s. 13 ban narrowly so that it was limited to extreme speech that stirred up hatred.[99] He reiterated that hatred involves "unusually strong and deep-felt emotions of detestation, calumny and vilification": It "allows for no 'redeeming qualities' in the person".[100]

There was, however, an important difference between the criminal and human rights bans on hate speech. Section 13, in contrast to the *Criminal Code* ban, did not require proof of an intention to spread hatred. As Chief Justice Dickson observed, the focus of the section "is solely upon likely effects, it being irrelevant whether an individual wishes to expose persons to hatred or contempt on the basis of their race or religion."[101] In *Keegstra*, Dickson CJ decided that the *Criminal Code* ban on hate speech was a justified restriction on freedom of expression, because it extended only to speech that *wilfully* promotes hatred. Nevertheless, in the *Taylor* decision, he held that the absence of an intention requirement did not undermine the constitutionality of section 13, because the purpose of human rights legislation is to "compensate and protect" the victim rather than to "stigmatize or punish" the person who has discriminated.[102] Even though "the section may impose a slightly broader limit upon freedom of expression than does section 319(2) of the *Criminal Code* . . . the

---

95 *Canada (HRC)* v. *Taylor* [1990] 3 S.C.R. 892.
96 The tribunal's order may be filed with the Federal Court and enforced as a court order: *CHRA* (n. 19) s. 57.
97 *Taylor* (n. 95) at para. 40.   98 *Taylor* (n. 95), at para. 40.
99 At the same time, he acknowledged that "the nature of human rights legislation militates against an unduly narrow reading of section 13(1)". (*Taylor*, n. 95, at para. 59.)
100 *Taylor* (n. 95), at para. 61.   101 *Taylor* (n. 95), at para. 66.   102 *Taylor* (n. 95), at para. 70.

conciliatory bent of a human rights statute renders such a limit more acceptable than would be the case with a criminal provision."[103]

As a practical matter, it is hard to imagine hatred being stirred up unintentionally or unwittingly. It seems likely that someone who expressed extreme views and succeeded in stirring up hatred intended to do so, or at least recognized this as the possible outcome of his or her speech. Indeed, in all of the cases in which the CHRT found a breach of section 13, the expression was so extreme that it is unlikely that the addition of an intention or knowledge requirement would have led to a different result. In many of these cases the call for violence against the target group – most often Jews – was explicit.[104]

In the more recent decision of *Whatcott* v. *Saskatchewan Human Rights Commission*, the Supreme Court of Canada found that the hate speech ban in the *Saskatchewan Human Rights Code* was, with one correction, compatible with the *Charter of Rights*.[105] Section 14 (1) (b) of the Saskatchewan *Code* prohibits signs and other forms of representation that "exposed or tended to expose to hatred . . . a person or class of persons based on one of the prohibited grounds" (which included race, ethnicity, gender, sexual orientation, and disability).[106] The section, though, also prohibits speech that "ridicules, belittles or affronts the dignity" of a person based on such grounds, and the Court decided that this element of the ban could not be sustained under the *Charter* and severed it from the rest of the section.

In upholding the remainder of the ban, the Court followed its earlier decision in *Taylor* v. *CHRC*.[107] Justice Rothstein, writing for the Court, noted that the harm of hate speech goes beyond the "emotional distress" caused to individual group members. Hate speech, he said, has a "societal impact": "If a group of people are considered inferior, sub-human, or lawless, it is easier to justify denying the group and its members equal rights or status."[108] In this way, hate speech "lays the groundwork for later, broad attacks on vulnerable groups [which] can range from discrimination to ostracism, segregation, violence and, in the most extreme cases, to genocide."[109] It "seeks to de-legitimize group members in the eyes of the majority, reducing their social standing and acceptance in society" and making it "easier to justify discriminatory treatment".[110]

Rothstein J. confirmed that the test for whether speech is likely to "stir up hatred", and therefore breach the code's hate speech ban, "is whether a reasonable person aware of the context and circumstances surrounding the expression, would view it as exposing the protected group to hatred."[111] His reliance on a reasonable person standard allowed him to avoid or obscure the two main challenges confronting any form of hate speech regulation: (i) the difficulty in establishing a causal link between

---

[103] *Taylor* (n. 95), at para. 61.   [104] Moon, *Report to the CHRC* (n. 15) at 35.
[105] *Whatcott* v. *Saskatchewan HRC* (n. 71). The facts of the case are discussed more fully in c. 5.
[106] *Saskatchewan Human Rights Code* (n. 24).   [107] *Taylor* (n. 95).
[108] *Whatcott* (n. 71), at para. 74.   [109] *Whatcott* (n. 71), at para. 74.
[110] *Whatcott* (n. 71), at para. 71.   [111] *Whatcott* (n. 71), at para. 56.

hate speech and the spread of hatred in the community (and the occurrence of harmful action) and (ii) the difficulty in distinguishing extreme speech, which is subject to restriction, from other, less extreme forms of speech. He recognized that it is unrealistic to expect proof of "a precise causal link" between the speech and harm and that instead common sense and experience (of the reasonable person) must serve to establish the connection in a particular case.[112] The decision-maker must look at the content and tone of the speech – the use of inflammatory and derogatory language – to determine whether the speech is likely to encourage hatred in the audience.

Justice Rothstein emphasized that the ban catches only a narrow category of extreme expression – speech that vilifies the members of a group, attributing to them "disgusting characteristics, inherent deficiencies, or immoral propensities".[113] The ban, said Justice Rothstein, does not extend to speech that merely discredits, humiliates, or offends the members of a group. Drawing on the jurisprudence of the CHRT, he identified certain "hallmarks of hate" (indicators of extreme speech), such as portraying a group as "a powerful menace that is taking control of the major institutions in society and depriving others of their livelihoods, safety, freedom of speech and general well-being", or "as preying upon children", or as responsible "for the current problems in society and the world", or "as dangerous or violent by nature, devoid of any redeeming qualities and ... innately evil", or as like "animals, vermin, excrement, and other noxious substances".[114] The various hallmarks of hatred set out by Rothstein J. involve claims about the inferiority or dangerousness of the target group that may encourage or reinforce hateful views among the audience, and lead to acts of violence and discrimination against the group's members. Despite Justice Rothstein's assertion that the ban does not target the "ideas" expressed but simply the "mode" of their public expression, these claims ("hallmarks of hatred") express extreme or hateful ideas about the members of certain groups.[115]

In both the *Whatcott* and *Taylor* decisions, there is a tension between the Supreme Court's broad description of the purpose of the human rights code ban on hate speech and its narrow definition of the scope of the ban. The purpose of the ban, according to the Court, is to prohibit speech that negatively affects the dignity or status of the members of an identifiable group and is tied to the code's larger purpose of "prevent[ing] the spread of prejudice and ... foster[ing] tolerance and equality in the community."[116] But if the purpose of the ban is understood in such broad terms, it is difficult to see why its scope should be confined to extreme or hateful expression. Speech that encourages feelings of dislike and suspicion may also lead to acts of discrimination. Group stereotyping, for example, may have a

---

[112] *Whatcott* (n. 71), at para. 132.   [113] *Whatcott* (n. 71), at para. 57.
[114] *Whatcott* (n. 71), at paras. 44, 45.   [115] *Whatcott* (n. 71), at para. 51.
[116] *Taylor* (n. 95), at para. 37.

damaging impact on the group's standing in the community and may encourage discriminatory treatment of its members.[117]

The Court in *Whatcott* tried in several ways to reconcile its narrow reading of the scope of the ban (limited to extreme speech) with its broad definition of the ban's purpose. According to the Court, less extreme forms of bigoted speech (such as stereotypes) may cause offense to the members of the targeted group, but do not contribute to the "objective" harm of discrimination. But offence and discrimination are not mutually exclusive injuries or effects – one is the subjective impact of the speech on the target group members and the other is the apparent (objective) impact of the speech on social relations in the community. The same speech act can both offend group members and disrupt social relations. Racial stereotypes are not just offensive to the members of the stereotyped group. They may also encourage or justify discriminatory treatment of the group's members. A second way in which the Court tried to confine the law's application to extreme expression was to describe the harm of hate speech in societal terms and assume that only extreme speech will have such a significant (society-wide) impact. And yet the opposite may be true. Extreme racist claims are dismissed by most people as bizarre and offensive. Such claims are less likely to spread throughout society and lead to systemic exclusion or discrimination. More moderate claims, on the other hand, may have a greater societal impact. Racial stereotypes about intelligence, for example, may shape the social perception of a particular group and contribute to its marginalization.

C Agency and Autonomy

There are two difficulties with the Canadian courts' attempt to reconcile the regulation of hate speech with the right to freedom of expression. The first concerns the claim that there is a causal link between the expression of hateful views and the spread of hatred (and acts of racial discrimination and violence) in the community. The second concerns the claim or assumption that it is possible to isolate for restriction a narrow category of extreme speech that reinforces, or contributes to, hatred in the community. In the Canadian courts' view, less extreme forms of speech may cause offence to the target group or encourage dislike of the group, but do not stir up hatred and so do not fall within the scope of the ban.

If some individuals are persuaded by views they hear or read and then act on these views, doing harm to others, then we might say that the expression has "caused" the harmful action. However, under most accounts of freedom of expression, the state is not justified in restricting expression simply because it causes harm in this way, by

---

[117] See Moon, *Report to the CHRC* (n. 15). A narrowly drawn ban on hate speech that focuses on extreme expression does not fit easily or simply into a human rights law that takes an expansive view of discrimination and emphasizes the effect of the action on the victim rather than the intention or misconduct of the actor.

persuading its audience. The listeners, as autonomous actors, are responsible for the judgments they make and the actions they take.[118] Indeed, as the courts recognize, it is difficult to prove the impact of expression on the attitudes and actions of audience members, who may understand, evaluate, and react to the communication in different ways based on their personal values and experiences. The familiar freedom of expression position is that ideas cannot be censored simply because we fear that some members of the community may find them persuasive, or that these ideas may negatively affect an individual's self-understanding or self-esteem. It is often said that we should respond to racist claims not with censorship, but by offering competing views (more speech) that make the case for equal respect, or by creating more avenues for marginalized groups to express themselves.

Faith in human reason underlies most accounts of freedom of expression and cannot simply be cut out and discarded from the analysis. Upon what is our commitment to freedom of expression based, if not on a belief in human reason and its power to recognize truth? What restrictions on expression are not acceptable once we have lost faith in human reason? If we are unwilling to trust, or give space to, individual judgment and public reason, then the question of censorship will turn simply on whether the particular expression conveys a good or bad message or whether the public acceptance of the message will have good or bad consequences. But this amounts to a rejection of freedom of expression as a political or constitutional principle. A commitment to freedom of expression means protecting expression for reasons more basic than our agreement with its message – for reasons independent of its content.

The censorship of hate speech rests on a concern that racist speech, and more particularly the advocacy of racial exclusion or violence, will not always fall on deaf ears. The courts are willing to treat the person expressing hateful views as responsible for the spread of hatred and for increases in racist violence because they are skeptical that the audience will always exercise rational judgment when assessing these views. We should not, said Chief Justice Dickson in the *Keegstra* decision, "overplay the view that rationality will overcome all falsehoods in the unregulated marketplace of ideas."[119] Dickson CJ thought that "the greater the degree of certainty that a statement is erroneous or mendacious, the less its value in the quest for truth."[120] The Cohen Commission had expressed a similar view in its report recommending the criminalization of hate promotion:

[W]e are less confident in the 20th century that the critical faculties of individuals will be brought to bear on the speech and writing which is directed at

---

[118] L.W. Sumner, *The Hateful and the Obscene: Studies in the Limits of Free Expression* (University of Toronto Press, 2004) at 34: "Even when it promises to be effective in preventing some significant social harm, censorship abridges personal liberty and deprives consumers of whatever benefits they may derive from the prohibited forms of expression."

[119] *Keegstra* (n. 1), at para. 92.   [120] *Keegstra* (n. 1), at para. 92.

them . . . While holding that over the long run, the human mind is repelled by blatant falsehood and seeks the good, it is too often true, in the short run, that emotion displaces reason and individuals perversely reject the demonstrations of truth put before them and forsake the good they know.[121]

The challenge for the courts is to determine when the risk of harm is so great – or when the space for independent judgment by the audience is so limited – that the speaker should be held at least partly responsible for the encouragement of bigoted attitudes and harmful actions.

At the core of hate speech is a claim that is false – that denies the equal worth or basic dignity of some individuals based on their race (or other identity or association), or, more often, that falsely attributes dangerous or undesirable traits to the members of such a group.[122] The claim that the members of a racial group are inherently inferior or dangerous is inconsistent with the principle of human equality that underpins political society and is entrenched in the constitution. Speech that challenges public values and commitments must, of course, be protected from censorship. This protection, though, should not be extended to speech that vilifies or stirs up hatred against the members of a group, and might lead to extreme or radical action against them.[123]

---

[121] Cohen Commission (n. 12), at 8: "The successes of modern advertising, the triumph of impudent propaganda such as Hitler's, have qualified sharply our belief in the rationality of man. We know that under strain and pressure in times of irritation and frustration, the individual is swayed and even swept away by hysterical, emotional appeals. We act irresponsibly if we ignore the way in which emotion can drive reason from the field". The Report continues: "The readiness with which millions can be reached with messages of every kind is a changed circumstance of importance. Radio, television, motion pictures, the pervasiveness of print are new elements in the 20th century which the classic supporters of free speech never had to reckon with".

[122] In *R. v. Zundel* [1992] 2 SCR 731 at 754, McLachlin J. claimed that lies may sometimes have value. Even if this is true, her examples of potentially valuable lies are troubling: "Exaggeration – even clear falsification – may arguably serve useful social purposes linked to the values underlying freedom of expression. A person fighting cruelty against animals may knowingly cite false statistics in pursuit of his or her beliefs and with the purpose of communicating a more fundamental message, e.g., 'cruelty to animals is increasing and must be stopped'. A doctor, in order to persuade people to be inoculated against a burgeoning epidemic, may exaggerate the number or geographical location of persons potentially infected with the virus. An artist, for artistic purposes, may make a statement that a particular society considers both an assertion of fact and a manifestly deliberate lie; consider the case of Salman Rushdie's *The Satanic Verses*, viewed by many Muslim societies as perpetrating deliberate lies against the Prophet." These lies may seem valuable to McLachlin J. because she is sympathetic to the ends the liar seeks to achieve. But, as is the case with all lies, they involve an injury to the listener and an undermining of the relationship of communication.

[123] The Court in *Whatcott* (n. 71) at para. 42 does not think that hate speech is necessarily false because the Court does not think that such speech involves a claim or proposition: "While hate speech often uses the device of inflammatory falsehoods and misrepresentations to persuade and galvanize its audience, the use of such tools is not necessary to a finding that the expression exposes its targeted group to hatred." Yet hate speech always involves a claim, either explicit or implicit, about the inferiority or undesirability of the members of a particular group. This claim must be viewed as false, if we are committed to the idea of human equality – and the basic dignity of all persons.

Hate speech is not restricted simply because its central claim or idea is untrue and contrary to equality values. The form of hate speech, the nature of its appeal, and the circumstances in which it most often occurs all contribute to the case for restriction. When expressed with great anger, the claim that a particular group represents a threat to society is more likely to stir anger and fear in the audience. This is the point made by Mark Freiman: "While a broad range, especially of political expression, may contain both intellectual and emotive content, what separates hate speech from other types of political communication, is that it is pitched to an emotion that is intrinsically dangerous."[124] The visceral appeal of hate speech may fuel anger and resentment and may discourage careful, dispassionate assessment of its claims by audience members.[125]

While the tone of the communication – the anger in its message or its appeal to fear – contributes to its impact on the audience, too great a focus on tone may encourage a misleading impression that the harm or wrong of hate speech is offence. Indeed, critics of hate speech regulation often describe the wrong in such terms (as offence to the target group's members) and then proceed to make the point that offence is a subjective matter and as such cannot be the basis for a legal ban on speech. Hate speech, though, is objectionable not because it is offensive (which it is) but rather because it contributes to the spread of hateful ideas in the community.

Hate speech law bans certain claims about the inferiority or dangerousness of a group when they are expressed in a way that stirs fear and anger and discourages independent judgment. The audience will be less critical of speech that provides a channel for its anxieties and resentments (e.g., about moral decay or terrorism) and purports to explain its economic and social difficulties. The idea of race – of significant natural group differences – is deeply embedded in our culture, its linguistic forms, and popular concepts. Hate speech builds on more mainstream, less extreme, forms of racist thought and speech. While most members of the community will dismiss the extreme claims of hate-mongers such as Keegstra and Taylor as bizarre and irrational, some individuals, already weighed down by prejudice, may see in these claims a plausible account of their social and economic disappointments and perhaps also a justification for violent action.

Hate speech generally occurs at the margins of public discourse, where the opportunity for response or engagement is limited. It is often directed at the members of a relatively insular racist subculture, who are uninterested in exposing themselves to other views.[126] When directed at such an audience, extreme speech may reinforce

---

[124] Mark Freiman, "Hate Speech and the Reasonable Supreme Court of Canada" (2013) 63 S.C.L.R. (2d) 295 at 304.

[125] Moreover, the growth of advertising as the model or norm for contemporary speech, in which the speaker makes a visceral or non-rational appeal and seeks to impact rather than persuade the audience, may have dulled our capacity or reduced our opportunity to reflect critically on the claims made.

[126] Moon, *Report to the CHRC* (n. 15), at 29 and Moon, *The Constitutional Protection of Freedom of Expression* (n. 32), at 142.

and extend bigoted views without being subjected to public criticism. Certainly, the assumption that the individual will be exposed to a range of views, enabling him or her to make an informed and independent judgment, seems increasingly strained with the growth in audience fragmentation – particularly on the Internet, which has become the principal vehicle for the expression of hate speech. L.W. Sumner notes that neo-Nazi and other racist material is often circulated through websites "not to contribute to a broad debate concerning Jews, blacks, or gays" but instead "to reinforce the shared ideology that binds the group together and to recruit new group members".[127] In such a community, the "ideology" is a "call to action" that does not "merely legitimize or endorse violence" against target groups, but may also "encourage or even instigate it."[128]

The Internet offers a low-cost way to communicate with a potentially large audience. It enables individuals and groups with common interests to connect with one another, even when they are geographically remote. Individuals can access material on the Internet easily and without personal risk. These attributes have made the Internet a key source of information for members of the public and an important communication vehicle for individuals who do not have the resources to reach an audience through the traditional media. The Internet has, because of these characteristics, been described as a democratic medium – and an important alternative to the traditional media. These characteristics have also made the Internet the preferred medium for hate promoters. The Internet's complex public and private character makes it a potent vehicle for the promotion and reinforcement of hateful views. Because the Internet audience is highly fragmented, it is easy for a particular website to avoid critical public scrutiny. While most websites are public in the sense that they are generally accessible, the audience for a particular site is often self-selecting and sometimes quite small. Smaller hate sites (or those that are less easily accessed, such as chat rooms) that link like-minded individuals are able to encourage a sense of intimacy and identity and to operate below the radar. These sites may be an effective means for individuals and groups who hold hateful views to encourage others to adopt more extreme views or to take radical action, without exposing themselves to a broad and potentially critical audience.[129] Speaking in a "safe place", free from challenge, may also encourage speakers to express more extreme views and even perhaps to believe more strongly in the views they are expressing.

The early proponents of hate speech bans in the post-WWII period recognized that a campaign of hate propaganda could lead to widespread violence against the

---

[127] Sumner (n. 118), at 162.   [128] Sumner (n. 118), at 163.

[129] Danielle Keats Citron, *Hate Crimes in Cyberspace* (Harvard University Press, 2014) at 63, referring to the work of Magdalena Wojcieszak, who interviewed a number of individuals who posted on neo-Nazi websites. She notes that "although extreme people tend to turn to radical groups in the first place, their participation in on-line hate groups nudges them to greater extremes". And at 63, "Learning that others share their worldviews boosts their confidence". See also Cass R. Sunstein, *Republic.com 2.0* (Princeton University Press, 2007) at 60.

members of a target group. The Nazi campaign against the Jews provided horrify-
ing evidence of this. The promotion of hatred against an identifiable group should
be prohibited, according to the Cohen Commission, because "in times of stress
such 'hate' could mushroom into a real and monstrous threat to our way of life".[130]
If the purpose of hate speech law is to prevent the spread of hateful views across
the community, then the size of the audience for a particular communication may
be a relevant, even significant, consideration in the ban's enforcement. The larger
the audience for the speech, the greater will be its potential for harm. Indeed,
hate speech prohibitions generally apply only to speech that occurs in "public", or in
the words of s. 319(2) of the *Criminal Code*, "other than in private conversation". On
this view, then, speech that occurs outside mainstream discourse (that takes place
at the margins), among a small, sympathetic audience, may have a limited impact
and its harm may be minor.[131]

Yet, in the next section, I will argue that hate speech law may be ineffective, and
perhaps even counter-productive, in suppressing widely expressed racist views.[132]
The irony of hate speech law is that it cannot effectively address bigoted views
that are part of mainstream discourse. The primary concern of contemporary hate
speech law must instead be to prevent the encouragement of "isolated" acts of violence against members of an identifiable group, acts such as gay-bashing or fire-
bombing a synagogue. Hate crimes are committed most often not by organized
groups, but by individuals who have immersed themselves in an extremist subculture that operates at the margins of public discourse, and principally on the Internet. If the purpose of hate speech law is (also) to prevent the expression of extreme
claims about racial or religious groups that may influence some to engage in violence against the members of these groups, then audience size is less important.
Indeed, hate speech will be more effective when directed at a smaller, selected
audience. While it is unlikely that a large group of individuals will be encouraged
by hateful/extreme speech to commit violent acts (the risk of many people being
influenced by this speech is low) the risk or likelihood of an individual – "a lone
wolf" – or small group taking action is significant. On this view, the requirement

---

[130] Cohen Commission (n. 12), at 24. A familiar civil libertarian argument against hate speech laws is
that such laws existed in the German Weimar Republic, yet did nothing to prevent the spread of anti-
Semitism and the Nazi rise to power. The Weimar Republic argument is made by the former General Counsel of the Canadian Civil Liberties Association, Alan Borovoy, in his book *When Freedoms
Collide* (Lester, Orpen Dennys, 1988) at 50.

[131] Michel Rosenfeld, "Hate Speech in Constitutional Jurisprudence: A Comparative Analysis", in Herz
and Molnar (n. 58), at 244: "it is primarily opponents of government and, in the majority of cases,
members of marginalized groups with scant hope of achieving political power that engage in hate
speech".

[132] Sumner (n. 118), at 194: "Because the groups most responsible for these messages operate clandestinely
on the margins of Canadian society, they are likely to have little influence on mainstream public
opinion. It might well be that the principal consequence of allowing them to voice their views openly
and frankly, without codes and subtexts, would be to marginalize and discredit them further."

included in most hate speech laws that the speech be public may not be an element of the wrong, but simply a constraint on the scope of legal regulation, based on concerns about state intrusion into private life.[133]

Hate speech does not simply or directly cause the audience to think and act in a hateful way towards others. However, a court may decide that a particular type or instance of bigoted speech creates a significant risk of harm (a risk that may be viewed as the speaker's responsibility) when it thinks that the audience's opportunity to critically assess the speaker's false and extreme claims is limited by the form of his or her speech and the circumstances in which it occurs.[134] The extreme claims that are caught by the ban on hate speech often play to fear and resentment – appealing to the audience on a visceral level. They are often directed at a sympathetic audience in a context that limits the opportunity for debate and reflection. In such circumstances, some in the audience may take seriously the message of hate speech and follow its logic to a violent conclusion.

D *Line Drawing and the Systemic Problem of Prejudice*

Even if we accept that hate speech encourages hateful views and actions in the community, it is difficult to see how a single/particular instance of bigoted or hateful expression might do so. If speech does "cause" harm – if it does in some sense lead audience members to hate others or to engage in acts of discrimination and violence – it can only do so as part of a systemic practice. No one instance of expression leads to hatred; but a wide range of bigoted representations (some extreme and some more temperate and even commonplace) may contribute to hateful attitudes and discriminatory actions in the community. It is difficult to imagine, for example, that the extreme views of Keegstra or Taylor would be taken seriously by anyone who was not already mired in prejudice. Hate speech will affect an audience only if it is able to build on more widely held racial stereotypes.

But if the spread of hatred is a systemic problem, it will be difficult to isolate a narrow category of *extreme* expression that causes or leads to hatred. Indeed, it is arguable that more moderate ("mainstream") forms of discriminatory speech may be more harmful because their audience is larger and their discriminatory message more insidious. For example, the claim or assumption that there are genetically based differences in intelligence between racial groups may have a significant impact on popular thinking and result in subtle and not so subtle acts of discrimination against a particular group and may, of course, also provide the grounding for more extreme claims about racial traits.

---

[133] The Internet makes possible a form of personal speech between strangers who may be like-minded but have no personal history or connection and may be geographically remote.

[134] An analogy is often made to pornography – but in fact the case is even stronger that pornography does not engage its audience in a way that justifies its protection as expression. For a discussion see Moon, *The Constitutional Protection* (n. 32), at 120–22.

Critics of hate speech law often point out how difficult it is to draw a line between extreme speech that should be restricted and other forms of speech (about race) that should be protected under freedom of expression.[135] Justice McLachlin, in her dissenting judgment in *Keegstra*, argued that the line separating hate speech from valuable forms of expression might be drawn in the wrong place so that expression that ought to be protected is not.[136] She further argued that even if the court managed to draw the line in the right place, the hate speech ban might have a "chilling effect" on legitimate expression: Some community members might be reluctant to publish material, even valuable material that should not, and probably would not, be restricted, because they are unwilling to take the risk that it might fall afoul of a criminal prohibition that does not have a clearly defined scope.[137] In support of her claim about the potential chilling effect of hate speech law, Madame Justice McLachlin noted that in the past, the criminal ban "had provoked many questionable actions on the part of the authorities".[138] For example, the novels *The Haj* by Leon Uris and *The Satanic Verses* by Salman Rushdie were investigated and temporarily interfered with under Canadian customs regulations.[139] Even though it was decided, following investigation, that neither book fell within the scope of the hate speech ban, McLachlin J. argued that the temporary interference with these books by customs officials illustrated the uncertain application of the restriction and helped to create a climate in which writers might have genuine concerns that their work could result in criminal punishment.

The way the line-drawing argument is stated, it sounds as if expression that has little or no value must be protected to ensure that valuable expression does not become vulnerable to censorship. The restriction of harmful or valueless expression puts at risk the protection of valuable expression. Keegstra's and Taylor's Jewish conspiracy claims must be protected, if we are to ensure that Leon Uris is not prevented or discouraged from publishing *The Haj*. But if Uris's expression is valuable and Keegstra's is not, why is it so difficult to draw a line between them? If hate speech has little or no value, then it should be possible to draw a line separating it from valuable forms of expression. I suspect that the line-drawing problem is not, as Justice McLachlin suggested, that the line between legitimate and illegitimate expression may be drawn in the wrong place by the police or the courts, or that, even if the line is drawn in the right place, it may have a chilling effect on legitimate expression. The

---

[135] The line-drawing argument often seems to substitute for a more direct claim that the freedom should protect the expression of all viewpoints, no matter how wrong or offensive.

[136] *Keegstra* (n. 1), at para. 283.

[137] For a critical discussion of the "chilling effect" doctrine see Lee C. Bollinger, *The Tolerant Society* (Oxford University Press, 1988). Bollinger goes on to argue that being required to tolerate extreme or anti-social speech will help to cultivate the social habit or public virtue of tolerance.

[138] *Keegstra* (n. 1), at para. 339.

[139] Leon Uris, *The Haj* (Corgi, 1984); Salman Rushdie, *The Satanic Verses* (Viking, 1988). These examples are taken from Borovoy (n. 130), at 43.

problem instead is that every act of expression may have value (contributing ideas and information and stimulating thought and judgment) but may also carry a risk of harm (as potentially misleading or manipulating). As earlier noted, in many freedom of expression cases, the courts must make a relative judgment about whether a particular form of expression (within a certain context) engages the audience in a way that ought to be protected – whether the speech encourages or discourages independent judgment.

There are differences between what Keegstra says and what Uris writes, but there are also some significant similarities. This is why the censorship of Keegstra's speech may put the writing of Uris at risk. Keegstra, in contrast to Uris, makes specific racist claims that are extreme and bizarre. But Uris's writing is most certainly not free of the taint of prejudice. Indeed, the writing of Uris builds ethnic/racial stereotypes into the characters and events of a fast-paced narrative. The Jewish characters in his book, *The Haj*, are heroic and honourable, while the Arab characters are cowardly and dishonest. In contrast to the Jewish characters, the Arabs in his story lie, cheat, rape, and attack for little or no reason. Yet these are just the attributes of the particular characters in a work of historical fiction. Uris seldom makes explicit claims about Jews and Arabs that are open to assessment or judgment by readers, although he does make a few, including the following: "The short fuse that every Arab carries in his gut had been ignited with consummate ease. Enraged mobs poured into the streets"; "The Bedouin was thief, assassin, raider and hard labour was immoral"; "So before I was nine I learned the basic canon of Arab life. It was me against my brother; me and my brother against my father; my family against my cousins and the clan; the clan against the tribe; and the tribe against the world".[140] Uris's writing supports and revitalizes ethnic/racial stereotypes not by argument or even assertion, but simply by weaving them into a "realistic" narrative that is read by a wide audience.

Is the answer simply to exclude both Keesgtra and Uris from the protection of freedom of expression? Keegstra makes racist claims that play on the fears and prejudices of some members of the community. Uris's narrative relies on ethnic and religious stereotypes that may encourage or reinforce racist attitudes. The line-drawing problem, however, is not resolved by redrawing the line in another place. The problem is much deeper than the unclear distinction between what Keegstra says and what Uris writes. Justice McLachlin has not simply chosen a bad example with *The Haj*. Racial and other stereotypes are so deeply entrenched in our culture, our language, and our thinking that it may be difficult to isolate clearly Keegstra's speech from mainstream discourse. A wide range of expression, both extreme and ordinary, conveys racist attitudes and contributes to the spread and reinforcement of racist opinion in the community. This is the real line-drawing problem.

Yet, at the same time, the recognition that line-drawing is a problem because racial and other stereotypes are pervasive may provide some support for the

---

[140] In *The Haj* (n. 139), at 89, 29, 25.

restriction of extreme speech. The line-drawing problem can be turned on its head once we understand why line-drawing is difficult. Keegstra's hate speech is continuous with (an extreme version of) the racial stereotypes that pervade mainstream discourse. His expression, though, may also be more dangerous because of the pervasiveness of these stereotypes. Keegstra's audience understands and evaluates his claims against this larger background of racist assumptions. The extreme claims of Keegstra build on the social background of racial stereotyping, of which Uris's novel *The Haj* is only a small part. Against this background, an extreme racist claim may seem plausible, even reasonable, to some in the audience. Extreme claims may resist critical evaluation because they give shape to popular, but inchoate, assumptions and attitudes. The prevalence of racist imagery and messages also means that the members of the target groups may have little space to define their public identity and to refute racist claims.

A narrowly drawn ban that prohibits only extreme speech may seem inadequate to those who are concerned about the persistence of prejudice and inequality in the community. Expression that stereotypes the members of a racial or other identifiable group is insulting and harmful to the group's members. Yet, because discriminatory views or assumptions are widely held and circulate generally in society, they cannot simply be removed through censorship. Any attempt to exclude all racial or other prejudice from public discourse would require extraordinary intervention by the state and would dramatically compromise the public commitment to freedom of expression. Because discriminatory speech is so commonplace, it is impossible to establish clear and effective rules for its identification and exclusion. Because discriminatory attitudes and assumptions are so pervasive, it is vital that they be confronted and contested in the public sphere – that they be treated as objectionable or erroneous political views that must be publicly addressed.

We must develop ways other than censorship to respond to expression that stereotypes or defames the members of an identifiable group. Even if we accept that ordinary or commonplace racist claims should be answered and not simply excised from public discourse, a sensitivity to the limits of reason, and to the insidious influence of racist stereotypes, should lead us to pay more attention to inequalities in communicative power. A laissez-faire approach to discriminatory speech fails the groups that are victimized and implicates the larger society in that victimization, because communicative power is so unevenly distributed in society. If more speech rather than censorship is the only viable response to mainstream forms of discriminatory expression, then we must ensure that there are effective opportunities to respond to this expression.[141]

Speech always carries the potential for harm. The difficult question is whether the speech is so harmful (or the risk of harm is so significant), and its value so limited,

---

[141] Groups within the community should have a real opportunity to respond to expression that is not so extreme that it violates criminal or human rights laws but may nevertheless affect their position within the larger community.

that it should be restricted, despite the public commitment to open debate and the practical limits of state censorship. Insults and threats directed at members of a target group – speech that harasses, denigrates, and humiliates – can be restricted for the kinds of reasons put forward by Jeremy Waldron.[142] Speech of this kind may offend, but it does more than that, particularly when it is part of a pattern of racist speech and violence. It undermines the group's standing or dignity within society and its ability to live within the community with any confidence about its safety or security. This speech is intended to abuse and intimidate rather than engage its audience. The scope of a restriction on this form of speech, though, is subject to a variety of practical limits based on concerns about state oversight of personal and public conversations and state policing of the conventions of social interaction.

However, a restriction on expression that is intended to persuade its audience that the members of a racial or other target group are dangerous or undesirable involves a more direct challenge to the public commitment to freedom of expression. It is not enough to assert that this speech may encourage or lead to the growth of discriminatory attitudes and actions. The argument for restriction must show that the speech is likely to stir up hatred, because it occurs in a form or context that discourages independent, critical judgment by the audience – that its appeal is more visceral than cognitive. The courts and other state actors must make a relative judgment about the character of the communicative engagement between speaker and audience – about whether the speech engages the audience in a way that deserves constitutional protection.[143]

The scope of the hate speech ban must be narrowly drawn so that it extends only to extreme speech – speech that either explicitly or implicitly advocates or justifies violent action against a particular group. Expression may be understood as justifying violence if its claims are so extreme that anyone who takes them seriously would reasonably conclude that violent action against the group was either necessary or appropriate. While it is unrealistic to expect that more familiar forms of discriminatory expression could be censored out of public discourse, the failure to ban the extreme or radical edge of prejudiced speech carries too many risks, particularly when it is directed at the members of a racist subculture or occurs in a context in which there is little opportunity for response. While the line will sometimes be difficult to draw, it is possible to identify factors that characterize extreme hate speech, the "hallmarks of hate", and to determine whether a particular instance of

---

[142] Waldron (n. 58). See also Bhikhu Parekh, "Is There a Case for Banning Hate Speech", in Herz and Molnar (n. 58), at 44: "[Hate speech] views members of the target group as an enemy within, refuses to accept them as legitimate and equal members of society, lowers their social standing, and in these and other ways subverts the very bases of shared life".

[143] They must mark the point (draw the line) at which speech ceases to appeal to independent judgment or conscious reflection and to be part of an open public discourse – the point at which speech no longer seeks to persuade or engage the audience. For a discussion see Moon, "Limits on Rights" (n. 48).

speech vilifies the members of a particular group and amounts to a call for violent or radical action against them. In contrast, it is impossible to know where, or even how, to draw a line separating racial (and other) stereotypes from ordinary public discourse, given the pervasiveness of racial and other forms of prejudice.

IV THE HATE SPEECH DEBATE

I am surprised sometimes by the fervour with which some individuals oppose all forms of hate speech regulation. In a few cases the opposition to hate speech regulation is simply a more palatable way of defending hate speech – the message it carries. Hatemongers have found it strategically useful to present themselves as defenders of free speech. The shift from advocate of hate to defender of free speech fits well with the hatemonger's self-understanding as a victim of state oppression and a defender of Western values against multiculturalism. More often, though, the opposition to hate speech regulation has a principled basis. There are many committed civil libertarians who regard hate speech as odious, but are nevertheless prepared to defend the right of others to engage in it. Their opposition to the restriction of hate speech rests on a commitment to individual liberty and a concern about the reach of state power. While I think that the civil libertarian position is mistaken, it is, of course, not without merit. What is perplexing though is the extraordinary energy that these advocates of free speech put into the fight against hate speech laws. They seem convinced that the integrity of the free speech edifice depends on holding the line here. Yet they seem indifferent to the more significant ways in which freedom of expression is being eroded in Western democracies. Whether by design or not, the obsessive opposition to hate speech regulation diverts our attention away from more fundamental free speech issues concerning the character and structure of public discourse, and more particularly the domination of public discourse by commercial messages and the advertising form (which seeks to influence audience behaviour without direct persuasion), the growth of audience fragmentation, and more generally the loss of discursive engagement in the community. But, of course, these are not issues that can be addressed by the courts, except in indirect ways, and that may partly explain the lack of attention they receive.

The public commitment to freedom of expression rests on a belief that humans are substantially rational beings capable of evaluating factual and other claims and an assumption that public discourse is open to a wide range of competing views that may be assessed by the audience. How should the courts and other public actors respond to concerns about the harm (and value) of hate speech, or commercial advertising, or pornography, or even political speech, when these assumptions about the rationality of discourse and the scope of communicative engagement seem increasingly to be eroded, not simply in limited situations of the sort described by Mill and other early defenders of free speech, but more broadly as the consequence of larger changes in the character of public discourse? What is the value of speech, if it serves only to reinforce the audience's existing views or to deceive or manipulate the audience, or to insult rather than persuade them? While the restriction of deceptive or hostile speech may not always be easy to reconcile with the commitment to free speech, simply carrying on as if we live in a world of rational discourse and open engagement may have considerable costs.

In the chapters that follow, I will explore the place of religion in the hate speech debate. Religion is almost invariably included as a protected ground in equality or anti-discrimination laws, including restrictions on hate speech. Religion, though, does not fit easily within the framework of such laws. The difficulty is that while religious membership may sometimes be viewed as a cultural or ethnic identity (and religious believers as a cultural community) that should be respected as a matter of equality, it may also be viewed as a personal commitment to a set of beliefs about what is true and right that must remain open to challenge and criticism, even that which is harsh in tone.

The focus in the next two chapters will be on the regulation of hate speech that targets a religious group or religious belief system and in particular Muslims and Islam. The final chapter of the book will consider the impact on hate speech law when religion is the source of views that are alleged to be hateful.

3

When Religious Groups are the Target of Hate Speech

Islamophobia and the Muslim Tide

INTRODUCTION

A *Religious Commitment and Identity*

Religion is viewed by the courts and other public institutions through two lenses. While religious commitment is sometimes viewed as an individual choice or judgment that is open to criticism and subject to revision, it is also, or sometimes instead, viewed as a cultural identity that involves rooted values and shared practices.[1]

The challenge for the courts (and other public institutions) has been to fit this complex conception of religious adherence (as a matter of both personal judgment and cultural identity) into a constitutional rights framework (and more broadly a liberal conception of rights) that draws a distinction between individual choices and commitments that should be protected as a matter of liberty (but subject to limits in the public interest), and individual or group attributes that should be respected as a matter of equality. The rights framework imposes this distinction between judgment and identity (choice and attribute) on the rich and complex experience of religious commitment.

Religious belief lies at the core of the individual's worldview. It orients individuals in the social world, shapes their perception of the natural order, and provides a moral framework for their actions. Religious commitment also ties individuals to a community of believers and is often the central or defining association in their lives. The individual adherent participates in a shared system of practices and values that may in some cases be described as "a way of life."

The idea of religion as a cultural identity lies behind the requirement that the state remain neutral in religious matters – a requirement that is understood to flow

---

[1] R. Moon, *Freedom of Conscience and Religion* (Irwin Law, 2014) and "Freedom of religion under the Charter of Rights: The limits of state neutrality" (2012) *UBC Law Rev.* 497.

from the commitment to religious freedom and that receives formal support in many or most liberal democracies.[2] If religious membership is viewed as an identity rather than a choice or judgment, then when the state treats the practices or beliefs of a particular religious group as less important or less true than the practices or beliefs of other groups, or when it marginalizes the group in some way, it is doing more than simply rejecting the group's beliefs; it is striking at the group's identity and denying the equal worth or standing of its members. Religious freedom, on this account, is a form of equality right that requires the state to treat religious belief systems or communities in an equal or even-handed manner. The state must not support or prefer the practices of one religious group over those of another (religious contest should be excluded from politics) and it must not restrict the practices of a religious group, unless this is necessary to protect a significant public interest (religion should be insulated from politics).

The difficulty with the requirement of state neutrality in religious matters and with the conception of religious membership as an identity is that religious beliefs involve claims about what is true and right that must sometimes be viewed as a matter of judgment (rather than cultural practice) and open to contest in the public sphere. The problem, though, is deeper than that. Because religious beliefs sometimes address public concerns – because they sometimes say something about the rights or interests of others in the community – they cannot simply be insulated or excluded from political decision making.

There are a variety of reasons why it might sometimes be appropriate to treat religion as a cultural identity, towards which the state should remain neutral. Religious commitments are often deep and religious associations are often strong. There may be concern that state *support* or preference for a particular religious belief system will generate political and social conflict, or that *restrictions* on religious practice will have the effect of excluding a religious group from full participation in society, and will negatively affect the members' identification or connection with the larger community. However, the courts have generally been unwilling to treat religious beliefs or practices as cultural rather than political (and insulated or excluded from democratic decision making) when these beliefs relate to civic concerns.

A religious practice/belief should be accommodated only when it does not directly address or significantly impact the rights and interests of others in the community. At issue in "religious accommodation" cases then is the line between the

---

[2] In Canada see, for example, *Mouvement laïque v. Saguenay (City)*, 2015 SCC 16. The Supreme Court of Canada said that the state should remain neutral in matters of religion and should not support or favour the practices of one religion over those of another – or religious views over non-religious views and vice versa. See also *Lautsi and Others v. Italy*, 18 March 2011, European Court of Human Rights [ECtHR] (Grand Chamber), n. 30814/06. Despite its formal commitment to a neutrality requirement, the ECtHR in *Lautsi* seemed to rely on a standard of non-coercion in deciding that the requirement that Italian schools place crucifixes in classrooms did not breach the *European Convention on Human Rights* [ECHR].

civic sphere (of government action) and the private sphere (of religious practice).[3] The courts may decide to exempt a religious practice from the application of ordinary law (and extend the "private" space for religious practice) if doing so will not have a significant negative impact on the public interest.[4] For example, the courts may sometimes exempt religious individuals from dress codes or religious organizations in their internal operations from anti-discrimination laws.[5]

Similarly, the courts in Canada and elsewhere have not interpreted the freedom of religion right as *excluding* religion entirely from the political sphere. The courts have recognized that religious practices have shaped the traditions or customs of the community and so cannot simply be erased from the public sphere or ignored in the formulation of public policy. They have not demanded that governments (literally or metaphorically) sandblast religious symbols and practices from physical and social structures, some of which were constructed long ago. According to the Supreme Court of Canada, "the state's duty of neutrality does not require it to abstain from celebrating and preserving its religious heritage".[6] Moreover, if a large part of the population is Christian, it is difficult to see how the state could not take the practices of this group into account, when, for example, selecting statutory holidays or establishing a "pause day" from work.[7] As long as religion remains an important part of private life, it is bound to affect the shape of public action. Of course, it may

---

[3] Nevertheless, in such cases, accommodation will seldom be more than minor or marginal. A court has no way to attach a specific value or weight to a religious practice. From a secular or public perspective, a religious practice has no necessary value; indeed, it is said that a court should take no position concerning its value. The practice matters only because it is important to the individual – because it matters deeply to him/her and to his/her group. There is no way, then, to balance this "value" against the purpose or value of the restrictive law.

[4] This fits with the idea that the requirement that the state remain neutral in matters of religion depends on the courts' ability to distinguish between the private sphere (of religious life) and the civic/secular sphere – even if the line between these two spheres often seems porous and movable. See Moon, *Freedom of Conscience and Religion* (n. 1), at 133.

[5] The courts have generally treated religious organizations as voluntary associations of individuals pursuing common ends. It is assumed that those who choose to become, or to remain, members of a religious group do not require protection from intragroup rules, even rules that are harsh and discriminatory. The state may sometimes decide to intervene in the affairs of a religious community characterized by hierarchy and insularity when the prevailing practices in that community are thought to be harmful to some of its members, even though the members have, in a least a formal sense, chosen to participate in those practices. The deep communal connections that are part of the value of religious life and commitment (a source of meaning and value for adherents) may also be the source of what the courts regard as harm – the lack of meaningful choice or opportunity open to the members of such communities or the oppression of vulnerable group members. A judgment about whether the state should intervene in the "internal" affairs of a religious community to protect members form harmful acts will depend not simply on the seriousness of the harm that may occur but also on whether the individual member is in a position to "exit" the community.

[6] *Mouvement laique* (n. 2) at para. 116. See also *Lautsi* (n. 2). In the United States see, for example, *Van Orden* v. *Perry*, 545 US 677 (2005), and *Marsh* v. *Chambers*, 463 US 783 (1983).

[7] R. v. *Edwards Book and Arts Ltd.* [1986] 2 SCR 713.

sometimes be difficult to determine when the use of religious symbols or practices by that state is simply an acknowledgment of the country's religious history or of the importance of religion in the private lives of citizens, and when it amounts to a contemporary affirmation by the state of the truth of a particular religious belief system. The Canadian courts have also said that while the state must not support or prefer the *practices* of a particular religious belief system, it is not precluded from relying on religious *values* when making political decisions. This is so, according to Chief Justice McLachlin, because "Religion is an integral aspect of people's lives, and cannot be left at the boardroom door."[8]

But even if the state is (sometimes) expected to treat religious beliefs and practices in a neutral or even-handed way, individuals are not required to do so. An individual (or group) is free to adopt, or identify with, a particular religious belief system and to follow its practices, subject, of course, to limits in the public interest. The individual may seek to persuade others of the truth or wisdom of his or her beliefs and may criticize the beliefs of others. This is a reminder that the requirement of state neutrality is based not on a skeptical view of religion, but instead on more practical concerns – notably that the alignment of religion and politics may result in significant social conflict, or may contribute to the marginalization of some groups in the larger community.[9] And so, even if there is reason for the *state* (sometimes) to remain neutral in matters of religion (to treat religion as a cultural identity), religious beliefs, because they address important questions, must be open to debate and criticism in the public sphere.

B *Hate Speech: Belief and Believer*

In hate speech regulation, a distinction is generally made between an attack on a (religious) group, which if sufficiently hateful or extreme may amount to hate

---

[8] *Chamberlain* v. *Surrey School District No 36*, 2002 SCC 86 at para. 19. The distinction the Canadian courts seem to rely on, if only implicitly, is between, on one side, the elements of a religious belief system (religious "values") that address civic issues and are concerned with individual rights or public welfare, and on the other, religious "practices" or beliefs – those elements of a belief system that address spiritual or otherworldly matters. Religious "practices" should not be supported by the state and should instead be viewed as personal to the individual or internal to the group. Religiously grounded "values", though, should not be excluded from politics and should instead be debated on their merits – on their conception of human good or public welfare. The line between the "civic" and "personal" or communal elements of a religious belief system (between value and practice) will be the subject of contest. Where the line is drawn in a particular case will reflect the decision maker's views about the nature of human welfare, the proper scope of political action, and perhaps also the appropriate forms of religious worship. For a discussion, see Moon, *Freedom of Conscience and Religion* (n. 1), at 52–65.

[9] As well, it may be important to preserve space for religious communities, because they are a source of value and meaning for their members – or (without embracing moral relativism) because space should be preserved for different moral perspectives or communal experiments. There is also an argument that the entanglement of religion with politics will have a corrupting influence on religion because politics demands compromise. See, for example, Mark DeWolfe Howe, *Garden and the Wilderness: Religion and Government in American Constitutional History* (University of Chicago Press, 1968).

speech, and an attack on the group's beliefs, which must be permitted, even when it is harsh and intemperate.[10] A ban on hate speech should apply only to assertions that the members of the group are less worthy or less human than others or that they necessarily share certain undesirable traits – that they are by nature dangerous, or dishonest, or violent and should be treated accordingly. Attacks on belief are a different matter. The criticism of an individual's or group's beliefs is understood to fall within the core of the protection granted by freedom of expression. Religious beliefs, including beliefs about God, or about human dignity and virtue, address issues of truth or right and so must be open to criticism of all kinds. As Iain Leigh observes, religion, as a belief system, "do[es] not have rights because ideas do not have rights".[11] Individuals and groups are free to advance their religious views in the public sphere and to engage in proselytization activities, but they must also be prepared to receive criticism of those views.

There are, however, two difficulties with this distinction between attacks on belief and attacks on believers that stem from our complex conception of religious adherence, as both personal judgment and cultural identity.

The first has to do with the relationship between the individual and the religious tradition with which he or she identifies or associates. Hate speech, when directed at a religious group, often falsely attributes a dangerous or undesirable belief to the members of the group, presenting the belief as an essential part of the religious tradition. The implication is that the members of a group that holds such a belief must themselves be dangerous or undesirable. In attributing a belief that may be held (if at all) by only a fringe element of the group to all its members – to all those who identify with the belief system or tradition – the speech elides the space for judgment and disagreement within the tradition and ignores the diversity of opinion and attachment within the religious community. In effect, it "racializes" the group (or essentializes its belief system), treating the attributed belief as an aspect of the identity or character of each of the group's members. An attack on a particular (attributed) belief becomes an attack on the members of the religious group – and may amount to hate speech, if the falsely attributed belief is sufficiently extreme.

The second difficulty with this distinction between attacks on belief and attacks on the believer is that, because religious beliefs are deeply held, an attack on the individual's beliefs (on the beliefs he or she actually holds) may be experienced by the believer profoundly and personally. The members of a religious group may

---

[10] European Commission for Democracy through Law (Venice Commission), "Report: On the Relationship between Freedom of Expression and Freedom of Religion: The Issue of the Regulation and Prosecution of Blasphemy, Religious Insult and Incitement to Religious Hatred", Oct 23, 2008, para. 49.

[11] I. Leigh, "Damned if they do, damned if they don't: The European Court of Human Rights and the protection of religion from attack", 17 *Res Publica* 55 (2011) at 68. See also Jeremy Waldron, *The Harm of Hate Speech* (Harvard University Press, 2012) at 120: "But the basic distinction between an attack on the body of belief and an attack on the social standing and reputation of a group of people is clear. In every aspect of democratic society we distinguish between the respect accorded to a citizen and the disagreement we might have concerning his or her social and political convictions".

regard certain persons and rituals as sacred – as deserving respect or veneration. To those outside the group, these "sacred" matters may be regarded as part of the group's cultural identity or its internal spiritual life. Recognition of the deep connection between believer and belief (or adherent and practice) has led some to argue that religious beliefs or sacred objects or symbols should be insulated from intemperate criticism or gratuitous insult.[12]

I HATE SPEECH AND RELIGIOUS MEMBERSHIP

A *The Attribution of Belief*

In its most familiar form, hate speech makes the claim that the members of a racial or other identifiable group are less human or less worthy than others or that they share a dangerous or undesirable trait. Hate speech directed against a religious group often takes this standard form, falsely attributing traits such as dishonesty or cruelty to the group's members – presenting these traits as genetically based or culturally determined, particularly when group membership is regarded as a matter of inheritance.

Anti-Semitism, at least in the modern era, has generally taken this form, involving claims about the undesirable biological characteristics of Jews. While the roots of anti-Semitism were religious, based on Christian scripture and teaching, in the early to mid-1800s the content of anti-Semitism shifted from claims about the beliefs and practices of Jews to more "scientific" claims about the group's racial characteristics.[13] Jews were portrayed as innately corrupt and dishonest – traits that were said to be manifested in their business practices and more disturbingly in the Jewish plot to undermine Christian society by acquiring control of its cultural, economic, and political institutions. This "plot" was "exposed" in *The Protocols of the Elders of Zion*, a booklet that was forged in Russia at the very beginning of the twentieth century, and that still circulates today.[14] The anti-Semitic speech of Keegstra, Taylor, Zundel, and others, described in Chapter 1, fits easily into the model of racist hate speech, attributing to Jews, as a group, certain undesirable or dangerous traits that are assumed to be deeply rooted, and perhaps even genetically inherited.[15]

However, the attribution of undesirable traits to the members of a religious group is often less direct than this. The speaker may associate the members of a group not with an undesirable biological trait, but instead with a dangerous belief – a

---

[12] *Otto Preminger Film Institute* v. *Austria* (13470/87) [1994], ECHR 26.

[13] Robert S. Wistrich, *Anti-Semitism: The Longest Hatred* (Pantheon, 1991) at 47.

[14] *The Protocols of the Elders of Zion* (1903). For a discussion see Stephen Eric Bronner, *A Rumor about the Jews: Reflections on Antisemitism and the Protocols of the Learned Elders of Zion* (St. Martin's Press, 2000).

[15] Michael Whine, "Expanding Holocaust denial and legislating against it," in Ivan Hare and James Weinstein (eds.), *Extreme Speech and Democracy* (Oxford University Press, 2009) at 538.

belief that may (or may not) have some grounding in the group's scripture or may (or may not) be held by a fringe element of the religious tradition. Hate speech, when directed at a group, such as Muslims, attributes an undesirable or dangerous belief to the group as a whole and treats the belief as an aspect of each believer's worldview. A belief (e.g., that violence is justified to advance the faith), which may be held by a fringe element of the tradition, is falsely attributed to all the group's members – to anyone who identifies as a member of the group. While the attack focuses on a particular belief, the clear implication is that the members of a religious tradition that includes such a belief are dangerous and deserving of contempt or hatred. The objectionable belief is presented as an essential and rooted part of group membership. In this way, the belief serves the same role as a falsely attributed racial characteristic: To be a member of the group is to think and act in a particular way.[16]

If an individual is committed, along with others, to objectionable views, he or she may be criticized for these views. It might also be said that an individual (or group of individuals) who holds such views is morally or rationally deficient. The beliefs we hold reveal something about us, either because we have chosen them or because they define us in some way. But it is also true that within any religious community or tradition there is an enormous diversity of belief and practice. Disagreement within a religious community about the correct reading of scripture or the proper form of worship will often be deep and may sometimes be severe. It sometimes seems that the differences in belief and practice within a religious community or tradition are as great as the differences between religious traditions. An individual may think of himself or herself as a religious group member, or may identify with a religious tradition, without sharing exactly or even approximately the same beliefs as other members – and indeed it may be difficult to identify a shared core of group belief except in very abstract terms. The followers of a religious tradition may interpret scripture or apply the practices of the tradition in different ways, and yet still understand themselves to be members of that tradition – to be Christians or Jews or Buddhists.[17] They may identify with a religious tradition or belief system in different ways, with different levels of commitment and degrees of involvement. This is a reminder of the way in which religion is a matter both of cultural identity and of personal commitment – that it is a system or tradition that individual members understand, and identify with, in particular or personal ways.

---

[16] Alana Lentin and Gavan Titley, *The Crisis of Multiculturalism: Racism in a Neoliberal Age* (Zed Books, 2011), at p. 5: "culture can be reified and essentialized to the point where it becomes the fundamental equivalent of race".

[17] Charles Taylor, *Dilemmas and Connections* (Harvard University Press, 2011) at 261: "Many people have placed distance between themselves and their ancestral churches without altogether breaking off. They retain some of the beliefs of Christianity, for instance, and/or they retain some nominal tie with the church and still identify in some way with it; they will reply, say, to a poll by saying they are Anglican or Catholic. Sociologists are forced to invent new terms, such as *believing without belonging*, or *diffusive Christianity* to come to grips with this." In some cases, though, the individual's connection might be better described as "belonging without believing".

Elision of the space between the individual adherent and the larger religious tradition or group may occur in one of two ways, each of which is illustrated in recent anti-Muslim/Islam writing – or what is sometimes referred to as "Muslim Tide" or "Eurabia" literature. The first involves a simple and direct claim about what Muslims believe and how they behave. A central claim in the Eurabia writing is that "they" (Muslims) support, or are sympathetic to, the use of violence to advance their faith – to impose their beliefs on others. Even when it is acknowledged that perhaps not all those who describe themselves as Muslim are committed to the use of violence, it is suggested that non-violent or "moderate" Muslims are prepared to support or acquiesce in the use of violence by others in the group or that "moderate" Muslims, who are opposed to violence, are exceptional. The second way in which the distinction between adherent and tradition is elided involves a claim about the core tenets of Islam. The claim is that a simple and true reading of the Quran reveals that violence is a central component of Islam. It follows then that a real Muslim, a true believer, must be committed to the use of violence to advance the faith. Those who call themselves Muslims, but do not support the use of violence, are not true adherents of the faith and indeed, by associating with the tradition, may be giving legitimacy to its promotion of violence. From either of these perspectives – Muslims as violent or Islam as a violent religion – the members of the group (those who identify as Muslim or as adherents of Islam) are seen as holding dangerous beliefs and practices.

B *Eurabia and the Muslim Tide*

In the last few decades a growing body of writing – books, articles, and blogs – has contributed to the spread in Europe, and elsewhere in the West, of fear and anger towards Muslims.[18] Much of this writing has sought to raise the alarm about what it sees as the Muslim takeover of Europe, which is said to be occurring through high levels of immigration from Muslim countries and higher birth rates in Muslim families that have settled in the West.[19] Jytte Klausen observes that, in the Eurabia writing, "[f]alse facts about demographic trends are seamlessly interwoven with cultural stereotypes and religious prejudice to spin tales about the failure of assimilation and Muslims propensities for totalitarian behavior because of their faith."[20]

---

[18] See, for example, Christopher Caldwell, *Reflections on the Revolution in Europe* (Anchor Books, 2010); Bruce Bawer, *While Europe Slept: How Radical Islam Is Destroying the West from Within* (Anchor Books, 2007).

[19] For example, Bawer (n. 18) at 33: "The number of Muslims will increase dramatically, partly through continued immigration and partly through reproduction (the fertility rate of Muslims in Europe being considerably higher than that of non-Muslims)." Caldwell (n. 18) at 17: "Immigration is not enhancing or validating European culture; it is supplanting it. Europe is not welcoming its newest residents but making way for them."

[20] Jytte Klausen, *The Cartoons That Shook the World* (Yale University Press, 2009) at 61. Others have shown the flaws in these demographic claims. See, for example, Matt Carr, "You are now entering

Muslims, it is claimed in this writing, wish to impose Sharia law (which is described as a comprehensive set of spiritual and political rules) on the European countries in which they reside, and are prepared to use a variety of means to achieve this end, including violence.[21] Islamic or Muslim values are presented as fundamentally incompatible with the values of the West, making inevitable a "clash of civilizations".[22] Hard-won rights and freedoms are said to be under threat from a group that adheres blindly to a regressive religious belief system.[23] It is claimed that Muslims are opposed to gender equality, sexual orientation equality, free speech, religious liberty, and, more generally, secular democracy.

Christopher Caldwell describes Islam "as a mighty identity, shaping every aspect of a believer's life and reducing lesser allegiances to unimportance".[24] Muslim culture is, on this view, rooted, static, and homogenous and will not be transformed or moderated by the surrounding liberal-secular culture. Matt Carr, a critic of this writing, notes that the Eurabia writers present Islam as "a hermetically sealed monolithic bloc, whose adherents are theologically incapable of coexistence with other cultures or religions" – unable or unwilling to assimilate into liberal-democratic societies.[25] While Muslim communities in Europe often "live precarious, besieged

---

Eurabia", 48 *Race and Class* 1 (2006); Doug Saunders, *The Myth of the Muslim Tide* (Knopf, 2012); and Philip Jenkins, *God's Continent* (Oxford, 2007): "European cultural and social arrangements have, it seems, gutted the continent's Christian heritage; yet prophets of Muslim dominance of Europe assume that Islam will somehow be immune to these same overwhelming pressures. In fact, both Christianity and Islam face real difficulties in surviving within Europe's secular cultural ambience in anything like their familiar historic forms" (3).

[21] Bawer (n. 18) at 3 speaks of the European Muslims' anticipation of "the establishment in Europe of a caliphate government according to sharia law" and their regard for "Islamic terrorists as allies in a global jihad... dedicated to that goal". Robert Spencer, *The Complete Infidels' Guide to the Koran* (Regnery, 2009), at 227: "Islam has always been not just a religion in the Western sense, but a political and social system that acknowledges no legitimate distinction between the sacred and secular realms, and mandates religious law as the only legitimate system of law and governance." But as Klausen (n. 20) at 133 observes, "Many European Muslims adamantly oppose the view that Islamic law should be incorporated in the civil code, arguing that they have left behind a theocratic state and have no desire to re-empower Islamic law. Alternatively, some observant Muslims sometimes argue that they are better served by a secular state that does not get involved with faith matters."

[22] Samuel Huntington, *The Clash of Civilizations and the Remaking of World Order* (Simon and Schuster, 2011 [1996]). For an early critique see E.W. Said, "The Clash of Ignorance", *Nation*, October 2001, www.thenation.com/article/clash-ignorance/: "Huntington... wants to make 'civilizations' and 'identities' into what they are not: shut-down, sealed-off entities that have been purged of the myriad currents and countercurrents that animate human history, and that over centuries have made it possible for that history not only to contain wars of religion and imperial conquest but also to be one of exchange, cross-fertilization and sharing. This far less visible history is ignored in the rush to highlight the ludicrously compressed and constricted warfare that 'the clash of civilizations' argues is the reality."

[23] Mark Steyn, *America Alone* (Regnery Press, 2006) at xxv: "A significant strain of Islam is incompatible with the rough and tumble of a free society". Bawer (n. 18) at 27 declares that it was always plain to him "that fundamentalist Islam was on the march in Europe and wasn't adapting itself to democratic values. It seemed clear that there'd be a confrontation – or capitulation".

[24] Caldwell (n. 18) at 129. [25] Carr (n. 20) at 12.

existences", Carr points out that the Muslim Tide writing reverses things "in order to present the dominant 'Christian' or 'secular' culture as under siege" by existing Muslim minorities and "by the hypothetical majorities of the future that will subject the rest of Europe to servile dhimmitude".[26]

The Eurabia writers are less explicit about what should be done to address the Muslim "threat". They sometimes call for political action, but more often seem to accept that such action will be futile. Robert Spencer, like many Muslim Tide writers, calls for a ban on Muslim immigration: "Since there is no completely reliable way to tell if any given Muslim believer takes the Koran's dictates about warfare against Infidels literally, immigration of Muslims into the United States should be halted".[27] Bruce Bawer ominously points out that European states have it within their power to prevent the Muslim take-over: "They have armies. They have police. They have prisons."[28]

Just as Muslims are viewed as a more or less homogenous group that is opposed to liberal democratic values, "native" Europeans (and "old-stock" Canadians, perhaps) are presented as uniformly committed to these values. The process of distinguishing Muslims from Europeans or Muslim values from the values of the West (establishing a "clash of civilizations") also requires the elision of difference within mainstream culture, which is said to include a commitment to gender equality, freedom of expression, and secularism, with no acknowledgement of the significant variation in opinion on these issues.[29] Anxiety about European identity, based on demographic changes, globalism, consumerism, and loss of faith, is expressed in

---

[26] Carr (n. 20) at 15.

[27] Spencer (n. 21) at 230. Donald Trump adopted a similar position: "If Donald Trump were campaigning in Canada could he be charged with hate speech?" *National Post*, Dec 9, 2015.

[28] Bruce Bawer in a 2007 blog that is quoted in Doug Saunders, *The Myth of the Muslim Tide* (n. 20) at 14.

[29] These values – and in particular the commitment to secular politics – are sometimes said to have emerged from the Christian tradition: See for example the decision of the ECtHR in *Lautsi* (n. 2). For a discussion of the *Lautsi* decision and the link between Christianity and European identity see Richard Moon, "Christianity, multiculturalism, and national identity: A Canadian comment on Lautsi and Others v. Italy", in Jeroen Temperman (ed.), *The Lautsi Papers: Multidisciplinary Reflections on Religious Symbols in the Public School Classroom* (BRILL/Martinus Nijhoff, 2013): "In the *Lautsi* decision, religion and politics come together in the definition of national identity and civic obligation... This link between religion and politics is seen as necessary to the maintenance of political community – reinforcing the connection between its members and the foundation of its core principles. A Christian or post-Christian public morality may serve as a civil religion that inspires and binds citizens. It may contribute to a richer or more substantial form of national identity than one based simply on a shared commitment to democratic principles. At the same time, the link between Christian morality and national identity or political community serves to exclude some. And indeed, it appears that the exclusion of non-Christians, or those who do not identify with Christian public morality, is not just a regrettable side-effect of the attempt to bolster civic union and national identity" (259–60). "The remarkable claim by the Italian courts that Christianity is uniquely tolerant and inclusive and lies at the foundation of the modern liberal/secular state, is significantly a claim about other religions, and [Islam] in particular" (263).

both the creation of the regressive Muslim "other" and the invention of the European as liberal, democratic, and egalitarian.[30] Islam, says Oliver Roy, is "a mirror in which the West projects its own identity".[31] John Bowen suggests that attacking Islam for its opposition to gender and sexual orientation equality "can be a psychologically useful way of reworking one's own heritage", which encompassed views similar to those ascribed to Muslims.[32] In France, gender equality has become part of the "national creed" that all citizens are expected to uphold, while in the Netherlands, the toleration or acceptance of sexual diversity has become part of what it means to be Dutch and "a salient part of the critique of Islam".[33] Jytte Klausen observes that the protection of free speech, and in particular "corrosive and profane humor", has become the "symbol of essential Danish values that are placed at risk by religious Muslims".[34]

The Eurabia authors are suspicious of the use of law (either hate speech laws or human rights codes) by Muslims to protect the interests of their community (or, according to these writers, to gain a foothold for Sharia law and to suppress criticism of Islam). Conservative Christians may seek the protection of blasphemy laws, or exemption from anti-discrimination bans, without their commitment to the political community or the democratic process being questioned – or at least without all those who identify as Christian being viewed as politically regressive. In the Eurabia writing, these same actions performed by individual Muslims provide evidence of the ultimate objective of Islam and the true character of Muslims.

Reliance on law by Muslims is viewed not as an acceptance of the norms of democratic community (as citizen-like behaviour), but as confirmation of the anti-democratic character of Islam – as a repudiation of Western values such as freedom of expression and religious freedom. Geert Wilders describes this use of law as "'legal jihad' or 'lawfare' – a process in which Muslim litigants exploit Western laws and legal systems to attack their critics and threaten them with suppression or other forms of retribution."[35] As these terms are meant to suggest, litigation – legal jihad – is viewed as coercion or violence by other means, or in Geert Wilders's words, as "a weapon of war".[36] Litigation is just another strategy – another weapon – in the Muslim arsenal, which is employed when it might be more effective than violence in furthering the goal of Muslim domination of Europe. The Eurabia writers believe that as long as Muslims are a minority in Europe, they will seek to pass themselves off as good Europeans and engage in "legal jihad" as the most effective way to advance their ends. For example, "new-atheist" Sam Harris asserts that

---

[30] Jenkins (n. 20) at 247: "The urgency of the religious confrontation has forced European thinkers to define their beliefs far more explicitly and to specify the core values that newcomers should accept, however implausibly these can be presented as 'fundamentally European'".

[31] Oliver Roy, *Secularism Confronts Islam* (Columbia University Press, 2007) (trans. George Holoch).

[32] John R. Bowen, *Blaming Islam* (MIT Press, 2012) at 40.   [33] Bowen (n. 32) at 40.

[34] Klausen (n. 20) at 61.   [35] Geert Wilders, *Marked for Death* (Regnery Publishing, 2012) at 182.

[36] Wilders (n. 35) at 182.

Muslims in the West have adopted religious tolerance as a "practical strategy", while they wait until their numbers increase and they achieve "political ascendancy".[37] In support of this claim, critics of Islam, such as Wilders, point to a passage in the Quran, which they say instructs Muslims to use deception to advance the faith. The idea of *taqiyya* – the permission to deny one's faith under extreme duress – becomes, for Wilders and other Eurabia writers, "lying for the sake of Allah – allow[ing] a believer to conceal his true intentions in order to advance the cause of Islam."[38]

The Eurabia writers accuse the "elites" of European society of complicity in the Muslim takeover of Europe.[39] They argue that the elites' support for multi-culturalism and open immigration has exposed Europe to the threat of Muslim domination.[40] Multiculturalism, on this view, rests on a commitment to moral relativism – tolerance for the intolerant – or on a mistaken assumption that Muslim immigrants will assimilate to Western values.[41] Many of the Eurabia writers also argue that the aging European population (which has invited Muslim immigrants into Europe to make up for lower birthrates and a shrinking workforce) has neither the will nor the strength to resist the ideological determination of the followers of Islam.[42] Some of these writers have a grudging admiration for the moral clarity and resolve of the Muslim community and a contempt for the weakness of "native" Europeans, who have been coddled for too long by the welfare state.[43] The anti-Muslim position then is often tied to a neo-conservative view about the collapse of the West, which has been weakened by the welfare state and a culture that lacks moral foundations.

---

[37] Sam Harris, *The End of Faith* (W.W. Norton, 2005) at 130.

[38] Wilders (n. 35) at 87. See also Spencer (n. 21) at 202: "Islam is the only religion with a developed doctrine of deception".

[39] Steyn (n. 23) describes these elites as "dopey enablers" (xxv) and "western appeasers" (xvi). Bowen (n. 32) at 39: These populist attacks on the elites resonate with "the forgotten working class".

[40] A more bizarre account is offered in Bat Ye'or's (Giselle Littman's) book, *Eurabia: The Euro-Arab Axis* (Fairleigh Dickson University Press, 2005). Ye'or, who coined the terms "Eurabia" and "dhimmitude", asserts that following the 1973 oil crisis the European elites agreed with the Muslim nations to permit mass Muslim immigration and the Muslim domination of the West in return for continuing access to oil. Bawer (n. 18) at 102 adopts Ye'or's historical account. Carr (n. 20) at 6 describes the Ye'or conspiracy theory as "flat-out barking gibberish".

[41] Bawer (n. 18) at 3 and at 233: "In the end, Europe's enemy is not Islam, or even radical Islam. Europe's enemy is itself – its destructive passivity, its softness toward tyranny, its reflexive inclination to appease, and its uncomprehending distaste for America's pride, courage, and resolve in the face of a deadly foe".

[42] Steyn (n. 23) at xxi: "forces in the developed world...have left Europe too enfeebled to resist its remorseless transformation into Eurabia". Confronted with the violent acts of Muslims, Europeans – "Too sedated even to sue for terms...capitulate instantly" (xxxv); Bawer (n. 18) at 34: "when Christian faith had departed, it had taken with it a sense of ultimate meaning and purpose – and left the Continent vulnerable to conquest by people with deeper faith and stronger convictions".

[43] Bawer (n. 18) at 149 speaks of the "deadly pattern of passivity" in Europe "that derives from a habit – born of life in a welfare state – of expecting the government to take care of things." Caldwell (n. 18) at 286: "When insecure, malleable, relativistic culture meets a culture that is anchored, confident, and strengthened by common doctrines, it is generally the former that changes to suit the latter."

Claims about the Muslim Tide or the rise of Eurabia are often expressed in a visceral way – in a form we associate with hate speech. In *R. v. Harding*, for example, a Christian pastor described Muslims in a series of flyers as "wolves in sheep's clothing", who are seeking to undermine Christian society and are prepared to use violence to do so.[44] Mr. Harding was convicted of willfully promoting hatred under the *Criminal Code*, because, in the court's view, the pamphlets he distributed conveyed the message "that Muslims are detestable people, deserving our contempt" and invited readers "to take defensive action against the threat of violence posed by Muslims".[45] Much of the Eurabia writing, though, is less vitriolic in tone and is superficially more reasonable in its presentation. This writing sometimes even takes the form of journalistic reporting or academic argument. The courts and other public actors have so far been unwilling to see this writing as hate speech.

C Mark Steyn and Muslim Violence

Mark Steyn, a Canadian contributor to the Eurabia writing, asserts that we are at "the dawn of a new Dark Ages" in which much of Europe will be "re-primitivized" by Muslims.[46] The goal of the "Islamists", says Steyn, is "the re-establishment of a Muslim caliphate, living under sharia, that extends to Europe."[47] The Western world, he tells us, "will not survive this century"; it may not even endure "beyond our lifetimes".[48] He sees an unbridgeable divide between Muslim culture and the culture of the West: Muslims simply cannot be assimilated into liberal-democratic society.[49]

Steyn regards Islam as a "political project", an "ideology", and as different in that respect from other religions.[50] His critique, though, focuses on Muslims, on what they say and do in the civic sphere, rather than on the religious tenets or spiritual practices of Islam. He rejects any suggestion that Muslims are a racial group, whose members share certain biological traits. He notes that in a place such as the Balkans the Muslims and non-Muslims "look exactly the same, race-wise".[51] He complains about what he describes as "the fetishization of reductive notions of race which makes us so ill-equipped to understand what is really going on".[52] If Muslims are not a race, then, in Steyn's mind, a critique of their beliefs and actions – of their 'culture' – cannot be described as racist: "To claim [Islam] is a 'race' is so

---

[44] *R. v. Harding* (1998) O.J. No. 2603, affirmed in Ontario Court of Appeal, 160 CCC (3d) 225; 48 C.R. (5th) 1. See the description of the case in c. 1. See also *Norwood v. UK* (ECtHR), Application No. 23131/03), Nov 16, 2004.

[45] *Harding* (n. 44) at 10.   [46] Steyn (n. 23) at xxiv.

[47] Steyn (n. 23) at 38.   [48] Steyn (n. 23) at xxiv.

[49] George M. Frederickson, *Racism: A Short History* (Princeton University Press, 2002) at 9: "In all manifestations of racism from the mildest to the most severe, what is being denied is that the racializers and the racialized can coexist in the same society, except perhaps on the basis of domination and submission."

[50] Steyn (n. 23) at 62.   [51] Steyn (n. 23) at xx.   [52] Steyn (n. 23) at xx.

breathtakingly stupid as to give the game away – and to confirm that 'Racist!' is now no more than the cry of a western liberal who can't stand his illusions being disturbed".[53]

But even if Islamic belief or Muslim culture is not an inherited trait, it is, for Steyn, something almost as deep and rooted in the life of a Muslim. Islam, he observes, "forms the primal, core identity of most of its adherents in the Middle East, South Asia, and elsewhere".[54] It is "a powerful identity that leaps frontiers and continents", and "not something you leave behind in the old country".[55] Steyn seeks to avoid the charge of racism by distinguishing between race, which is immutable, and culture, which is changeable, and insisting that his critique is focused on the latter, but then proceeds to describe Muslim culture as deep-rooted, static, and generic. In Steyn's account, then, culture becomes the equivalent of race. As George M. Frederickson observes, "If we think of culture as historically constructed, fluid, variable in time and space, and adaptable to changing circumstances, it is a concept antithetical to that of race. But culture can be reified and essentialized to the point where it becomes the functional equivalent of race" – representing "unbridgeable and invidious differences" between groups.[56]

When complaining about the European media's unwillingness to identify Muslims as the perpetrators of violence, Steyn tells the following story:

> In June 2006, a 54-year-old Flemish train conductor called Guido Demoor got on the Number 23 bus in Antwerp to go to work. Six – what's that word again? – "youths" boarded the bus and commenced intimidating the other riders... Mr. Demoor asked the lads to cut it out and so they turned on him, thumping and kicking him. [N]one [of the other passengers] intervened to help the man under attack... leaving Mr. Demoor to be beaten to death. Three "youths" were arrested, and proved to be – *quelle surprise!* – of Moroccan origin.[57]

---

[53] Steyn (n. 23) at xxi.

[54] Steyn (n. 23) at xxxv. But see Amartya Sen, *Identity and Violence* (Penguin, 2006), at 42: It is a mistake to think that "seeing people exclusively or primarily in terms of the religion-based civilizations to which they are taken to belong is a good way of understanding human beings."

[55] Steyn (n. 23) at xxxviii. He continues, claiming that for many Muslims in the West, Islam has become "their principal expression" – "a pan-Islamic identity that transcends borders". This is also the view of Caldwell (n. 18) at 138: "The old identities didn't seem to go away. They were always ready to be tapped into at any time by second- or third generation Muslims somehow discontent with European culture". But Steyn and Caldwell seem to have things backwards. The adoption of a pan-Islamic identity, it turns out, involves leaving behind the Islam of the old country or of one's parents or grandparents, which was tied to local culture: See Oliver Roy, *Holy Ignorance: When Religion and Culture Part Ways* (Oxford University Press, 2013) (trans. Ros Schwartz).

[56] Frederickson (n. 49) at 7. This is sometimes referred to as "cultural racism" or the "new racism". Lentin and Titley (n. 16) at 5: "By effecting an ahistorical divide between ideas of (biological) 'race' and 'culture', it has become unacceptable to essentialize and scapegoat people on the basis of pseudo-science, but a refreshing and necessary form of truth-telling to do so on the basis of equally spurious understandings of culture."

[57] Steyn (n. 23) at 34–35. See also Bawer (n. 18) at 39: "In some urban areas of Europe, all order has broken down. Young men roam the streets in packs and commit crimes in the daylight". According to Bawer, these men rape and rob with impunity. A teenage girl who goes out without wearing a burqa is, in the eyes of these men, "admitting she's a whore and asking to be raped".

It seems unlikely that the young men involved in this incident were devout Muslims and even less likely that their assault on the bus driver was intended to advance the cause of Islam in Europe. They may have been raised in Muslim households or their parents or grandparents may have been adherents of Islam – although almost certainly followers of a culturally particular form of the faith. This, it appears, was another tragic instance of the violent behaviour in which alienated young men too often engage. Religion appears to have played no role in their actions.[58] Indeed, Steyn describes the men as Moroccan rather than Muslim, but his story is linked to a set of claims about Muslims and violence. In this way, he encourages the reader to make the short leap and equate Moroccan with Muslim – and to see the violent act of these young men as a manifestation of the violence of the larger Muslim culture. Steyn seems to attach the label "Muslim" to anyone who comes from (or more often whose parents or grandparents come from) a country in which the dominant religion is Islam.[59] As Oliver Roy observes, the terms "Islam" and "Muslim" are used in the Eurabia writing "to give unity to a complex array of demands, identities, activities" and are turned into an "essence" that "determines attitudes in very different contexts".[60]

Steyn also points to the riots in the French *banlieues* to support his case. These riots were described by the French authorities as popular revolts by young men, mostly of North African origin, driven by unemployment and discrimination.[61] In *America Alone*, Steyn acknowledges but then ignores the criticism of earlier claims he made about the role of Muslims in the riots:

> When I pointed out the media's strange reluctance to use the M-word vis-à-vis the rioting "youths," I received a ton of e-mails arguing there is no Islamist component, they're not the madrassa crowd, they may be Muslim but they're secular and Westernized and into drugs and rap and meaningless sex with no emotional commitment, and rioting and looting and torching and trashing, just like any normal

---

[58] There are of course young men who have been "radicalized". Young men who are angry and alienated have sometimes found in radical religious ideology a purpose or identity – a way to channel or fuel their resentment and anger. They may have been raised in ordinary Muslim homes or they may be converts – although in either case, their knowledge of Islam is probably very limited. For a discussion, see c. 5. Oliver Roy, quoted in Jenkins (n. 20) at 227: "The Young people in working class urban areas are against the system and converting to Islam is the ultimate way to challenge the system. They convert to stick it to their parents, to their principal . . . They convert in the same way that people in the 1970s went to Bolivia and Vietnam. I see a very European tradition of identifying with a Third World cause."

[59] Klausen (n. 20) at 2: "The term 'Muslim' is also problematic, if only because it refers to a religious identity – or, perhaps, a religious heritage that people sometimes choose to recognize as an identity – which is as complex and diverse as Christianity. The term is sometimes used, still more loosely, to describe an ethnicity or even geography."

[60] Roy (n. 55) at 77.

[61] Bowen (n. 32) at 62. Jenkins (n. 20) points out that, for many in France, Islam is a "cultural identity rather than a religious practice" (158) – that the vast majority of young Muslims adhere to none or few of the five pillars of the faith – and that the label "Islam" is often just "a convenient label for a more generalized disaffection that in slightly different circumstances could easily have been expressed in terms of class or race" (168).

healthy Western teenagers. These guys have economic concerns, it's the lack of jobs, it's conditions peculiar to France.[62]

He admits that not "everything's about jihad" but then says that "a good 90 percent of everything's about demography" – as if this confirms, somehow, his claim about the violent and backward nature of Muslim culture and the inevitable takeover of Europe by Muslims, through numbers and violence.[63]

At important points in his attack on Muslim immigration, Steyn seeks to avoid the charge of racism or hate speech by acknowledging that not all Muslims are committed to the use of violence. He offers what he calls "the obligatory 'of courses'", seeming to acknowledge (with a nudge and a wink to those who know what is expected in our "politically correct" society) the diversity of opinion within the religious community. Not all Muslims are inclined to violence, Steyn concedes; but then in baroque style he immediately inserts a counterpoint – qualifying the caveat or generalizing again about Muslims and the place of violence in their culture:

> Time for the obligatory "of courses": *Of course*, not all Muslims are terrorists – though enough are hot for jihad to provide an impressive support network of mosques from Vienna to Stockholm to Toronto to Seattle. *Of course*, not all Muslims support terrorists – though enough of them share their basic objectives (the wish to live under Islamic law in Europe and North America) to function wittingly or otherwise as the "good cop" end of the Islamic good cop/bad cop routine. But, at the very minimum, this fast moving demographic transformation provides a huge comfort zone for the jihad to move around in.[64] [emphasis in the original].

This caveat allows him to say that his criticism is directed only at those who support violence. Yet framed in this way, as a compulsory acknowledgement, Steyn's caveat is about as comforting as the statement that "not every Jew is dishonest" or "some gay men are not pedophiles". It is offered as the exception that supports the general rule about the group. He formally concedes that not everyone who identifies with the group holds such a belief, while suggesting that it is the prevailing or established view in the group.

This is a familiar strategy. When the speaker – in this case Steyn – is pressed (possibly even accused of engaging in hate speech), he pulls back and insists that he is only making a claim about those members of the group who hold this belief, while encouraging his readers in various ways to think that the number of believers is considerable. "What we still do not know", says Steyn, "is how deep the psychoses of jihadism reach within Islam in general, and the West's Muslim populations in particular".[65] Even if the number of violent "jihadists" remains

---

[62] Steyn (n. 23) at 34. [63] Steyn (n. 23) at 34. [64] Steyn (n. 23) at 33.

[65] Steyn (n. 23) at 88. And at 86, "[W]estern politicians and religious leaders tell us . . . incessantly that the 'vast majority' of Muslims do not support terrorism. Yet how vast is the minority that does? One percent? Ten percent? [There is reason to think] . . . it might be rather more." At 89, "The free world's Muslim populations are growing more radical with each generation." At 88, "It seems likely that the

unspecified in Steyn's account, once the association of Muslims with violence is made, it becomes easy to present Muslim moderates as exceptional. When the issue is how many Muslims support violence, then all are suspect and appropriately subject to scrutiny and perhaps even exclusion – since "we just can't be sure" which ones do and which ones do not support violence.[66] If the Islamic faith or Muslim culture is the common thread that connects these violent actors, then there must be something about the culture or religion that accounts for the prevalence of violence among Muslims – even if not every Muslim is violent.

At other times, Steyn argues that, even if Muslims are not all willing to commit acts of violence, they are at least united in their openness to violence. In Steyn's view, the diversity among Muslims is simply in the degree of their commitment to, or sympathy towards, violence as an instrument to achieve the "Islamification" of the West. He rejects what he refers to as the "black" and "white" account that draws a clear distinction between "the bomber" and everyone else:

> [T]he terrorist bent on devastation and destruction prowls the street, while around him are a significant number of people urging him on, and around them a larger group of cock-sure young male co-religionists gleefully celebrating mass murder, and around them a much larger group of "moderates" who stand silent at the acts committed in their name, and around them a mesh of religious and community leaders openly inciting treason against the state, and around them another mesh of religious and community leaders who serve as apologists for the inciters, and around them a network of professional identity-group grievance-mongers adamant that they're the real victims.[67]

A "moderate Muslim", says Steyn, may be "a Muslim who wants stoning for adultery to be introduced in Liverpool, but he's 'moderate' because he can't be bothered flying a plane into a skyscraper to get it."[68] In other words, he is moderate, according to Steyn, not because he is opposed to violence, but simply because he is unwilling to engage in it himself.

---

beliefs of Mohammed Atta are closer to the thinking of most Muslims than those of [Muslim critic and reformist Irshad] Manji are."

[66] Donald Trump, quoted in "If Donald Trump were campaigning in Canada could he be charged with hate speech?" *National Post*, Dec 9, 2015.

[67] Steyn (n. 23) at 196. He continues, "and around them a vast mass of elite opinion in the media and elsewhere too squeamish about ethno-cultural matters to confront reality, and around them a political establishment desperate to pretend this is just a managerial problem that can be finessed away with a few new laws and a bit of community outreach".

[68] Steyn (n. 23) at 77. He continues, "Huge numbers of Muslims – many of them British subjects born and bred – see their fellow Britons blown apart on trains and buses and are willing to rationalize the actions of mass murderers." Bawer (n. 18) at 180 wonders about the unwillingness of so-called "moderate Muslims" to condemn the hateful words and violent actions of those who purported to speak and act in the name of Islam. And at 229, "many European Muslims may themselves be moderates, yet may have a concept of religious identity that makes it difficult for them to side with infidels against even the most violent of their fellow Muslims".

Steyn shows some skill at moving between, on one side, an assumption that Islam is a cultural identity, fixed and rooted, and, on the other, a recognition that religion is a personal commitment or judgment and that those who describe themselves as Muslims may have different views about what their faith requires or what is spiritually true and right. In this way, he is able to blur the line between criticism of a particular belief (that may be held by some members of the religious tradition) and an attack on the entire religious group. The complex character of religious adherence as both cultural identity and personal judgment allows Steyn to associate all Muslims with violence – as almost a character trait – while superficially acknowledging that some Muslims may choose to reject or abstain from violence. He is aided in this by popular assumptions in the West about Muslims. Because non-Muslims tend to view Muslims as a more or less homogenous group, and often only hear about Muslims in connection with violence, they may associate all or most of the group's members with the beliefs and actions of a violent subgroup.

In a comment that appeared in the *National Post* the day after the November 2015 terrorist attack in Paris, Steyn again implicates the entire Muslim community in terrorist violence.[69] He says that "most" of the Muslims who have settled in Europe "don't want to participate *actively* in bringing about the death of diners, concertgoers and soccer fans, but at a certain level most of them either wish or are indifferent to the *death of the societies* in which they live – modern, pluralist, western societies" [emphasis added]. Despite his informal or folksy writing style, Steyn is very careful in his wording. He suggests but never quite says that all Muslims support violence. The suggestion in the first half of the quoted statement is that even if most Muslims do not actively support violence – the murder ("death") of non-Muslims – they may do so passively; yet in the second half he adjusts his claim, suggesting only that they wish for the "death" of liberal democratic society. The use of the word "death" first literally in relation to individuals and then figuratively in relation to society holds the two parts of the sentence together and serves to taint all Muslims with the violent acts of a few. In Steyn's account, even if most in the Muslim community do not actively aid and abet acts of terrorism, they are at least passively – culturally – complicit in these acts. This is the obvious message, when he goes on to say that the Muslim community provides "a very large comfort zone in which [the terrorist may] swim, and which the authorities find almost impossible to penetrate." His answer to the terrorist problem is "to end mass Muslim immigration". An ordinary reader will have no difficulty understanding this call for exclusion, and indeed the entire piece, as an assertion that Muslims – the vast majority of them – are supporters of violence. Coming as it does in the wake of a large-scale terrorist attack, when feelings of fear and anger are strong, the piece might stir some readers to action.[70]

---

[69] Mark Steyn, "The barbarians are already inside. There's nowhere to get away from them", *National Post*, Nov 15, 2015.

[70] Seeking to remind us of the West's deep and consistent commitment to democracy, equality, and freedom, in contrast to the Muslim world's repudiation of such values, Steyn ("The Barbarians")

D *Geert Wilders and the Violence of Islam*

While Steyn focuses on what he thinks are the political beliefs or cultural practices of Muslims, Geert Wilders looks at the religious source for these beliefs and presumes to determine the authentic or correct meaning of Islam. Wilders is a Dutch politician who has written and spoken extensively about Islam. He has also produced a short anti-Muslim/Islam film, *Fitna*, that was released on the Internet in 2008 and was the subject of an unsuccessful hate speech prosecution in the Netherlands.[71]

In his speeches and writings, Wilders claims that violence is a central element of Islamic doctrine.[72] According to Wilders, the violent character of Islam is apparent on a simple reading of its scripture: "[T]he Koran plainly sanctions violence in the name of Allah."[73] A true Muslim, insists Wilders, must accept the legitimacy of violence against the infidel: "Islam admonishes pious Muslims to prepare themselves for jihad, the holy war to bring the whole world under Allah's domination."[74] Wilders believes that Islam's call "for limitless warfare against non-Muslims throughout the entire world" makes it "fundamentally different . . . from all other religions."[75] He observes that "most people today, even most Christians, will acknowledge that many Christians throughout history committed terrible crimes in the name of Christ"; however, he insists that "such actions actually violate Christian doctrine".[76]

Wilders is, of course, selective in his references to scripture. And it seems plain that if his approach to scriptural interpretation were applied to Judaism or Christianity, similar conclusions might be reached about these traditions. Within any religious tradition, it is possible to find support for acts that most of us today would consider entirely unacceptable. A quick reading of the Bible will reveal

---

(n. 69) makes the incredible claim that the European imperial powers introduced and applied these values in their colonies: "[T]hese are not 'universal values'", says Steyn, "but values that spring from a relatively narrow segment of humanity. They were kinda sorta 'universal' when the great powers were willing to enforce them around the world and the colonial subjects of ramshackle backwaters such as Aden, Sudan and the North-West Frontier Province were at least obliged to pay lip service to them. But the European empires retreated from the world, and those 'universal values' are utterly alien to large parts of the map today."

[71] The film is described in c. 1. The film is composed of a succession of images from news reports of terrorist attacks punctuated with English translations of verses from the Quran that appear to justify violence against non-believers.

[72] Geert Wilders, *Marked for Death* (n. 35), at 19–20. (The introduction to Wilders's book was written by Mark Steyn.) American writer and blogger Robert Spencer adopts a similar approach, presenting the Quran as a manifesto of hatred and violence: "There is no traditional, mainstream sect of Islam or school of Islamic jurisprudence that does not teach warfare against and the subjugation of non-believers." (Quoted in Nathan Lean, *The Islamophobia Industry* (PlutoPress, 2012) at 61.)

[73] Wilders, (n. 35) at 20. He says also that the "true faith of Islam" settles disagreements with violence – with "the axe" (4).

[74] Wilders (n. 35) at 78. See also Spencer (n. 21) – for example, at 232: "Despite the inclusion of verses that ostensibly counsel tolerance, the Koran's overall message is that Infidels should be converted to Islam, subjected as legal inferiors to Muslims, or killed."

[75] Wilders (n. 35) at 20.   [76] Wilders (n. 35) at 19.

numerous passages that may be understood as supporting violence against outsiders to the religious community, but, of course, the Bible, like the Quran, also, and centrally, affirms the values of peace, tolerance, and respect.[77] Philip Jenkins reminds us that the "hard sayings" in the Quran "that can lend themselves to promoting the hatred of Jews or unbelievers" are no more troubling than passages in Jewish and Christian scripture "which a determined reader could take as ordering genocide or prohibiting racial marriage on pain of inciting the wrath of God."[78]

Wilders's answer to those Muslims who say that Islam is a religion of peace is that they are wrong – that they are misreading the Quran or perhaps not reading it at all (or they are lying about its meaning).[79] Those who call themselves Muslims, but do not believe in the use of violence, are deviating from the true meaning of the faith. There may be moderate Muslims, says Wilders, "but there is no moderate Islam."[80] He adopts the words of Oriana Fallaci:

> A moderate Islam does not exist. It does not exist because there is no difference between good Islam and bad Islam. There is Islam and that is the end of it. Islam is the Koran, and nothing other than the Koran. And the Koran is the *Mein Kampf* of a religion that desires to eliminate others – non-Muslims – who are called infidel dogs and inferior creatures.[81]

---

[77] Jonathan Sacks, *Not in God's Name* (Schocken, 2015) at 2017: "Religions, especially religions of the books have hard texts: verses, commands, episodes, narratives that if understood literally and applied directly would... offend our moral sense... There are many examples in the Hebrew Bible. There is the war of revenge against the Midianites. There is the war mandated against the seven nations in the land of Canaan. There is the book of Joshua with its wars of conquest, and the bloody revenge against the Amalekites in the book of Samuel."

[78] Jenkins (n. 20) at 200. But Eurabia writer Spencer (n. 21) downplays these "sayings" at 10: "This lazy moral equivalency overlooks the glaring fact that there is hardly a single organization today that commits violent acts and justifies them by quoting the Bible and invoking Christianity". See also Keith Ward, *Is Religion Dangerous?* (Wm. B. Erdmans, 2006) at 36: "[B]ecause religion was founded in opposition to preceding mores and beliefs, and because from time to time it had to fight to preserve its integrity or its very existence... there are texts and traditions that justify the use of violence in self-defence, and that castigate enemies of the faith.... Such texts exist [in Judaism, Christianity, and Islam], but the real question to ask is what makes people pull them out and make them decisive texts to be literally applied in the very different circumstances of the modern world... [E]ach tradition has developed sophisticated ways of overriding those texts with other and usually later interpretations that stress what is quite clearly more basic – the command of God to have compassion and mercy."

[79] This is also the view of Sam Harris (n. 37) at 110: "While there are undoubtably some 'moderate' Muslims who have decided to overlook the irrescindable militancy of their religion, Islam is undeniably a religion of conquest. The only future devout Muslims can envisage – as Muslims – is one in which all infidels have been converted to Islam, subjugated, or killed." And at 117, "If you believe anything like what the Koran says you must believe in order to escape the fires of hell, you will, at the very least, be sympathetic with the actions of Osama bin Laden". These things, Harris tells us at 230, can be known "with something approaching mathematical certainly" from a reading of the Quran.

[80] Wilders (n. 35) at 163.

[81] Wilders (n. 35) at 26. He elaborates, claiming that "[T]he political ideology of Islam is not moderate – it is a totalitarian cult with global ambitions".

The view that Islam has a fixed and clear meaning that includes support for violence as a means to advance the faith is one that Wilders shares with the extremist fringe of the tradition.[82] He also agrees with the extremists that those who call themselves Muslims, but eschew violence, are not true Muslims – are not fully committed to Islam. In an interview in the *National Post*, Wilders insisted that "Islam itself has only one form" and that the "[t]otalitarian ideology contained in the Koran has no room for moderation". It is arguable, says Wilders, that "'moderate' Muslims are not Muslims at all" because the Quran says that a Muslim must adhere to all of its verses and will be considered an apostate if he or she fails to do so.[83]

Even though Wilders is an outsider to the tradition, he believes he has discovered the true, indisputable meaning of the Quran and so of Islam.[84] He has no interest in the discussions within the Muslim community about the best reading of scripture. Indeed, he believes that such discussions are ruled out in the Islamic tradition: "Since Allah authored the entire Koran, there is no room to re-interpret its commandments – they must simply be followed, unquestioningly, in their most literal sense".[85] And so, in Wilders's account, there is no space for doctrinal debate or for competing interpretations of scripture. As outsiders to a tradition or community sometimes do, Wilders sees Islamic doctrine as clear and fixed (and the Muslim community as more or less homogenous), in contrast to Christian doctrine, which "is subject to passionate discussion and interpretation."[86] Of course, it is the availability of different readings of the Quran or the Islamic tradition (including a fringe reading that accepts the use of violence) that gives Wilders's claim about the violent character of Islam its plausibility to a non-Muslim audience, which often only hears about Islam in connection with terrorist attacks or violent protests.

Within the Muslim community (or communities) – among those who identify with the Islamic tradition – there are different views and vigorous debate about the proper understanding of the tradition and its doctrine (even among those who believe that the Quran must be understood literally). An individual who identifies as a Muslim will seek to adopt the correct or best reading of the Quran, and more

---

[82] Roy (n. 55) at 42: "[T]o define Islam as a body of closed norms and Muslims as making up a community excluding membership in any other group is precisely to adopt the fundamentalists' definition of Islam. This is a reference to an imaginary Islam, and not the real Muslim world, and the fundamentalists are made into authentic representatives of Islam, even if this means speaking with benevolent condescension about the poor liberals who cannot make themselves heard."

[83] "Geert Wilders' problem with Islam", interview by Jonathan Kay, *National Post*, May 8, 2011. ISIL agrees with Wilders on this and issued a fatwa calling for the death of a number of "moderate" Imams in the West: Stewart Bell, "Canadian imams on ISIL hit list for preaching against extremism and steering Muslims 'away from jihad'", *National Post*, Apr. 13, 2016. http://news.nationalpost.com/news/canada/canadian-imams-on-isil-hit-list-for-preaching-against-extremism-and-steering-muslims-away-from-jihad.

[84] Wilders often seems to give agency to Islam – treating the religion as an actor in the world: for example, when he says that "Islam is waging an offensive to conquer Europe" (Wilders, n. 35, at 163). This enables him to ignore the diversity of belief among Muslims.

[85] Wilders (n. 35) at 58.   [86] Wilders (n. 35) at 58.

generally of the Islamic tradition. Extremists, for example, may assert that those who do not support the use of violence against outsiders are bad Muslims or have misread the tradition. Similarly, those who eschew violence and believe that Islam is a religion of peace may claim that the members of the violent fringe are not true Muslims – that they have adopted a twisted version of the faith. Disagreement or debate like this occurs "within" all faith traditions – among those who identify with the tradition. These debates will involve claims not just about what is the right or best interpretation of the faith's scripture or tradition but also about who is a true believer and can properly be described as an adherent – about who is a (good) Muslim or Jew or Christian.[87]

Yet there is something odd, and misconceived, about an outsider to the tradition, an individual like Wilders who makes no claim to be a Muslim and indeed has contempt for Islam, making definitive claims about Islamic doctrine. To assert that someone is or is not a true Muslim or that a particular reading of doctrine is or is not correct is to speak as an insider to the tradition. It is to hold a view about the right or true reading of the revealed word of God – and, more generally, of the tenets of a complex and rich tradition.[88] Wilders is entitled to his opinion about what the words in the Quran mean – although his reading of a translation from Arabic is uninformed by any knowledge of the context in which the cited passages were revealed. But to claim, as he does, to have objectively determined the correct or proper interpretation of the Quran, and to dismiss as erroneous the interpretations of others, is to fail to understand what is involved in the personal and shared search for the "truth" – in the interpretation of what is understood by Muslims to be the word of God. The debate among Muslims (an interpretative community) is about the true meaning of the Quran – about what God has revealed through the Prophet Mohammad. The relevant question, for Wilders and others outside the tradition, who do not believe that the Quran is the revealed word of God or expresses any form

---

[87] Many religious traditions do not have a designated authority or agreed upon process for determining issues of doctrine – for deciding who is or is not a member of the faith or what is or is not proper belief. Some will assert (argue) that they are true believers and others are not. Even scripture does not provide a decisive basis for the resolution of such disputes – since the debate among those who identify with the tradition is often about the role of scripture or the proper way to read it. The issue may be different – although perhaps not dramatically so – in the case of a religious community that has an authority structure for determining doctrine, such as the Roman Catholic Church or the Church of Latter Day Saints (LDS). Yet even if the Roman Catholic Church has decided, for example, that homosexuality is sinful, this doctrine is disputed or ignored by many who understand themselves to be Roman Catholics.

[88] The claim that ISIL is not truly Islamic is also a claim from within the tradition. When political leaders such as Barack Obama (who is not a Muslim) state that Islam is a religion of peace, they must be understood as speaking not as participants in theological debates about Islam, but rather as outsiders, who are observing that the vast majority of those who describe themselves as Muslims reject violence: Ruth Gledill, "Obama: Islam is a religion of 'peace, charity and justice'", *Christian Today*, Feb. 8, 2016, www.christiantoday.com/article/obama.islam.is.a.religion.of.peace.charity.and.justice/79033 .htm.

of spiritual truth, should not be "What is the objective meaning of the Quran?" but should instead be "How is the Quran understood by Muslims?" And, of course, it is apparent that the text is read in many different ways by those who identify as Muslim. Regardless of what the critics may think Islam requires of its adherents, what matters is what Muslims – those who actually believe Islam requires something of them – think it requires.

In the case of other religious traditions, it is generally accepted that their adherents interpret religious doctrine in various ways. For example, in *Owens* v. *Saskatchewan*, a case I will discuss at greater length in Chapter 5, the Saskatchewan Court of Appeal recognized that the Bible is open to a variety of interpretations.[89] Mr. Owens had published an advertisement in the Saskatoon newspaper opposing same-sex relationships. The ad included a number of scriptural references. One of these, from Leviticus in the Old Testament, declares that when a man lies with another man he should be put to death.[90] The Court, though, accepted that it was unlikely that the ad's audience would understand this passage literally – or that Mr. Owens, a believing Christian, intended his ad to be a call to violence. It is possible that in deciding that most of the ad's readers would not interpret the passage literally, the judges were speaking from within the Christian tradition, relying on their own understanding of the best reading of scripture.[91] But even if the judges in the case were not themselves practicing Christians, they were close enough to the Christian tradition to recognize that the Bible is interpreted in different ways by those who identify as Christian and indeed is interpreted by most Christians as calling for love and tolerance towards others.

Wilders maintains that he is simply attacking beliefs. Muslims should be excluded, he says, not because of who they are, or where they come from, but because of what they think and do. He avoids making any explicit claims about Arab, or Muslim, biology – or about the deep-rooted cultural practices of Arabs or Muslims. He insists that he is "talking about the ideology of Islam, not about individual Muslim people", although he is not always faithful to this distinction and speaks sometimes of the "Muslim problem".[92] He declares that anyone who rejects the Islamic faith, and embraces the secular values of the Netherlands, whatever their background, is welcome to remain in the country. Formally, then, he

---

[89] *Owens* v. *Saskatchewan (HRC)* [2006] S.J., No. 221 (Sask CA).

[90] Lev. 20:13 (New International Version).

[91] This may be difficult to avoid for insiders to the tradition who perform a public role. See, for example, the decisions of the Italian courts described in *Lautsi* (n. 2). In claiming that Christianity, in contrast to Islam, is a non-violent, non-oppressive belief system, the Italian courts dismissed the Crusades and the Inquisitions as un-Christian and as based on an incorrect reading of the Bible. In making such a claim, the judges were speaking from inside the Christian tradition as members of the spiritual community.

[92] Wilders (n. 35) at 26. See Jeroen Temperman, *Religious Hatred and International Law* (Cambridge University Press, 2015) at 114.

maintains space between the believer (the individual) and the religious belief system or group.

Wilders does not directly claim that everyone who calls him- or herself a Muslim is committed to violence, and this helps him to evade the charge of hate speech. Nevertheless, he asserts that "a significant and growing minority" of Muslims follow the Quran's violent teaching.[93] And like Steyn, he believes that many of those who describe themselves as Muslims, even if they do not themselves engage in violence or publically advocate violence, may quietly support its use by others to advance the faith. Even "moderate" Muslims, who do not support violence, may be implicated in the violent acts carried out by faithful Muslims. In Wilders's view, the moderates, by calling themselves Muslims, by identifying with the Islamic tradition, and by adhering to many of its practices, give legitimacy to a belief system that is violent and anti-democratic. They help to obscure the true (violent) character of the faith. Moderate Muslims then are not just mistaken about the meaning of their religion; they are complicit in the violence of Islam.

E *The Dismissal of the Complaints Made against Steyn and Wilders*

Both Steyn and Wilders were accused of engaging in hate speech. A complaint was made against Steyn under s. 7(1) (b) of the BC *Human Rights Code*, which prohibits the publication or display of any notice, sign, statement, or other representation that "is likely to expose a person or a group or class of persons to hatred or contempt".[94] Wilders was charged, among other things, with inciting hatred against a group based on their religion, under Art. 137d of the *Criminal Code* of the Netherlands 1881.[95] In both cases, the complaints were dismissed following a hearing.[96] Steyn was able to respond that he was making a claim not about all Muslims, but only about a "core" group of Muslims that is committed to the use of violence to advance their religion. Similarly, Wilders was able to say that he was simply attacking "beliefs" – the core of Islam. Both Steyn and Wilders could acknowledge formally the distinction between the individual and the religious tradition or community with which he or she

---

93 Wilders (n. 35) at 26.

94 BC *Human Rights Code*, RSBC 1996, c. 210, s. 7. A complaint against Steyn and *Macleans*, made under the *Canadian Human Rights Act*, R.S., 1985, c. H-6 [CHRA], was dismissed prior to adjudication. A complaint was also made to the Ontario Human Rights Commission, but the Commission determined that it did not have jurisdiction to consider the complaint, since the *Ontario Human Rights Code*, RSO 1990, c. H19, does not include a ban on hate speech.

95 Art. 137d, *Wetboek van Strafrecht (Sr.)*. Following a public speech several years later, Wilders was found to have incited discrimination against Dutch Moroccans.

96 The complaint against Steyn was dismissed following a hearing before the B.C. Human Rights Tribunal (*Elmasry v. Roger's Publishing and MacQueen (No. 4)*, 2008 BCHRT 378 [*Elmasry*]. In Wilders's case, the Dutch courts found that his film and related communications did not breach the criminal ban (Amsterdam District Court, Wilders, Case no. 13-425046-09 (23 June 2011)). For a discussion, see Temperman (n. 92) at 116.

identifies (and the space for disagreement or contest within the religious tradition) at important moments in their arguments, while effectively communicating the idea that to be a Muslim is to be committed to (or supportive of) the use of violence.

The hate speech complaint against Steyn was also dismissed because the tone of his article did not appear to be hateful or vitriolic.[97] The B.C. Human Rights Tribunal [BCHRT] found that the article did not rise "to the level of detestation, calumny and vilification necessary to breach . . . the Code."[98] It may have generated fear, but, according to the Tribunal, "fear is not synonymous with hatred and contempt".[99] As noted in the previous chapter, the angry or vitriolic tone of a particular instance of speech may discourage careful or critical judgment of its message by the audience, and so is a relevant consideration in determining whether the speech may contribute to the spread of hatred. Yet too great an emphasis on tone or style may encourage the mistaken impression that hate speech laws are intended to protect individuals from offence or hurt feelings, rather than from the spread of dangerous misinformation about their group in the larger community. The central question the courts must decide in these cases is whether the false claims made about Muslims are so extreme that they are likely to generate hateful views and encourage extreme action. Despite his glib and sometimes humorous style, Steyn's purpose seems to be to alert his "Western" audience to the threat posed by Muslims.

The complaint against Steyn was also dismissed because, according to the BCHRT, his expression contributed to public discussion: "[R]ead in its context, the Article is essentially an opinion on issues which in light of recent historical events involving extremist Muslims and the problems facing the vast majority of the Muslim community that does not support extremism, are legitimate subjects for public discussion".[100] While Steyn may have engaged in "exaggeration", said the tribunal, he did so in order to rally public opinion.[101] The question that was not asked by the tribunal in this case is what Steyn was hoping to achieve through his false and exaggerated claims – what exactly was he asking of his readers? In his column in *Macleans*, a popular national news magazine, and in his other writing, Steyn does not often call for political action; indeed, he sometimes says that political action will be futile in the current climate. Similarly, in Wilders's case, the Dutch authorities declared that his speech should be seen as part of an ongoing debate about immigration and terrorism. Wilders, of course, is the leader of a Dutch political party that has had some electoral success.[102]

---

[97] *Elmasry* (n. 96) at para. 151.   [98] *Elmasry* (n. 96) at para. 156.   [99] *Elmasry* (n. 96) at para. 154.

[100] *Elmasry* (n. 96) at para. 150. Steyn was not charged under the *Criminal Code*; however, it is worth noting that the ban on hate speech in the *Criminal Code* does not apply "if the statements were relevant to any subject of public interest, the discussion of which was for the public benefit, and if on reasonable grounds he believed them to be true" (s. 319(3)(c)). This may not be a true exception, since the false and extreme claims of hate speech are not based on "reasonable grounds" and are not for the public benefit.

[101] *Elmasry* (n. 96) at para. 156.   [102] Temperman (n. 92) at 116.

Because the view that Muslims are willing to use violence to advance their faith is no longer a fringe view, Steyn's claims about Muslims and Wilders's assertions about Islam are more likely to be viewed as support for political action rather than advocacy of extra-legal violence and discrimination. But, of course, the political action that is called for is the oppression or exclusion of Muslims. The involuntary deportation of Muslims from the West would require state violence that is too awful to imagine. Bruce Bawer in a 2007 blog post compares Muslims in contemporary Europe to the Nazis in the Weimar Republic and tells his readers that "European officials have a clear route out of this nightmare . . . They have armies. They have police. They have prisons".[103]

One of the ironies of hate speech law is that it may only be effective in dealing with speech that occurs at the margins of public discourse – that lies outside the scope of mainstream opinion and general debate.[104] As argued in the previous chapter, the purpose of a ban on hate speech cannot be to eradicate bigotry and discrimination in the community, but must instead be more narrowly defined – to prevent the encouragement of "isolated" acts of violence against the members of a targeted group and perhaps also to stop the extreme from becoming mainstream.

When Islamophobic speech is more widely expressed, not only will it be seen as encouraging political action rather than the incitement of extra-legal violence, but also it will be less recognizable as extreme – less likely to be read by its audience as calling for radical or violent action (state or extra-legal). Because anti-Muslim speech is more and more commonplace, because it is often made in public view and therefore exposed to debate and refutation, and because it may increasingly be understood as calling for (democratic) political action, there may be no alternative but to debate it. Nevertheless, if the claims of Steyn, Wilders, and others can be read as justifying (state or private) violence against Muslims, then they should be considered hate speech. To assert that Muslims, as a group, are violent is to vilify them and to (implicitly) advocate their forceful oppression. The real issue in these cases then is not whether the claim that Muslims are violent amounts to hate speech. It is whether Steyn and Wilders have made such a broad claim (about all Muslims) or have instead made a more limited claim that some Muslims are committed to the use of violence to advance their faith. Each of them in their writing tries to blur the distinction between these two claims.

The complaint against Steyn may also have been dismissed because there was no clear link between his expression and the spread of hatred or the occurrence of violence against Muslims. The Tribunal thought that Steyn's expression was not "likely to expose" Muslims "to hatred". Because the view that Muslims (or at least some of them) are dangerous is widely held and expressed, we are less likely to link violent action against the group's members to a particular writing or writer. Most of those who read the words of Steyn or Wilders will not engage in anti-Muslim

---

[103] Bruce Bawer in 2007 blog post quoted in Saunders (n. 28) at 14.   [104] See the discussion in c. 2.

violence. Doug Saunders, in his book *The Myth of the Muslim Tide*, observes that for most readers, the Muslim Tide literature serves as "reassurance" rather than "a call to arms": It helps to explain "the bewildering appearance of visibly different Muslim communities in their cities, and the near-simultaneous eruptions of Islamist violence that marked the first years of this century".[105] Yet, as Saunders also recognizes, "[a] small minority of readers have been inspired to support a new type of politics" and, I would add, to engage in oppressive and even violent action against Muslims.[106] Nevertheless, when an individual, a so-called "lone wolf" such as Anders Breivik, commits an act of violence after absorbing the Eurabia message, his extraordinary action can be attributed to his moral deficiency or mental illness.

In contrast, the Canadian, American, and European publics seem less inclined to view an act of violence as "isolated" or as the manifestation of mental illness when it is committed by an individual who has latched onto the message of ISIL terrorist propaganda. The two men who, in separate incidents a few years ago, murdered Canadian soldiers (in a shopping mall parking lot in a small Quebec town and at the cenotaph in Ottawa) were often described not as "lone wolves", but as agents of radical Islam acting on the direction of extremists from abroad, or as apostles of the violent ideology of radical Islam.[107] They were viewed in this way despite their limited knowledge of Islam and lack of connection to any radical organization and their personal histories of petty crime, drug abuse, and mental illness.[108]

Speech that attributes dangerous or undesirable traits to a group that has in the past been the target of a campaign of violence is more likely to be seen as hate speech – as causing, or creating a risk of, significant harm. We are more likely to discern a link between a particular instance of hateful speech and the spread of hatred or the occurrence of violence when there is a pattern or history of hatred and violence against the group. Moreover, as noted in the previous chapter, because phrases such as "the solution to the Jewish problem" or symbols, such as the swastika, evoke the Holocaust, it is easy to attribute a violent purpose to an individual who uses them. Because the act of burning a cross evokes the violent oppression of blacks in North America, it is easy to understand it as a call to violence (or as a threat of violence) and to connect its use to violent action. Yet, in the case of harsh, vitriolic statements made about other identifiable groups that do not have the same recent history of organized violent persecution, it may be harder to discern a violent purpose or effect. We are less likely to see speech as a call or prelude to violent action when violence seems remote or infrequent.

The question now is whether recent acts of violence against Muslims, including fire bombings of mosques, street assaults, and notably the mass murder in Norway committed by Anders Breivik, make it more likely that the claims of Steyn and

---

[105] Saunders (n. 20) at 23.   [106] Saunders (n. 20) at 23.
[107] "Attack on Ottawa: PM Harper cites terrorist motive", *Globe and Mail*, Oct 22, 2014.
[108] See discussion in c. 5.

others will be viewed as hate speech – as encouraging the violent oppression of Muslims. Breivik, who had "drenched" himself in anti-Islam writing by far right commentators from Europe and the United States, set off a bomb in the government district in Oslo, which killed 8 people.[109] He then travelled to the island location of a camp for youth members of the governing Social Democratic Party, where he shot and killed 69 young people.

Steyn was embarrassed by the references to his work in Anders Breivik's manifesto. Initially he responded by pointing out that Breivik's attack was directed against "native" Norwegians and not Muslims. Breivik's action, said Steyn, was not an "'Islamophobic' mass murder [because as] far as we know not a single Muslim was among the victims".[110] In his quick and defensive response, Steyn omitted to mention that a central theme in his writing is that the "liberal elites", who support immigration and multiculturalism, are complicit in the Muslim takeover of Europe. Breivik's attack was directed at the people (and their children) who Steyn claimed were appeasing radical Muslims. Breivik presented himself as a "saviour and redeemer of a white, Christian European Civilization" and intended his attack to be a wakeup call to his fellow Europeans.[111]

Steyn's other attempt to distance himself from Breivik's violence was to note that Breivik's manifesto referred to a wide range of authors, including major figures in European political theory, such as John Locke and Edmund Burke: "When a Norwegian man is citing Locke and Burke as a prelude to gunning down dozens of Norwegian teenagers, he is lost in his own psychosis."[112] Yet it was the writing of Steyn and other Eurabia authors that persuaded Breivik of the urgent need to respond to the threat to European civilization posed by Muslims. "Of course", Steyn cannot be blamed for eccentric readings of his words. But how should Breivik have read Steyn? If Steyn meant what he said, and Breivik was persuaded by his claim, what should Breivik have concluded? Steyn claimed that the European nations are about to succumb to the single-minded determination of the Muslim inhabitants of Europe, who are an "enemy within", prepared to employ coercive and violent means to impose their faith on others. Political action seems futile, said Steyn. The political elites of Europe are unable or unwilling to address the problem. Breivik appears to have drawn the logical conclusion from Steyn's claims. His "psychotic" actions may

[109] Bowen (n. 32) at 6. In January 2017, after this manuscript was completed, a lone gun attacked a mosque in Quebec city and shot and killed six of its members. For a thoughtful examination of the Breivik case and its impact in Norway, see Sindre Bangstad, *Anders Breivik and the Rise of Islamophobia* (Zed Books, 2014). Bangstad at 109: "Behring Breivik spent considerable time on the internet, so much so that one could well see his radicalization as a classic case of 'internet radicalization' mirroring that of a number of young European Muslims who turned to radical Islamism in the aftermath of 9/11."

[110] Mark Steyn, "Islamophobia and mass murder", *National Review*, July 25, 2011.

[111] Bangstad (n. 109) at 9. Bangstad also notes that Breivik would have had some difficulty finding a similar – concentrated – target composed of Muslims, who make up less than 2.5% of the population of Norway and are a diverse group, coming from a variety of cultural or national backgrounds.

[112] Steyn, "Islamophobia" (n. 110).

be seen as a "rational" response to Steyn's assertions. Perhaps Steyn never intended anyone to act on the views he expressed. Perhaps his claims were mostly hyperbole and meant simply to catch attention, generate controversy, sell books, and put him in the public eye. Yet Steyn's claims were offered as serious analysis and are understood by many readers as such. He should not be surprised then when some readers decide to act on his claims. His concluding words in *America Alone* were these: "We have been shirking too long, and that's unworthy of a great civilization. To see off the new Dark Ages will be tough and demanding. The alternative will be worse".[113]

Wilders similarly sought to distance himself from the actions of Breivik, by describing him as "a violent, sick, psychopath".[114] Wilders "abhors" these acts of violence – of murder – and instead favours the forced (violent) deportation of Muslims from Europe (on a grand scale), unless they recant their religious beliefs. Bruce Bawer described Breivik as "both highly intelligent and very well read in European history" and believed that Breivik had "a legitimate concern about genuine problems" even if his solution was "evil".[115] Bawer, though, insists that these serious concerns ought to be "forcefully addressed by government leaders".[116] In other words, Bawer thinks that the right response is state, rather than private, violence. American anti-Muslim blogger and activist Pamela Geller seemed to defend Breivik's actions, when she said, "Breivik was targeting the future leaders of the party responsible for flooding Norway with Muslims who refuse to assimilate, who commit major violence against Norwegian natives, including violent gang rapes, with impunity, and who live on the dole . . . all done without the consent of the Norwegians".[117]

---

[113] Steyn, *America Alone* (n. 23), at 214.
[114] Quoted in Doug Saunders, "'Eurabia' opponents scramble for distance from anti-Muslim murderer", *Globe and Mail*, July 25, 2011.
[115] Bruce Bawer in 2007 blog post quoted in Saunders (n. 20) at 14.
[116] Bruce Bawer in 2007 blog post quoted in Saunders (n. 20) at 14.
[117] Pamela Geller, quoted in Nathan Lean (n. 72) at 169.

4

The Ridicule and Insult of the Sacred

INTRODUCTION – THE SATANIC VERSES AND THE DANISH CARTOONS

The second difficulty with the distinction between attacks on a belief system (which should not be restricted) and attacks on an individual believer or a community of believers (which may sometimes be restricted) is that religious beliefs or commitments are sometimes so deeply held that an attack on the individual's beliefs, and on the objects, persons, or practices that he or she regards as sacred, affects the believer very personally and powerfully. Religion, when understood as a personal commitment to a set of truth claims, must remain open to criticism, even if it is harsh; but when religion is viewed as a cultural identity, attacks on its beliefs or sacred objects may be seen as a failure to respect the basic dignity of its adherents and may lead to the alienation of the group from the larger community.

The publication of Salman Rushdie's book *The Satanic Verses* in 1988 generated protests in England and elsewhere in the West.[1] The book was thought by many Muslims to be contemptuous of their faith and their community – ridiculing important elements of Islamic doctrine and defaming the Prophet Mohammad and other important figures in the tradition. The protests were initially peaceful, and so did not gain much attention. However, a group of protesters was advised by a community lawyer that they might be more successful in calling attention to their concerns if they held a book burning and invited the press to attend.[2] This advice was followed and the event did indeed generate publicity, almost all of which was negative. To some Britons, the protest confirmed that many Muslims did not understand free speech and other Western values.

Members of the Muslim community brought a complaint against the book's publisher under English blasphemy law. However, the complaint was dismissed because, according to the court, the blasphemy ban extended only to the

---

[1] Salman Rushdie, *The Satanic Verses* (Viking, 1988).
[2] Bhikhu Parekh, *Rethinking Multiculturalism* (Harvard University Press, 2000) at 299.

intemperate criticism or ridicule of the *Christian* faith – an inequity noted by the Muslim community in England. The book was eventually noticed in Muslim-majority countries, which led to large-scale protests and finally to a fatwa issued by the spiritual leader of Iran, Ayatollah Khomeini, calling for the death of Salman Rushdie and others involved in the book's publication.[3]

In September 2005, the Danish newspaper *Jyllands-Posten* printed twelve cartoons depicting the Prophet Mohammad. In an editorial accompanying the cartoons, the paper said that it had published these images of the Prophet as a defence of free speech against "[t]he Islamic spiritual leaders [who] feel called upon to gripe and an army of intellectually underequipped followers [who] respond and do what is interpreted as the Prophet's command and ultimately kill the offenders."[4] When first published, the cartoons caused no particular stir. Disappointed by this silence, the newspaper contacted a number of local imams to get their reaction. Even then the response from Danish Muslims was muted. It was only after a Danish-based imam delivered the cartoons (along with a few even more offensive images that were not part of the publication and indeed were not even created as images of Mohammad) to religious and political leaders in Saudi Arabia and elsewhere in the Muslim world that protest began – abroad rather than in Denmark. The cartoons were later reprinted in a variety of European publications, including *Charlie Hebdo* in France, ostensibly as an affirmation of the European commitment to freedom of expression.[5] A prosecution was initiated against the newspaper *Jyllands Posten* under Denmark's criminal ban on religious insult.[6] The court, however, dismissed the claim because, in its view, the cartoons were a form of social criticism that did not amount to a religious insult under the criminal law.[7]

There are different ways to understand the objections raised to the "Danish Cartoons" and to Salman Rushdie's book, *The Satanic Verses*.[8] One objection to the

---

[3] The fatwa against Rushdie was understood by many as an attempt by Khomeini to stabilize his position following the devastating Iran–Iraq war and to claim a leadership role in the Muslim world. To some extent he was successful. Muslims in the West, who often felt marginalized and ignored, gained a stronger sense of identity, community, and confidence: For a discussion, see Parekh (n. 2) at 300 and Kenan Malik, *From Jihad to Fatwas: The Rushdie Affair and Its Aftermath* (Melville House, 2014) at 17.

[4] Jytte Klausen, *The Cartoons That Shook the World* (Yale University Press, 2009) at 13.

[5] *Charlie Hebdo* produced many of its own cartoons, which were viewed as offensive to some Muslims. The magazine was the target of an attack in January 2015 that killed twelve people. For a discussion of *Charlie Hebdo* and the misreading of many of its cartoons, see Susan Benesch, "Charlie the free thinker: Religion, blasphemy and decent controversy", 10 *Religion and Human Rights* 244 (2015).

[6] Section 140 of the Danish Criminal Code prohibits public mockery or scorn of the beliefs of a recognized Danish religious community or faith.

[7] Jeroen Temperman, *Religious Hatred and International Law: The Prohibition of Incitement to Violence or Discrimination* (Cambridge University Press, 2015), at 106. The Danish law had last been applied in 1938 to Nazi anti-Semitic leaflets that claimed that the Talmud sanctioned the rape of Gentile women (Klausen, n. 4, at 144). Complaints made in other European jurisdictions were also unsuccessful.

[8] Klausen (n. 4) at 1 observes that there was no consensus among the protestors about why the cartoons were objectionable or what was to be achieved through the protests. And at 130, "The Muslim point

cartoons, in particular, was that they breached the religious prohibition against creating an image of the Prophet – a "graven image". But even if there was agreement among Muslims that representations of the Prophet Mohammad are prohibited and that this prohibition applied to both Muslims and non-Muslims – and it appears that there is no consensus on this – it is a religiously based prohibition and as such cannot be the basis for state action.[9] The Danish Cartoons and *The Satanic Verses* were also regarded by some Muslims as blasphemous, in the original sense of the term – as an insult to God and/or His Prophet that might lead to divine punishment against the community that tolerates these works. But again, state law must be based on secular or civic concerns.

Another argument, which is at least cognizable within a secular moral/political framework, is that the cartoons and Rushdie's book reinforced stereotypes of Muslims – that they represented Muslims as violent and backward to a predominantly non-Muslim audience. Bhikhu Parekh notes that many Muslims thought that Rushdie's book "gave a totally inaccurate account of Islam" and "demeaned and degraded" Muslims, reinforcing "traditional stereotypes", and presenting Muslims "as barbarians following a fraudulent religion created by a cunning manipulator and devoid of a sound system of morality".[10] For many Muslims, says Kenan Malik, the book "was part of the ancient tradition of Orientalism – the Western traducing of Islam."[11]

In an essay entitled "In Good Faith", Rushdie describes his object in writing *The Satanic Verses* as the creation of "a literary language and literary forms in which the experience of formerly colonized, still disadvantaged peoples might find full expression."[12] The novel, according to Rushdie, offers a "migrant's eye-view of the world . . . written from the very experience of uprooting, disjuncture and metamorphosis . . . that is the migrant condition, and from which . . . can be derived a metaphor for all of humanity."[13] Rushdie expresses frustration at the failure of so many to see that his novel is a work of fiction – rather than "a work of bad history [or] an anti-religious pamphlet".[14] He points out that virtually all of the alleged "insults and abuse" in the book occur in dreams that are painful to the dreamer and represent a form of punishment for the dreamer's loss of faith.[15] Rushdie insists

---

was not that the Danes could not make pictures of the Prophet but that the pictures said inflammatory things about Muslims."

[9] For a discussion of this see Anver Emon, "On the Pope, cartoons, and apostates", 22 *Journal of Law & Religion* 303 (2006–2007). Klausen (n. 4) at 8 observed that "few Muslims cited religious law for their protest".

[10] Parekh (n. 2) at 298–99. He continues, "As a Muslim as well as scholar of Islam, Rushdie owed it to his culturally besieged community to counter 'myths' and 'lies' spread about them or at least to refrain from lending them his authority."

[11] Malik (n. 3) at 153.

[12] Salman Rushdie, "In Good Faith", in *Imaginary Homelands* (Granta, 1992) at 394.

[13] Rushdie, "In Good Faith" (n. 12) at 394.   [14] Rushdie, "In Good Faith" (n. 12) at 393.

[15] Rushdie, "In Good Faith" (n. 12) at 398. Several other "insults" occur in a portrayal of persecution of spiritual followers. Rushdie wonders how a book could portray persecution "without allowing the persecutors to be seen persecuting?" (401).

that while the novel sought to explore the authority and authorship of the Quran, it was never intended to insult Islam or Muslims.[16] Rushdie's celebration of "hybridity, impurity, intermingling" is not easy to reconcile with the idea that some matters are sacred.[17] But even if the novel might be seen by some as blasphemous, the openness of its meaning makes it difficult to classify as hate speech – as intended to stir up hatred against Muslims.

The Danish Cartoons were also viewed by some as a form of group defamation. Strong objection was taken, in particular, to the cartoon in which the prophet Mohammad's turban was made to look like a bomb. This image was seen by many as linking Muslims to violence, a not unreasonable view given that claims about Muslim violence were being expressed with increasing frequency. The creator of the cartoon, though, insisted that the image was meant to be a comment on the violent fringe of the Muslim community and not on the community as a whole – and was not intended to suggest that Islam is a violent religion.[18] The debate around the Danish Cartoons seemed to confirm the openness of their meaning and the uncertainty of their impact on viewers.

The principal complaint about the cartoons and Rushdie's book seemed to be that matters sacred to a religious community were mocked or ridiculed, causing hurt or offence to the members of that community. Or, at least, that is how the complaint was understood by members of the mainstream community – some of whom were sympathetic to the complaint and others of whom were not.[19] According to Ziauddin Saddar, "The life of the Prophet Mohammad is the source of Muslim identity"; "Muslims relate to him directly and personally" with the result that "every word, every jibe, every obscenity in *The Satanic Verses*" was felt "personally".[20] Some Christians have objected for similar reasons to certain depictions of Jesus, such as "Piss Christ", a photograph that shows a plastic crucifix immersed in a jar of the

---

[16] Some Muslims might consider such an exploration, if it raised any doubt about the divine origin of the revelations, to be an insult to their faith (without necessarily thinking that such insults should be proscribed by law). For a discussion see c. 3.

[17] Rushdie "In Good Faith" (n. 12) at 394.

[18] Kurt Westergaard, "Why I drew the cartoon: The 'Muhammad Affair', in retrospect", *Princetonian*, Oct 1, 2009.

[19] For a survey of opinion see Lisa Appignanesi and Sara Maitland (eds.), *The Rushdie File* (Syracuse University Press, 1990).

[20] Ziauddin Saddar, quoted in Malik (n. 3) at 6. See also Saba Mahmood, "Religious reason and secular affect: An incommensurable divide?" in Talal Asad, Wendy Brown, Judith Butler, and Saba Mahmood, *Is Critique Secular? Blasphemy, Injury, and Free Speech* (Doreen B. Townsend Center for the Humanities, UC Berkeley, 2009) at 75: "Muhammed is regarded as a moral exemplar whose words and deeds are understood not so much as commandments but as ways of inhabiting the world, bodily and ethically." And at 77–78: "The sense of moral injury that emanates from such a relationship between the ethical subject and the figure of exemplarity (such as Muhammed) is quite distinct from one that the notion of blasphemy encodes. The notion of moral injury I am describing no doubt entails a sense of violation, but this violation emanates not from the judgment that the law has been transgressed but that one's being, grounded as it is in a relationship of dependency with the Prophet, has been shaken."

photographer's urine,[21] or the poem in the *Whitehouse* v. *Lemon* case, which is discussed below, that describes a homosexual encounter involving Jesus as well as sex acts performed on his crucified body,[22] or the film in the *Otto Preminger* case (also discussed below) that depicts Mary as a loose woman and God as senile.[23] The ridiculing or degrading of sacred matters is deeply hurtful to believers. This experience of offence or hurt may also lead to alienation and social tension, resulting in the additional and more tangible harm of public disturbance or communal violence.

The impact of religious insult may be greater when the targeted group's members already feel marginalized and view the speech as reinforcing their subordinate position in the broader community. Indeed, in such cases it may be difficult to distinguish – to disentangle – the personal offence that individuals feel when sacred symbols or venerated persons are ridiculed and disparaged from their concern or anger that their religious community is being represented as backward or barbaric. Kenan Malik notes that "political despair about belongingness and identity . . . stoked-up" the negative feelings in the British Muslim community about *The Satanic Verses* and the Danish Cartoons.[24] These depictions of Islam and Muslims may not have been clear in their meaning or sufficiently extreme in their content to be considered hate speech. Nevertheless, concerns about the defamation or misdescription of the Muslim community and its beliefs, combined with upset about the ways in which the novel and the cartoons insulted or blasphemed the Islamic faith, generated a strong, if sometimes unfocused, opposition to both works. Some members of the Muslim community also believed that the political and legal responses to Rushdie's novel and the Danish Cartoons revealed the double standard of European law, which prohibited the disparagement or defamation of the Jewish and Christian communities but refused to extend the same protection to Islam and Muslims.

It is worth noting, though, that most of those who objected to *The Satanic Verses* had not actually read the book. They had heard from others about its most objectionable passages, although they knew little about the narrative context from which

---

[21] A gallery in the Australian state of Victoria, which displayed the photograph, was the subject of an unsuccessful blasphemy prosecution: *Pell* v. *Council of Trustees of the National Gallery of Victoria* (Unreported, Supreme Court of Victoria, Harper J., 9 October 1997). According to the art critic and Roman Catholic nun Sister Wendy Beckett, in an interview with Bill Moyers on PBS in 1998, the Piss Christ photograph should be seen as a comment on contemporary society's treatment of Christ: "I thought he [the artist] was saying, in a rather simplistic, magazine-y type of way, that this is what we are doing to Christ, we are not treating him with reverence. His great sacrifice is not used. We live very vulgar lives. We put Christ in a bottle of urine – in practice. It was a very admonitory work. Not a great work; one wouldn't want to go on looking at it once one had already seen it once. But I think to call it blasphemous is really rather begging the question: it could be, or it could not be. It is what you make of it, and I could make something that made me feel a deep desire to reverence the death of Christ more by this suggestion that this is what, in practice, the world is doing." www.youtube.com/watch?v=L9pAKdkJh-Y.

[22] *Whitehouse* v. *Gay News Ltd* [1979] AC 617 (HL).

[23] *Otto-Preminger-Institut* v. *Austria*, No. 13470/87, [1994] ECHR 26.   [24] Malik (n. 3) at 95.

these passages were taken.[25] The person who led the campaign to have the novel banned in India said that he "did not have to wade through a filthy drain to know what filth is".[26] It seems more likely that those who were opposed to the cartoons had viewed them, although it would have been easy to avoid seeing them, since one had to either buy a newspaper that had published them, or search for them online. The offence or injury the critics experienced arose then not from the shock of seeing or hearing a work that disparaged sacred persons or objects, but instead from the simple knowledge that someone had produced and someone else had read/viewed, or might read/view, such a work. And so, despite the "secular" description of the injury as personal offence, the critics' objection was either to the public misrepresentation of their religion (or community) or to the ridicule of a sacred or venerated person (based on a more traditional understanding of blasphemy) – wrongs that did not depend on the direct personal experience of the objectionable speech.

I BLASPHEMY LAW

Blasphemy, as originally understood, involved insults directed at God (or other sacred figures) that might provoke divine retribution against the general community. The ban on blasphemy, at least within the Christian tradition, also came to include the public repudiation of the central truths of the established faith, or what might more properly be described as heresy. This early conception of blasphemy is apparent still in the arguments of conservative Christians such as Jerry Falwell and Pat Robertson, who claim that America's toleration of homosexuality has provoked God to act against the nation – through natural disasters such as Hurricane Katrina – or to withdraw *His* protection of the nation from man-made events, such as the 9/11 attacks.[27]

The justification for the blasphemy ban, at least in the English common law world, took a more worldly or political form in the seventeenth century, when its focus shifted from the protection of religious truth or the honour of religious figures

---

[25] Many readers – both Muslim and non-Muslim – took issue with what they saw as a distorted or simplified reading of the book. See, for example, Malik (n. 3) at 153 describing the novel as "a strikingly new literary exploration of race and religion in the postmodern world". Anne Norton, *On the Muslim Question* (Princeton University Press, 2013) at 16 thought *The Satanic Verses* was "a curious target" for religious protest, since it was a work of fiction "marked by elaborate fantasy sequences". Jeremy Waldron, *Liberal Rights* (Cambridge University Press, 1993) at 14 read the book as seeking "to make sense of human experience", as "touch[ing] on some of the problems that Islam addresses".

[26] Quoted in Leonard W. Levy, *Blasphemy* (University of North Carolina Press, 1995) at 561.

[27] "Falwell: Blame abortionists, feminists and gays", *The Guardian*, Wednesday, Sept 19, 2001, www.theguardian.com/world/2001/sep/19/september11.usa9. "The Rev Jerry Falwell and Pat Robertson ... asserted on US television that an angry God had allowed the terrorists to succeed in their deadly mission because the United States had become a nation of abortion, homosexuality, secular schools and courts, and the American civil liberties union. ... Mr Falwell's and Mr. Robertson's remarks were based in theology familiar to and accepted by many conservative evangelical Christians, who believe the Bible teaches that God withdraws protection from nations that violate his will."

to the defence of public morality and the legal order. The English courts decided that because religious beliefs and practices formed the basis for the legal/social system, any criticism of the established religion might undermine public respect for that system and should therefore be banned.[28] For Lord Chief Justice Hale in *Taylor's Case* "to say, religion is a cheat, is to dissolve all those obligations whereby the civil societies are preserved, [because]...Christianity is parcel of the laws of England...[T]o reproach the Christian religion is to speak in subversion of the law".[29]

In the late 1800s, the scope of the blasphemy ban was significantly narrowed. While blasphemy law in the West had previously banned public criticism of Christianity or the repudiation of its principal tenets, the law came to be interpreted more narrowly as a ban on intemperate attacks on the Christian faith. The purpose of the ban was no longer to defend the Christian foundations of the legal/social order, but was instead to protect the religious feelings or sensibilities of community members and to prevent public conflict and disorder. Lord Chief Justice Coleridge in *R. v. Ramsay and Foote* declared that "if the decencies of controversy are observed, even the fundamentals of religion may be attacked without the writer being guilty of blasphemy."[30] It was permissible at law for an individual to criticise the established religion, provided the criticism was civil or respectful in tone.

While the blasphemy ban had some life in England in the early part of the twentieth century, there were no prosecutions from 1922 until 1977, when the case of *Whitehouse* v. *Gay News* came before the courts.[31] In that case, a poem that was published in *Gay News* was found to breach the common law ban on blasphemy. The poem, which was titled "The Love That Dare Not Speak Its Name", described homosexual relations between Jesus and his disciples and sexual acts performed on the crucified body of Jesus.[32] The readers of *Gay News* made no complaint about

---

[28] Even if political unity and social peace did not require religious conformity, they were understood to require a degree of respect for the official or dominant religion.

[29] *Taylor's Case* (1676), 86 Eng. Rep. 189; 3 Keb. 607, 621.

[30] *R. v. Ramsay & Foote* (1883), 15 Cox Crim. Cases 231 (QB) at 238. Earlier in *R. v. Bradlaugh*, 15 Cox Cr. Cases 215 (1883) at 225, Coleridge LCJ. had said that expression was blasphemous only if it was "intended to insult the feelings and the deepest religious convictions of the great majority of the persons amongst whom we live". This view of the law was affirmed by the House of Lords in *Bowman* v. *Secular Society* [1917] AC 406 (HL).

[31] *Whitehouse* v. *Lemon* (1978) 67 Cr. App. R. 70 (CA); *Whitehouse* v. *Lemon* [1979] 2 WLR 281(HL); or *Whitehouse* v. *Gay News Ltd.* [1979] AC 617 (HL). An application under the ECHR was dismissed in *Gay News Ltd. and Lemon* v. *UK* [Eur Comm HR] 5 EHRR 123 (1982), App. No. 8710/79. In 1967 the *Blasphemy Act of 1698* was repealed by the UK Parliament (*Criminal Justice Act*, 1967). The courts, however, decided that this did not have the effect of abolishing the common law prohibition on blasphemy (Levy, n. 26, at 536).

[32] See also *Wingrove* v. *The United Kingdom* (19/1995/525/611), 25 November 1996 in which the ECtHR declined to interfere with the decision of the British Board of Film Classification (and the Video Appeals Committee) to refuse to issue a classification certificate to a video (entitled *Visions of Ecstasy*) that it judged to be blasphemous. Without such a certificate, the video could not be shown. The video depicted St Teresa of Avila experiencing sexual raptures stimulated by an image of the crucified Jesus.

the poem; however, three months after its publication, Mary Whitehouse, the head of an organization called the National Viewers' and Listeners' Association, learned of the poem and initiated a prosecution against the publisher under the blasphemy ban. The author, James Kirkup, a poet of some repute, said that he had written the poem "to portray strong deep emotion and intense passion (in both senses of the word), to present a human, earthly, and imperfect Christ symbolising my own outcast state and that of all outcasts in society."[33] He intended to create a work of art, he said, and not to commit a blasphemy, although he recognized that his poem would "dismay and shock some people". The courts, though, held that the relevant intention, under the blasphemy ban, was not whether the accused magazine intended to blaspheme but simply whether it intended to publish the blasphemy. A jury found that the poem breached the ban because it insulted Christians and aroused their resentment. The conviction of the publisher was upheld on appeal to both the Court of Appeal and the House of Lords.[34]

In his concurring judgment in the House of Lords decision in *Gay News*, Lord Scarman suggested that the blasphemy ban should be enlarged to protect the religious feelings of the followers of all faiths and not just the established religion. This was not an issue the Court had to resolve in *Gay News*, since the poem in that case involved blasphemy against the Christian faith. The scope of the English blasphemy ban, however, was directly at issue in the *Choudhry* case, which involved a private prosecution for blasphemy brought against the publisher of *The Satanic Verses*.[35] The Court of Queen's Bench held that the case against the publisher could not succeed because protection from intemperate criticism extended only to the established faith (the Church of England or perhaps generally the Christian faith) and not to Islam and other non-Christian faiths – a vestige of the law's earlier role in defending religious truth or protecting the integrity and stability of the nation's political and social institutions. The courts were unwilling to address this inequity, because they thought it was up to Parliament to make such a fundamental change to the law, and perhaps also because they were reluctant to extend the scope of a law that was increasingly viewed as problematic.[36] Indeed, Parliament subsequently repealed the English common law ban on blasphemy and enacted in its place a prohibition on the incitement of religious hatred.[37]

---

[33] James Kirkup, quoted in Levy (n. 26) at 537.   [34] *Whitehouse* (n. 31).

[35] R. v. *Chief Metropolitan Stipendiary Magistrate, Ex parte Choudhry* [1991] 1QB 429.

[36] For a criticism of Lord Scarman's proposal see Robert Post, "Cultural heterogeneity and law: Pornography, blasphemy, and the First Amendment" (1988) 76 *Cal. L. Rev.* 297.

[37] In 1981, the UK Law Commission had recommended the repeal of the common law crime. (UK Law Commission, *Offences against Religion and Public Worship* (Her Majesty's Stationer, 1985)). *Racial and Religious Hatred Act*, 2006, s. 29B: "A person who uses threatening words or behaviour, or displays any written material which is threatening, is guilty of an offence if he intends thereby to stir up religious hatred." In fact, the new ban was enacted shortly before the repeal of the blasphemy offence – but was understood to be a condition for the repeal.

In Canada, a ban on the publication of "blasphemous libel" was included in the *Criminal Code* that was enacted by the federal government in 1892, shortly after Confederation.[38] The *Code* provision incorporated contemporaneous changes in the English blasphemy jurisprudence, and so did not extend to expression of "an opinion on a religious subject" that is made "in good faith and in decent language". Between 1901 and 1936, there were five reported prosecutions under the *Criminal Code* ban, with "[n]one before and none since".[39] Four of these cases resulted in conviction. In each of these cases the attack was directed at the doctrine and clergy of the Roman Catholic church or one of the Protestant churches. It might be thought then that the Canadian blasphemy ban, in contrast to the English ban, protected all religious groups from insult or offence and not just the "established" or dominant faith community. More likely, though, the protection of both the Protestant and Catholic belief systems in Canada reflected the reality that Protestantism and Catholicism were once the dominant, or de facto "established", religions in different parts of the country – Catholicism in Quebec and Protestantism in English Canada.[40] Jeremy Patrick has argued that because "the Canadian statute on its face is not explicitly limited to protecting Christianity[,] Jews, Muslims, and others who feel aggrieved by a publication have at least a plausible argument for invoking the statute in their defence."[41] Certainly any principled reading of the ban today would require that it extend to intemperate attacks on both Christian and non-Christian religious belief systems. This, though, assumes that the law might have some form of contemporary life. Yet no cases have been brought under the provision for more than eighty years.[42] And it is accepted by many (including Patrick) that if the ban were to be invoked today, it would be struck down under the *Charter of Rights*, as an unjustified restriction on freedom of expression and/or religious freedom.

Blasphemy bans have been struck down by US courts under the First Amendment. For example, in 1952, the U.S. Supreme Court, in *Joseph Burstyn* v. *Wilson*, held that a New York statute that prohibited "sacrilegious" films breached the First Amendment, because it would inevitably be applied in a way that favoured "one religion over another" and in particular "the most vocal and powerful orthodoxies".[43] Several European jurisdictions maintain some form of blasphemy or religious insult law that formally protects all religious belief systems from ridicule or intemperate

---

[38] *Criminal Code*, R.S. 1985, c. C-46, s. 296. An individual found to have breached the ban is "liable to imprisonment for a term not exceeding two years".

[39] Jeremy Patrick, "Not dead, just sleeping: Canada's prohibition on blasphemous libel as a case in obsolete legislation", (2008) 41 *UBC Law Rev*. 193, para. 55.

[40] Richard Moon, *Freedom of Conscience and Religion* (Irwin Law, 2014) at 4.

[41] Patrick (n. 39) at para. 34.   [42] Patrick (n. 39) at para. 1.

[43] *Joesph Burstyn Inc.* v. *Wilson*, 343 US 495 (1952) (USSC). Clark J. for the Court, "In seeking to apply the broad and all-inclusive definition of sacrilegious . . . the censor is set adrift upon a boundless sea amid a myriad of conflicting current of religious views, with no charts but those provided by the most vocal and powerful orthodoxies."

criticism.[44] While these laws have seldom been enforced, they have not been entirely dormant either, as illustrated by some of the cases referred to in Chapter 1, such *Otto Preminger* and *IA Turkey*.[45] It is notable that in almost all of the successful blasphemy or religious insult prosecutions brought under these laws, the protected religious belief system is that of the majority community.

In *Otto Preminger*, a film institute in Salzburg planned to show a film entitled "Das Liebeskonzil" (Council of Heaven). The institute provided advance notice of the film's screening, with a description of its plot. The film, which was based on a play that had been the subject of a blasphemy prosecution in the nineteenth century, showed a performance of the play, along with scenes from the blasphemy trial of the playwright. In the play (and film) God decides, on the advice of the devil, to punish the Church for its corruption and debauchery by releasing a disease – syphilis – among the members of the papal and royal courts. The play depicts Mary as a loose woman, God as senile, and Jesus as cretinous. Before it could be shown, the Austrian authorities seized the film and commenced an action against the film institute under a provision of the penal code, which prohibits the disparagement of religious doctrine. The action was later dropped, but the film was not returned to the institute. The institute appealed the film's seizure to the ECtHR, arguing that it violated the freedom of expression provision of the *ECHR*. The Court, though, dismissed the complaint, holding that the state had a legitimate role in protecting religious believers from insult to their religious feelings. In the Court's view, speech that was "gratuitously" insulting could legitimately be restricted by the state, even when, as in this case, only those who chose to attend the screening would have seen the film and been directly exposed to its "insult".

In more recent cases, though, the ECtHR has been unwilling to uphold findings of blasphemy or religious insult by domestic European courts. In *Giniewski* v. *France*, for example, a journalist, who criticized the Roman Catholic Church – and a particular papal encyclical – for promoting a doctrine that in his view contributed to anti-Semitism and the Holocaust was fined by the French courts for defaming Christian belief.[46] The ECtHR found that the journalist's claims were

---

[44] For example, as noted in c. 1, the Austrian Penal Code makes it an offence to disparage religious doctrines (Austrian Penal Code, Art. 188, *Strafgesetzbuch* (StGB)); the Swiss Penal Code includes the offence of maliciously offending or ridiculing the religious convictions of others or to disparage a person's convictions, objects of veneration, places of worship, or religious articles (Swiss Penal Code, Art. 261, Strafgesetzbuch (StGB)); the Dutch Penal Code prohibits insulting a group because their religion or their life philosophy, as well as other grounds (Art. 137d *Wetboek van Strafrecht* (Sr.)); the German Criminal Code, Art. 166, makes it an offence to insult a religious worldview (*Weltanschauung*) publicly (*Strafgesetzbuch, StGB*).

[45] *Otto-Preminger-Institut* v. *Austria* (n. 23). In *I.A.* v. *Turkey*, No. 42571/98 (13 Sept. 2005), the ECtHR declined to overturn the conviction of a Turkish author for blasphemy. The Court agreed with the Turkish authorities that the book *God, the Religion, the Prophet, and the Holy Book* amounted to an abusive attack on the Prophet Mohammad and was not simply offensive or provocative.

[46] *Giniewski* v. *France*, Application No. 64016/00 (Eur. Ct. H.R. Jan. 31, 2006).

not "gratuitously offensive" and could be viewed as a contribution to debate. The Court concluded that the journalist's conviction in the domestic courts breached the Convention's freedom of expression and religious freedom protections.[47]

The ECtHR's increasingly restrictive interpretation of these laws reflects a growing commitment to freedom of expression in religious matters in a "secular age". In the European jurisdictions in which blasphemy laws remain on the books, the law is rarely enforced.[48] Claims by Muslim groups to the protection of blasphemy and religious insult laws may also have contributed to the repeal of such laws or to a narrowing of their scope. Many in the larger community were already troubled by the occasional use of religious insult or blasphemy laws to protect the sensibilities of historically dominant religious groups, viewing these laws either as anachronistic or as appropriately applied only in exceptional cases of extreme insult. The problems with these laws may have become more apparent to the larger community once non-Christians sought to invoke their protection. Some in the Muslim community have complained about "double standards" in the application of these laws – and there is certainly some merit in these complaints. Jytte Klausen, however, argues that such laws have seldom been enforced in the last thirty or forty years and that the obstacle to Muslim complaints is not double standards but rather "changing norms", noting that "[c]ourts and law-makers have increasingly refused to subordinate free speech to religious prohibitions."[49]

Yet the demise, or decline, of blasphemy laws in Europe may be connected to the construction of the Muslim "other" in the ideological clash of civilizations in which Muslims are viewed as opponents of free speech, who wish to suppress any criticism of their beliefs and practices, while seeking also to impose their faith on others.[50] "Native" Europeans (either Christians or those from a Christian background) are assumed in this account to be uniformly committed to liberal democratic values such as free speech. In other words, separating "us" from "them" requires not just that "they" (Muslims) be seen as opposed to free speech, but also that "we" ("native" Europeans, in a Christian-inspired culture) be seen as united in "our" commitment to freedom of expression and other liberal values. That blasphemy laws remain on the books in some countries, and are sometimes still enforced, is an embarrassment to this story about European enlightenment and its opposition to a regressive Muslim culture.

---

[47] See also *Klein* v. *Slovakia*, Application No. 72208/01 (31 Oct 2006) and *Aydin Tatlav* v. *Turkey*, App. No. 50692/99 (2 May 2006) (ECtHR).

[48] The Republic of Ireland seems to be moving against this trend with its enactment of a blasphemy ban in 2009: *Defamation Act*, 2009 s. 36 (Republic of Ireland). However, there is now a significant movement in the Republic to repeal the ban.

[49] Klausen (n. 4) at 146. See also Hilary Power, Nazila Ghanea, and Marc Limon, "Fighting religious intolerance and discrimination: The UN account", 11 *Religion and Human Rights* 21 at 58 (2016), noting that such laws are rarely applied and that "the last formal prison sentence for blasphemy [in Europe] was in 1922".

[50] See the earlier discussion in c. 3 of claims in the "Eurabia" writing that the utilization of religious insult laws by Muslims is illegitimate and amounts to "soft jihad" or "stealth jihad" or "lawfare".

II PROHIBITING RIDICULE AND GRATUITOUS INSULT

Whether in the form of an updated blasphemy law, a broadly interpreted hate speech law, or a law directly aimed at preventing insult to religious beliefs or practices, there appears to be at least some (albeit declining) support for a ban on the ridicule or intemperate criticism of religion, in order to protect religious believers from insult to their deepest convictions. A ban on such criticism may be seen as a middle position that recognizes that religious adherence is not only a personal commitment to certain truths that must be open to debate and criticism, but also a cultural identity that should be treated with respect. Criticism must be permitted, but not when it "gratuitously" injures or offends the deep commitments of others or threatens to disrupt public order.

This middle ground, however, is unworkable for several related reasons. First, it is difficult to define enforceable standards of civility in public discourse, and nearly impossible to do so when religion is the subject of debate. Second, if a restriction on intemperate criticism of religious belief rests on the idea that religion is deep-rooted, then it seems unlikely that temperate or reasoned criticism of religion will have much of an impact on religious adherents. We might instead see a greater role for ridicule and harsh criticism in disrupting entrenched religious views. Third, religious beliefs often have public implications and so must be open to criticism that is deeply felt and sometimes very harsh.

A *Civility Standards*

Expression or communication is a relationship between speaker and audience that may be compromised or undermined by manipulation, deceit, and incivility – including insult and ridicule. As noted in Chapter 2, restrictions on speech that intimidates or harasses others, have been upheld by the courts as justified limits on freedom of expression. However, requirements of civility or respect in discourse – (beyond restrictions on threats and harassment) are more difficult to define and to reconcile with the public commitment to freedom of expression.

Civility standards are conventional or cultural and therefore not easy to establish in a multicultural, multifaith society. Different individuals or groups within the larger community will have very different views about what is civil or respectful.[51] Moreover, freedom of expression must to some extent protect challenges not only

---

[51] Joss Marsh, *Word Crimes: Blasphemy, Culture, and Literature in Nineteenth-Century England* (University of Chicago Press, 1998), which makes the case that blasphemy in the nineteenth century was a class crime – in which the decision to convict often turned on class differences in the way criticism of religion or religious institutions was expressed. See also Levy (n. 26) at 484, quoting Mathew Arnold: "It seems to us painfully clear that there must be something wrong in a law of blasphemy which punishes the vulgar man for saying in coarse language what it never thinks of punishing the refined man for saying in keen, sarcastic language".

to conventional opinion but also to the conventions of communicative engagement and social respect. As Robert Post observes, public discourse aspires to be reasoned and non-coercive, in other words, to adhere to norms of civility, and yet at the same time to "be free from the constraints of existing community norms".[52]

A degree of tension or conflict in communicative relationships is unavoidable and not always undesirable. While the audience may not always want to hear a message that it regards as harsh and even hostile, freedom of expression is understood to protect the communication of deeply felt views, even those that are unpleasant or confrontational in character. The courts have accepted that an important dimension of expression is its emotional force – the manifestation of anger, outrage, and other strong emotions. In *Handyside* v. *UK*, the ECtHR said that freedom of expression protects speech that may "offend, shock or disturb the State or any sector of the population".[53] This was also the view of the U.S. Supreme Court in *Cohen* v. *California*, in which it was noted that "linguistic expression" often "serves a dual communicative function: it conveys not only ideas capable of relatively precise, detached explication, but otherwise inexpressible emotions as well."[54] As many have noted, to say something in a different way, with less emotion or anger, for example, is to say something different.

Hate speech laws are sometimes presented as a form of civility regulation, which like blasphemy laws proscribe speech that is offensive or hurtful to others. Robert Post, for example, argues that hate speech laws "are driven as much by the need to eliminate the objective harms of discrimination as by the urgent need to suppress speech that violates social norms of respect".[55] It is a mistake, though, to see the "harm" of hate speech as personal offence, resulting from the emotional force or

---

[52] Robert Post, *Constitutional Domains* (Harvard University Press, 1995) at 147. And at 313, "If the state were permitted to enforce civility rules, it would in effect exclude from public discourse those whose speech advocated and exemplified unfamiliar and marginalized forms of life. But if the state were to suspend the enforcement of civility rules, it would endanger the possibility of rational discourse by permitting the dissemination of abusive and coercive speech. This tension between the requirement that self-government respect all of its citizens 'as free and equal persons', and the requirement that self-government proceed through processes of rational deliberation, creates the paradox of public discourse."

[53] *Handyside* v. *United Kingdom*, 1 Eur. HR Rep. 737 (1976).

[54] *Cohen* v. *California*, 403 U.S. 15 (1971) at p. 26. The Court in that case held that the First Amendment protected an individual's right to wear in public space a jacket carrying the message "Fuck the Draft". In the Court's view, "the State has no right to cleanse public debate to the point where it is grammatically palatable to the most squeamish among us . . . [W]hile the particular four-letter word being litigated here is perhaps more distasteful than most others of its genre, it is nevertheless often true that one man's vulgarity is another's lyric" (25). In the United States see also *Hustler Magazine* v. *Falwell*, 485 US 46 (1988), in which the U.S. Supreme Court held that an intentionally offensive (perhaps even outrageous) parody of a public figure, such as the Rev. Jerry Falwell, was protected under the First Amendment. See also *Snyder* v. *Phelps*, 562 US 443 (2011), which is discussed in c. 5.

[55] Robert Post, "Hate Speech", in Ivan Hare and James Weinstein (eds.), *Extreme Speech and Democracy* (Oxford University Press, 2009) at 135. He continues at 136, "We may tell a story about the connection between hate speech and violence, but the actual shape of the law suggests that we are instead using law to enforce norms of propriety in sensitive areas like race, nationality, and ethnicity". Admittedly this may describe the way hate speech laws are sometimes interpreted and applied.

uncivil tone of the expression. As noted in Chapter 2, hate speech laws, when applied to threats or insults, are intended to protect the audience not from offence or hurt feelings, but instead from intimidation or harassment. Hate speech laws, though, are most often applied to speech that seeks to persuade members of the general community of the dangerousness or undesirability of a particular racial, religious, or other group. In such cases, the purpose of the hate speech ban is to prevent the spread of falsehoods that may encourage radical or violent action against some community members. The anger with which these false claims are often communicated may facilitate their spread, but is not the gravamen of the wrong.

Hate speech, either explicitly or implicitly, claims that the members of an identifiable group should not be regarded as full members of the community and/or that they share dangerous or undesirable traits – that they are by nature violent or corrupt, for example. Whether the speech takes the form of a threat directed at the members of a particular group or a claim about the group that is made to the members of the general community, its message is that the target group's members are inferior or immoral and should be treated accordingly. Such claims of natural or inherent inferiority run contrary to the commitment to human equality that underpins civil society. Equality norms must, of course, remain open to public discussion and challenge; however, when the challenge to these norms takes the form of a threat against the members of a particular group, or the encouragement of others to take violent action against the group, it should be restricted.

The regulation of harsh or mocking criticism of a religion is very different from the regulation of hate speech. The state, it is generally said, should take no position on the truth of a particular religious belief system. It should remain neutral on the question of whether a particular faith is true or false. The restriction of religious criticism or ridicule then must be based entirely on the impact it has on the feelings or self-esteem of the adherent, either because it is wrong to insult or offend an individual or because those who have been offended might disrupt public order. The state cannot make judgments about religious truth or the correct forms of worship, but must instead try to grasp the significance of the belief to the believer, and the injury he or she experiences when the "sacred" is ridiculed or the "truth", as he or she understands it, is treated with contempt.

There are several difficulties raised by a subjective test of this sort. First, the believer's experience of injury is tied to belief in the truth of what is being ridiculed. The believer does not object to the ridicule of his or her faith because he or she feels hurt by it. He or she is hurt by it and objects to it because it mocks or disparages that which should be venerated or treated as sacred. While the wrong is framed in subjective terms, as offence or insult to dignity, the believer's subjective experience is based on his or her commitment to a particular conception of spiritual truth.[56]

---

[56] Levy (n. 26) at 573 argues that even though heresy is no longer a crime, "blasphemy cannot be prosecuted unless some implicit standard of heresy exists, thus aggravating the abridgment of freedom of speech and religious liberty." Another way to make this point is to note that while the experience of

The protection of religious sensibilities is in effect, then, the protection by the state of what the individual regards as religious truth.[57] This is perhaps why (as earlier noted), in cases such as *Otto Preminger* or *Gay News* (or the complaints against the Danish Cartoons and *The Satanic Verses*), it did not seem to matter that the complainants were not directly confronted with the objectionable words or images and often had no personal exposure to them.

Second, and more practically, it is unclear how the state is to determine when the experience of offence is sufficiently great that the speech ought to be restricted. To describe something as "sacred" is to say that it should be treated with respect. (Or to describe something as part of the individual's or group's identity – the secular acknowledgement of the sacred – is to say that it lies outside the scope of ordinary debate and challenge.) But then even the most temperate criticism of a group's religious beliefs, including a simple denial of their truth, might be viewed by some of the group's members as disrespectful and unacceptable.[58] Different religious traditions (and groups within each tradition) have different understandings of the obligations of those inside and outside the religious community to respect the sacred.[59] And, of course, because individual believers relate to their religious traditions/belief systems in various ways, they will not experience religious criticism or ridicule of the sacred in exactly the same way. Finally, some in the religious community may read a particular representation or statement as ridiculing a sacred object or symbol, even though that may not be the intent of the speaker/creator and may not be how others understand the speech. The standard for the restriction of criticism, then, cannot be based simply on the reactions or feelings of adherents or their reports of their feelings. It must rest instead on a view about what is the reasonable or ordinary subjective reaction to religious criticism. But there can be no agreement on this. There is simply no vantage point outside the faith tradition, or the individual's experience of it, from which a secular public decision maker, such as a judge, can decide what is intolerable or unacceptable offence.

offence is not a legally cognizable injury, it can sometimes be understood as the subjective dimension of a harm or wrong, such as intimidation or harassment, that may be proscribed by law. The problem in this case, though, is that the only identifiable wrong – insulting or undermining religious truth – does not fall within the domain of secular law.

[57] As noted later, in prohibiting religious offence, the law is siding with the believer against the critic, who may be using ridicule or mockery to question the very idea that religious belief has merit or truth.

[58] Rex Adhar and Ian Leigh, *Religious Freedom in the Liberal State* (Oxford University Press, 2005), at 373: "One reason not to expand the ambit of the offence is the significant risk of blasphemy law becoming the locus of religious controversy, with opposing groups claiming a right to be protected against offence caused to them by the mere expression of others' beliefs."

[59] Jeremy Waldron, *Liberal Rights* (n. 25), at 138–39: "What is serious and what is offensive, what is sober and what is mockery – these are not neutral ideas ... [D]ifferent religions define them in different ways." The Venice Commission in its 2008 Report at 51 observes that "What is likely to cause substantial offence to persons of a particular religious persuasion will vary significantly from time to time and from place to place" (the European Commission for Democracy through Law (the "Venice Commission"), which is the Council of Europe's advisory body on constitutional matters).

It has been suggested that religious criticism may be restricted when it has no other purpose than to offend or injure the audience. Temperate or reasoned critique of religion is intended to engage believers, to encourage them to rethink or · justify their views, and to generate debate in the community. Intemperate criticism, on the other hand, may be intended only to offend and so makes no contribution to public discourse. In the *Otto Preminger* case, for example, the European Court of Human Rights suggested that ridicule or mockery of religion could properly be restricted by the state because (or when) it is "gratuitous".[60] The Venice Commission Report similarly distinguishes between "genuine 'philosophical' discussion about religious ideas and gratuitous insults against a believer of an 'inferior' faith."[61] I will return to this claim shortly, but for now it may be enough to say that to the critic, who sees a particular religion or all religions as irrational and perhaps even socially harmful, there is nothing gratuitous or excessive about mocking religion. Indeed, it may seem to the critic that this is the only sensible reaction to such beliefs.

The restriction of religious criticism (and more particularly, the distinction between acceptable/temperate and unacceptable/intemperate criticism) is sometimes said to depend on whether the criticism is likely to lead to a breach of the peace – to disrupt public order. The protection of public order appears to offer a more objective standard for the restriction of such speech. The problem, though, is that if speech can be restricted whenever violence occurs (or is threatened), there will be an incentive for opponents of the speech to respond violently. When the state indicates that it will restrict expression that is likely to lead to a breach of the peace, some in the community will routinely react to speech they find objectionable by threatening to disrupt public order, resulting in what is sometimes referred to in the United States as the "heckler's veto".[62] As well, if the object of the ban on intemperate criticism is to prevent public disorder from occurring, the courts must determine in advance whether the speech at issue is of a kind that is likely to lead to a breach of the peace – relying principally on past events when making this determination. Yet when human behaviour is the subject of prediction, past practice may be of limited value. Any claim that an attack on the beliefs and rituals of some members of the community will lead to disorder is bound to be speculative. In practice, then, the courts must decide whether the disruption of public order would be a reasonable or understandable reaction to a particular form of speech; but once again, there is no basis for such a judgment. Finally, there is always the risk that state authorities will be tempted to use the real or imagined threat of disorder as an excuse to shut down unpopular speech.

---

[60] *Otto Preminger* (n. 23) at para. 49.   [61] Venice Commission (n. 59) at 61.

[62] "Heckler's veto" was a term coined by Harry Kalven, Jr., in *The Negro and the First Amendment* (University of Chicago Press, 1965). It was employed by Justice Black in *Gregory* v. *Chicago*, 394 US 111 (1969).

If "risk of public disorder" is the test for determining whether religious criticism goes too far and should be restricted, then it may be easier to justify the restriction of intemperate criticism directed at the beliefs of the majority community. Attacks on the dominant religious tradition may cause a significant public reaction. Yet it could just as plausibly be argued that the members of the majority community, confident in their status, will feel no need to take violent action in response to harsh criticism, while minority group members, who feel marginalized and politically powerless, may be more likely to respond to ridicule with anger and violence. In both the *Otto Preminger* and *Gay News* decisions, religious insult or blasphemy laws were used to protect the sensibilities of the majority community or the integrity of the dominant religious tradition.[63] In each of these cases, there is a hint of the pre-Enlightenment idea that social stability or cohesion requires a level of religious conformity or at least the suppression of vocal challenge to the dominant religion.[64] In this way, these decisions run against the contemporary view that stability in the community is more reliably achieved through religious tolerance and open debate about religion rather than the enforcement of religious conformity or the suppression of religious dissent.

If the restriction of harsh criticism or ridicule of religious belief is based on the deep offence experienced by religious adherents, then perhaps other symbols or beliefs that matter deeply to individuals or groups (to which the individual or group may feel attached) should be protected from ridicule. Some Americans take great offence to the mistreatment of the US flag, which they regard as a near-sacred symbol of the country to which they feel a profound, perhaps even spiritual, attachment.[65] It is for this reason that laws against flag burning have been enacted in some American states. Yet, at the same time, the symbolic role of the flag means that its destruction or denigration may serve as a powerful protest against the policies and practices of the country. This is why US courts have held that laws banning flag burning violate the First Amendment right to free speech.[66]

---

[63] *Otto Preminger* (n. 23) and *Whitehouse* v. *Gay News* (n. 31).

[64] Just as some countries, such as Greece, have in the past restricted the proselytization activities of different groups in order to preserve a national religious identity or to limit social conflict, so too a country might decide that social stability requires the restriction of religious criticism. The ECtHR ruled that Greece's general ban on proselytization breached the *ECHR* in *Kokkinakis* v. *Greece* (Application No. 14307/88) (May 25, 1993).

[65] For a discussion, see William T. Cavanaugh, *Migrations of the Holy* (Wm. B. Eerdmans, 2011), at 120: "But what remains when humans attempt to clear a space of God's presence is not a disenchanted world but a world full of idols. Humans remain naturally worshipping creatures, and the need for liturgy remains a motivating force . . . in a supposedly 'secular' space". See also Paul W. Kahn, *Political Theology: Four New Chapters on the Concept of Sovereignty* (Columbia University Press, 2011). Other examples might include criticism of the state of Israel or of the monarchy in countries such as Thailand, which seem to retain a divine aura.

[66] In *Texas* v. *Johnson*, 491 US 397 (1989), the U.S. Supreme Court struck down a state law prohibiting the desecration of the US flag. In his dissenting judgment, Justice Rehnquist wrote that "The flag is not simply another 'idea' or 'point of view' competing for recognition in the marketplace of ideas.

B The Effectiveness of Rational Criticism

The reinterpretation of English blasphemy law in the nineteenth century, so that it caught only intemperate attacks on the Christian faith, rested on the view that religious beliefs could (even should) be subject to reasoned criticism – that the "truth" does not need to be protected from thoughtful debate.[67] Milton (and later Mill) argued that "man" was endowed with the capacity for reason and that in a "free and open encounter", between Truth and falsehood, we should not doubt the strength of the former.[68] Debate about issues of common interest, including religion (the existence of God and the afterlife), should take place on the ground of reason.[69] Milton thought that intemperate attacks on belief (religious, political, etc.) might distort the search for truth, displacing reason and judgment, and so have no claim to protection. If the principal justification for freedom of expression is its contribution to the realization of truth, then its protection should extend only to expression that is temperate and that appeals to reason rather than emotion.

However, in the contemporary context, the protection of free expression is no longer limited to speech that is dispassionate and respectful. Free expression now protects harsh and intemperate criticism of belief and opinion. As already noted, the emotional dimension of expression (including anger, outrage, and disgust) is considered to be important and deserving of protection. The restriction of ridicule or intemperate criticism of *religious* beliefs and practices, then, can no longer be explained as simply part of a more general exclusion of intemperate speech from the scope of freedom of expression. The contemporary claim that *religious* beliefs should be protected from such criticism must instead be based on the view that these beliefs are different from other beliefs. The argument now is that religious beliefs are deeply held and faith-based, a matter of identity rather than judgment, and so should be specially protected from ridicule or intemperate criticism. Even if political, moral, and other beliefs must remain open to harsh criticism or mockery, religious beliefs are different and should be insulated from attacks of this kind.

The conception of religious belief that underlies the contemporary argument for the restriction of intemperate criticism, then, is entirely different from that which lay

---

Millions and millions of Americans regard it with an almost mystical reverence regardless of what sort of social, political, or philosophical beliefs they may have." For a more general account of the "sacredness" of the US flag see Carolyn Marvin and David W. Ingle, *Blood Sacrifice and the Nation: Totem Rituals and the American Flag* (Cambridge University Press, 1999).

[67] See the earlier discussion of the evolution of blasphemy law in England, notably the judgments of *Ramsay & Foote* (n. 30) and *R. v. Gott* (1922), 16 Cr App R 87.

[68] John Milton, *Aeropagitica and Other Prose Works* (JM Dent, 1927 [1644]).

[69] While some in the Enlightenment period thought that Christianity could not survive critical scrutiny, others insisted that the truth of Christianity could be demonstrated through the application of reason. Locke, for example, sought to detail and defend what he understood to be a rational form of Christianity: John Locke, *The Reasonableness of Christianity, as Delivered in the Scriptures* (CreateSpace Independent Publishing Platform, 2014 [1695]).

behind the revision of blasphemy law in the nineteenth century. Religious believers are thought to experience attacks on their beliefs in a profound and personal
way – in a way that is different from attacks on their political or moral beliefs (on
beliefs that relate to social and civic issues). Intemperate attacks on religion should
be proscribed not because they might interfere with reasoned public deliberation
but because religious commitment is an aspect of individual or group identity that
should be treated with respect – and as outside the scope of ordinary public debate.
Yet, as earlier noted, this argument for the insulation of religion from harsh and
intemperate criticism may be difficult to contain, and could just as easily justify the
restriction of any criticism of religion. If religion is viewed as an identity, then any
criticism, no matter how politely expressed, might be hurtful or upsetting to individual adherents. As Jeremy Waldron observes, "there are some who hold their beliefs
so devoutly that even the most sober and respectful criticism would count as mortal
insult to their personality".[70]

Even if it is accepted that only intemperate criticism of religion is sufficiently
injurious to require restriction, it is not clear what role temperate criticism can or
should play in the public discussion of religion. If religion is a matter of identity, or
is deep-rooted (which is the basis for the restriction of intemperate criticism), then
why would we imagine that an individual's beliefs might be altered or affected by
calm, rational criticism? In the words of Jonathan Swift, "It is useless to attempt to
reason a man out of a thing he was never reasoned into."[71] Could we not then turn
the argument (for the restriction of intemperate criticism) on its head? If rational
critique is unlikely to be effective (if religion lies outside the scope of reasonable
debate or lies at its edge, as some believe)[72] then perhaps protection should be given
to the ridicule, or intemperate criticism, of religious belief. It may be that only these
forms of criticism will have any impact. Critics of a particular religion may seek to
confront or shock – to shake believers from their unreflective acceptance of certain
views or values – or they may simply wish to express to the holders of such views, or
to the larger world, their outrage and frustration at what they see as an irrational and
regressive belief system.[73]

---

[70] Jeremy Waldron, *Liberal Rights* (n. 25), at 139.
[71] Attributed to Jonathan Swift in Maturin Murray Ballou, *Treasury of Thought: Forming an Encyclopæ-
dia of Quotations from Ancient and Modern Authors* (Houghton Mifflin, 1872), at 433.
[72] See the discussion in c. 5.
[73] The Law Commission (UK), *Criminal Law: Offences against Religion and Public Worship* (n. 37), at
26: "Some religious tenets or practices may deserve criticism or ridicule in the sharpest terms; abuse
or insult cannot be excluded from the weapons of such criticism; and the purpose of the critic of such
matters may indeed be to shock or outrage his readers by the use of abuse or insult, the better to realise
the effect of that criticism". See also Post, *Constitutional Domains* (n. 52), at 139: "Outrageous speech
calls community identity into question, practically as well as cognitively, and thus it has unique power
to focus attention, dislocate old assumptions, and shock its audience into the recognition of unfamiliar
forms of life".

C *The Public Significance of Religion*

The third difficulty with a restriction on intemperate criticism is that religions often say something about the way we should treat others and about the kind of society we should work to create. While religion is sometimes regarded as a cultural identity (that should be treated with equal respect), when it addresses, or touches upon, civic matters (the rights and interests of others) it must be viewed as a political or moral judgment by the individual or group that is open to public criticism, even when this is harsh and intemperate.

Some members of the general community may have a strong reaction to religious beliefs that address their interests or status. For example, gays and lesbians may feel anger about the anti-gay teachings of some churches and the impact of these teachings on their ability to live lives that are full or even safe. A poem about Jesus engaging in same-sex relations with his disciples, although offensive to many practicing Christians, may offer, in a provocative way, a more inclusive reading of the Christian tradition, or it may simply express anger about the anti-gay beliefs and actions of some Christian churches.[74] Playwright Tony Kushner, writing in *The Nation*, said that Pope John Paul II's condemnation of homosexuality amounted to an "endorse[ment] of murder".[75] This may have been an intemperate remark, but it was made in reaction to the brutal murder of Matthew Shepard, a young gay man, in Wyoming.

"New atheists" such as Christopher Hitchens and Richard Dawkins believe not just that there is no God, but that belief in God (and religion more generally) is damaging and dangerous – that it inhibits the moral growth of individuals and encourages them to behave irrationally and sometimes even violently. Dawkins has described religion as "one of the world's great evils, comparable to the smallpox virus."[76] Christopher Hitchens similarly declared that religions are not simply untrue but "positively harmful" in their effects.[77] Critics seeking to show the absurdity or regressive character of religion may think that ridicule is the most effective way to do this. From their perspective, there is nothing gratuitous about the harsh criticism or ridicule of religion. As Charles Taylor points out, "The idea that one might suppress a book because blasphemous, on the ground that the sentiment offended deserves some stronger protection than that whose expression is inhibited ... fails to take unbelief seriously, as though the 'blasphemer'

---

74 As earlier noted, James Kirkup, whose poem was the subject of the successful blasphemy prosecution in *Gay News* (n. 37), wanted to see Jesus "in terms of modern sexual liberation" as a "real human being" with "the same lusts, failings, ecstacies and sexual equipment" as others (Levy, n. 26, at 537).

75 Kushner, quoted by Philip Jenkins, *The New Anti-Catholicism: The Last Acceptable Prejudice* (Oxford University Press, 2003), who roundly criticises him.

76 Richard Dawkins, "Is science a religion?" *The Humanist*, January/February 1997.

77 Christopher Hitchens, *Letters to a Young Contrarian* (Basic Books, 2001), at 55.

just wanted to let off steam...to vent his spleen, and didn't have a more serious purpose".[78]

The adherents of one religious tradition must be free to criticize the beliefs of another tradition. Given what is at stake in these disagreements – the most profound questions about the salvation of the soul, the will of God, etc. – this criticism may sometimes be deeply felt and harsh in tone. As Leonard Levy reminds us: "Inoffensive speech was not the hallmark of Elijah, Isaiah, or Jesus himself" or "of champions of the true faith" such as "Paul, Augustine, Luther, Calvin and Fox".[79] To this we might add that some of the harshest, and most intemperate, criticism of a particular religious community or belief system comes from individuals who have a personal connection with the particular community or tradition, whose identity has been shaped by it, and who may be struggling to separate themselves from it – the ex-Mormon or the ex-Catholic, for example. They may have a powerful reaction to a religious tradition or community that is part of who they are. Furthermore, because the boundaries of a religious group are always contested, it may be difficult to distinguish internal from external religious critique. Some "members" may describe others as bad Muslims or as not true to Islam, or they may say that others are mistaken in their interpretation of Christian doctrine or are not proper Christians. The state is not supposed to involve itself in internal religious disputes; but a restriction on (intemperate) criticism of a religious practice or doctrine may sometimes draw the state into debates within the religious community about church doctrine or about the boundaries of the community or tradition, and involve it in the suppression of dissent and the reinforcement of orthodoxy.

Perhaps we can go farther than this and say that in any religious tradition that claims universality – that believes there is a truth that can be known by all and seeks to spread that truth across the nations – there can be no meaningful distinction between external and internal debate and criticism. Most religious groups seek to appeal to non-believers, who they hope will come to see the "truth". These non-believers may be "people of the book", who have not yet recognized the final revelation given to the Prophet Mohammad. Or they may, in the words of conservative commentator Ann Coulter, be "imperfect Christians" – Jews who have failed to recognize Jesus as the Messiah.[80] If an individual or group is free to persuade others of

---

[78] Charles Taylor, "The Rushdie controversy", 2 *Public Culture* 118 (1989) at 119. Taylor notes also at 121 that there is "something uniquely powerful about religious language and symbols which make even those who reject them need them in order to explore their own universe. These symbols are as indispensible to those who want to negate them as they are to those who live by affirming them".

[79] Levy (n. 26) at 572.

[80] http://thecaucus.blogs.nytimes.com/2007/10/11/coulter-christians-as-perfected-jews/?_r=o.   Coulter was severely criticized when she said that "Jews need to be perfected", and there is little doubt that her choice of wording was meant to cause offence and to gain public attention. But from a Christian perspective her claim was truthful. Had Jews recognized Jesus as the Messiah, whose coming was foretold in the Old Testament, they would be Christians.

the truth of their spiritual beliefs, then they must also be open to the rejection or criticism of their beliefs by others.

To take religion seriously, as something that matters, is to see its claims about truth and right as important and worthy of consideration. But it also means that these claims, whether they relate to spiritual or civic questions, must be open to criticism. Because religion is important, its discussion may be intense and uncomfortable. Jeremy Waldron makes the point: "The great themes of religion matter too much to be closeted by the sensitivity of those who are counted as pious."[81]

III ON THE OTHER HAND

A *Self-Censorship and Personal Restraint*

The law may permit the ridicule of religious faith, but that is not itself a reason to engage in such speech – to express oneself in a way that may upset or offend others. Indeed, there may be good reason to refrain from religious ridicule or attack when the group at the receiving end feels marginalized and powerless.

Violent responses to religious criticism or ridicule, although exceptional, have been widely publicized in the media. These responses have led some individuals to self-censor and others to do the opposite and engage in, or support, the creation of offensive imagery – ostensibly as a vindication of free speech against the threat from "outsiders". Free speech, though, can be defended without re-enacting the injury to a group that feels misunderstood and marginalized. As Islamic scholar Emran Quereishi observed in an op-ed in the New York Times, while "[t]he answer is not more censorship", "it would be nice if Western champions of freedom of speech didn't trivialize it" and view it "much as Muslim fundamentalists do – simply as the ability to offend – rather than as a cornerstone of a liberal democratic polity".[82] Often the defence of free speech is simply cover for the more direct goal of ridiculing Islam and provoking Muslims.[83] Some proponents of the Eurabia position have republished the Danish Cartoons (or generated new cartoons of the Prophet Mohammad) in the hope of stirring a reaction in the Muslim community, and thus proving their claim that Muslims are anti-democratic. And indeed, fringe elements of the Muslim community have sometimes responded by taking violent action, appearing then to provide confirmation of what the Eurabia writers see as the Muslim habit of violence.[84] The reality, of course, is that the overwhelming

---

[81] Jeremy Waldron, *Liberal Rights* (n. 25) at 142.

[82] Emran Qureishi, "The Islam the riots obscured" (op-ed), *New York Times*, Feb. 12, 2006.

[83] See R. Moon, "The Hate Speech Diversion", in Shelagh Day, Lucie Lamarche, and Ken Norman (eds.), *14 Arguments in Favour of Human Rights Institutions* (Irwin, 2014) at 279: Sometimes "the opposition to hate speech regulation is simply a more palatable way of defending hate speech – the message it carries."

[84] A cartoon drawing event, sponsored by the American Freedom Defense Initiative, an anti-Muslim group directed by Pamela Geller and Robert Spencer, was attacked by two gunmen, both of whom

majority of Muslims in Canada, the United States, and Europe, some of whom may feel deeply hurt or offended by the ridicule or mockery of their faith, would never contemplate responding to these images in a violent way.

B *A Captive Audience*

While religion must, as a general matter, be open to challenge that is harsh and intemperate, there may be particular situations in which it is appropriate for the state to protect religious adherents from intemperate criticism or ridicule of their beliefs.

First, it may be argued that a captive audience should be protected from expression that is deeply hurtful. For example, the burning of a Quran on the sidewalk outside a mosque at the end of Friday prayers involves a direct and unavoidable confrontation with the members of the community. Even Christopher Hitchens acknowledges that there may be limits to anti-religious speech: "I am not asking for the right to slaughter a pig in a synagogue or mosque or to relieve myself on a 'holy' book".[85] As earlier noted, members of the Muslim community did not have to read *The Satanic Verses*, or view the "Danish Cartoons", and generally did not do so. Their objection was to the creation and publicity of such works and not to the personal trauma or hurt of being directly confronted by them. However, the recognition that religious commitment is deep-rooted may support a limited and location-based restriction on the ridicule or denigration of religious rituals or symbols. There will of course be difficulties in defining the scope of such a restriction. The focus of any restriction should be on ridicule and insult that the believer cannot easily avoid seeing or hearing.

Public spaces cannot and should not be cleansed of speech that may cause offense to others; yet at the same time expression has often been restricted to protect privacy or dignity interests in otherwise public spaces.[86] Concerns about affront to the dignity or the sensitivities of a captive audience have led to the legal enforcement of

---

were shot and killed by police. The event featured Geert Wilders as a keynote speaker. "Two shot dead after they open fire at Mohammed cartoon event in Texas", CNN, Monday, May 4, 2015, www .cnn.com/2015/05/03/us/mohammed-drawing-contest-shooting/.

[85] See also Christopher Hitchens, "Cartoon debate: The case for mocking religion", *Slate*, Feb. 4, 2006, www.slate/com/articles/news_and_politics/fighting/words/2006/02/cartoon_debate.html.

[86] See *R. v. Labaye*, 2005 SCC 80, in which the Supreme Court of Canada describes the harm of public indecency at para. 40: "One reason for criminalizing indecent acts and displays is to protect the public from being confronted with acts and material that reduce their quality of life. Indecent acts are banned because they subject the public to unwanted confrontation with inappropriate conduct. This harm is conceptually akin to nuisance ... The harm is not the aesthetic harm of a less attractive community, but the loss of autonomy and liberty that public indecency may impose on individuals in society, as they seek to avoid confrontation with acts they find offensive and unacceptable. The value or interest protected is the autonomy and liberty of members of the public, to live within a zone that is free from conduct that deeply offends them".

buffer zones around abortion clinics and funerals.[87] The recognition of such a limitation on speech (on protest) is bound to be controversial, though, given the view of some in the community that religion is necessarily foolish or harmful. Critics of religion may think that religious belief should not be insulated from criticism in any circumstance – just as those who believe that abortion involves the taking of an innocent life do not accept that a woman who has decided to have an abortion should, at any point in the process, be protected from challenge – even on the steps of a clinic.

C *The Incapacity of the State*

Second, as noted in Chapter 2, a commitment to freedom of expression means that we do not ordinarily hold the speaker responsible for the actions of the audience. The audience must be free to hear different views and to make its own judgment about the merits of those views. If a listener agrees or disagrees with the message of the speaker and then takes action (either following or opposing the advice of the speaker), he or she alone is responsible for the action. However, again as earlier noted, this depends on a number of assumptions or conditions. Underlying the commitment to freedom of expression (and the refusal to treat speech as a cause of audience action) are the belief that humans are substantially rational beings capable of evaluating factual and other claims and the assumption that public discourse is open to a wide range of competing views that may be assessed by the audience. The protection of freedom of expression (and the absolving of the speaker from responsibility for the actions of the audience) may also depend on the state's ability to regulate the audience's response – to either prevent or punish wrongful action by the audience.

It would be a mistake not to recognize that at some times and in some places speech that ridicules what some in the community regard as sacred may have very dangerous consequences. While we must be careful to avoid the "heckler's veto" (when the threat of violence by others is used by the state as a reason to shut down

---

[87] Buffer or access zones around abortion clinics have been established in a variety of jurisdictions. For example, in British Columbia, the *Access to Abortion Services Act*, Revised Statutes of BC, c. 1, s. 2 prohibits a variety of activities, such as protesting and besetting, within a certain area around a clinic. In *Madsen v. Women's Health Center, Inc.*, 512 U.S. 753, the U.S. Supreme Court upheld the constitutionality of a Florida court injunction establishing a buffer zone around an abortion clinic. The US courts have recognized in other cases the right of a "captive audience" to be protected from speech that is hurtful or offensive. See, for example, *Frisby v. Schultz*, 487 U.S. 474 (around a private home). But see *Snyder v. Phelps*, 562 U.S. 443 (2011), in which the U.S. Supreme Court found that a protest by members of the Westboro church, near the funeral of an American soldier, was protected under the First Amendment. However offensive or outrageous the "content" of the protestors' signs, their speech related "to public, rather than private, matters" such as the fate of the nation, homosexuality in the military, and scandals involving the Catholic clergy. The Court noted that the Westboro protestors remained some distance from the funeral and that the soldier's family "could see no more than the tops of the picketers' signs".

otherwise protected speech), and this is a serious concern, we must also recognize that the state will sometimes lack the effective power to prevent or punish a violent response to "offensive" speech, particularly when a situation arises suddenly and unexpectedly in a public space.[88] Perhaps then in exceptional circumstances the state may be justified in treating speech as a potential cause of harmful action that should be suppressed before it actually leads to injury. Yet, with that said, the risks of giving to the state the power to suppress speech in order to prevent a violent response may outweigh the risk to public order. The temptation of a government to prohibit provocative speech – and to use the risk of public disorder as an excuse to do so – may be too great to permit such an exception to the general protection of expression.

---

[88] Bhikhu Parekh, "Is there a case for banning hate speech?", in Michael Herz and Peter Molnar (eds.), *The Content and Context of Hate Speech: Rethinking Regulation and Responses* (Cambridge University Press, 2012), at 55. This recognition of the limits of state power lies behind US free speech exception doctrines such as "fighting words" and "imminent lawlessness", discussed in c. 2.

5

When Religion is the Source of Hate Speech

INTRODUCTION

A *The Difference Religion Makes*

There are at least two ways in which the religious source of speech (that is alleged to be hateful) may affect the application of a ban on hate speech. These two ways mirror the complications, described in the previous chapters, that arise when religion is the target of hate speech, and similarly stem from the complex connection between the individual and his or her religious community or tradition.

The first is the difficulty in determining an individual's meaning or intention when he or she invokes religious scripture to justify his or her criticism of a particular group. There is little doubt that when a speaker calls for the death of the members of a racial or other identifiable group, or attributes dangerous traits to the members of such a group, he or she will be found to breach the ban on hate speech, even though his or her views are rooted in a religious belief system. However, when a speaker makes positive references to scriptural passages that appear to demand or justify the killing of the members of a particular group, should he or she be understood, as encouraging hatred and violence towards the group? For example, when a believing Christian cites Lev. 20:13 in a newspaper advertisement that opposes gay marriage, should he or she be understood as calling for the death of gays? The biblical passage says that two men who "lie together" should be put to death.[1] Yet we know that Christians understand the doctrine and scripture of their faith in various ways, and, indeed, that many Christians do not adopt a literal reading of this and other scriptural passages. We cannot, then, simply attribute to the speaker the surface meaning of the passages he or she cites, or assume that the communication will be understood by other members of that particular faith group as calling for the death of gays.

---

[1] Lev. 20:13 (AV).

This mirrors the claim, made in Chapter 3, that the attribution of a dangerous belief to the members of a religious community (to each and every member) based on a literal reading of selected passages from scripture is unjustified and may amount to hate speech. Just as it is wrong, and sometimes a breach of hate speech law, to attribute dangerous or undesirable beliefs (that may have a scriptural source) to the members of a religious community, it is also wrong simply to attribute such a belief to a speaker, and to regard his or her speech as hateful, when it invokes scripture that may be read by some in the community as justifying hatred for a group.

A second complication, also stemming from the conception of religion as both a cultural identity (that should be treated with respect) and an individual commitment to a set of truth claims (that should be open to criticism), is that the courts may sometimes be reluctant to decide that the expression of sincerely held religious beliefs breaches the hate speech ban.[2] Specifically, the courts may be disinclined to interpret religiously based speech as carrying a hateful message – as sufficiently extreme to constitute hate speech – even if they are unwilling to excuse religious speech that is clearly hateful. This reluctance to view religious speech as hateful may explain in part the courts' non-literal reading of scriptural passages that call for violence against gays. Because religious beliefs are often deep-rooted and part of a shared culture, their censorship by the state may be experienced by believers as an affront to their dignity and to the standing of their group. In a sense, this is the mirror of the claim, discussed in the previous chapter, that an individual believer experiences injury when his or her beliefs are ridiculed or gratuitously insulted.

But just as the individual's (actual) religious beliefs and practices should not be insulated from critique, even that which is harsh and intemperate (as argued in the previous chapter), so too the expression of hateful views should not be insulated from state regulation simply because they are grounded in a religious belief system. When religion addresses civic issues – the rights or status of others in the community – and informs the believer's public action, it should not be treated as a cultural identity and insulated from the application of ordinary law.[3] If, as a democratic community, we have decided that a particular activity should be restricted as harmful, or that a particular policy should be supported in the public interest, why should the issue be revisited for an individual or group that holds a different view on religious grounds? An individual may choose to live her private life in accordance with her values. Or a community of believers – a religious association – may seek to operate

---

[2] Section 319 of the *Criminal Code* of Canada specifically provides that "a person shall not be convicted under the section ... if, in good faith, he expressed or attempted to establish by argument an opinion on a religious subject or on an opinion based on a belief in a religious text" (s. 319(3)(b)). The statement must be made in good faith but need not be reasonable. The Canadian cases discussed in this section were all brought under human rights code restrictions on hate speech; nevertheless, this exemption in the Code supports the claim that religious speech should only exceptionally be viewed as hate speech.

[3] Richard Moon, *Freedom of Conscience and Religion* (Irwin Law, 2014), at xiii.

in accordance with shared norms or practices that may be inconsistent with public norms. Accommodation, though, ought not be extended to beliefs that explicitly address civic matters and are directly at odds with democratically adopted public policies.[4]

The idea of religion as a cultural identity (and as faith-based and entrenched) may in another way bolster the argument for the restriction of religiously-grounded hate speech. As noted in Chapter 2, the commitment to freedom of expression rests on a belief that humans are substantially rational beings capable of evaluating factual and other claims and on an assumption that they will be exposed in public discourse to a range of different views. The courts, though, recognize that these assumptions may not always hold and have permitted the restriction of speech that occurs in a form and/or context that limits independent and informed judgment by the audience – that "incites" or "manipulates" its audience. When someone who holds a position of spiritual authority vilifies the members of an identifiable group, we may be justifiably concerned that this speech will unduly influence the thoughts and actions of an audience of believers. The persuasive force of hateful speech will be greater when it is delivered by a minister, imam, or other spiritual leader, is justified on religious grounds, and is directed at a religious audience. The power of such speech to influence will be even greater if the audience fears that the survival of their spiritual community is threatened by outsiders – by external forces of evil or corruption.

B *The Targets of Religiously Based Hate Speech*

1 The Religious Roots of Anti-Semitism

For centuries, European anti-Semitism was based principally on the Christian belief that the Jews were responsible for the death of Jesus. According to the Gospel of Matthew, when the Roman Governor, Pontius Pilate, considered releasing Jesus, a "blameless" man, the Jews present at the trial called for his death, saying "let his blood be on our heads and the heads of children".[5] With these words, the Jews were said to have accepted collective responsibility for the death of Jesus. Even though the foundations of Christianity lay in Jewish tradition and scripture, the Jews had repudiated the Messiah and so became enemies of the faith.[6] The Gospel of John seemed to confirm the evil character of Jews when it reported Jesus as saying to the Jews who rejected him, "You are of your father the devil, and your will is to do your father's desires".[7] Christian Europe in the Middle Ages maintained a deep

---

[4] In *Chamberlain* v. *Surrey School Board No. 36*, 2002 SCC 86, the Supreme Court of Canada held that public decision-makers could not be expected to leave their religious values at the doorstep when making political decisions.

[5] Matt. 27:25 (AV).

[6] George M. Frederickson, *Racism: A Short History* (Princeton University Press, 2002), at 18.

[7] John 8:44 (AV).

suspicion of Jews, who were thought to be responsible for the spread of diseases such as cholera and the Black Death and for the immiseration of many in the developing commercial economy.[8] Also, during this period, rumours circulated in England and elsewhere about Jews kidnapping and murdering Gentile children as part of a ritual that involved the use of the children's blood in the making of Passover matzo – what is referred to as the "blood libel".[9] The claim may not have had a scriptural basis, but it resonated with the original charge of deicide.

In the nineteenth century, anti-Semitic speech shifted from claims about the defective or immoral character of Jewish belief and practice to claims about the undesirable racial or biological characteristics of Jews – characteristics that were seen as distinguishing Jews from the rest of European society. Jews did not simply hold erroneous beliefs and adhere to false rituals; they were "intrinsically and organically evil", and so fell outside the human community – in religious terms, they were beyond redemption.[10] Yet even when framed in the more secular language of race and biology, the concern of anti-Semitic speech was that Jews were conspiring to undermine Christian civilization and its values.[11]

While anti-Semitism in the West may be less widespread and virulent than it once was, it remains part of the cultural landscape in Europe and North America. In many Western democracies, its force was dulled following WWII, when the Nazi atrocities against the Jews became widely known. More recently, it appears to have been further reduced as a result of changing attitudes among conservative Christians – a group once deeply suspicious of Jews but now more inclined to see them (and Israel) as an ally in a number of contests involving Muslims and atheists. Nevertheless, anti-Semitism persists in an extreme form at the margins of public discourse in many Western democracies, and more centrally in a number of Eastern European countries.[12]

Anti-Semitism in Muslim societies, much like that in predominantly Christian countries, has both a religious and a racial character. According to the Quran and Hadith, Jews, like Christians, are "people of the book", who worship the God of Abraham as the one true God, and so should be shown respect and granted a degree of autonomy within Muslim majority countries.[13] At the same time, the Islamic tradition includes an account of the betrayal of the Prophet Mohammad by some of the Jewish clans in Medina during the conflict between the nascent Muslim community and the merchant families in Mecca.[14] This account is now sometimes

---

[8] Robert S. Wistrich, *Antisemitism* (Pantheon, 1991), at 28.

[9] Frederickson (n. 6) at 20; Wistrich (n. 7) at 32.   [10] Frederickson (n. 6) at 19.

[11] For example, James Keegstra, in the case discussed in c. 2, taught his students that Jews were seeking to destroy Christian society.

[12] Wistrich (n. 8) at 169.

[13] Anver Emon, *Religious Pluralism and Islamic Law: Dhimmis and Others in the Empire of Law* (Oxford University Press, 2012).

[14] Karen Armstrong, *Fields of Blood* (Knopf, 2014), at 183, tells the story of Mohammad's relationship with the Jewish tribes in Medina. Some tribes are said to have breached their pact with Mohammad, while others remained faithful to it.

linked to the "racial" claim that Jews are duplicitous or conspiratorial – a claim that continues to have currency in Muslim majority countries, as evidenced by the popularity of *The Protocols of the Elders of Zion* in several of these countries.[15] In some countries, anti-Semitism is also fueled by the Israel/Palestine conflict and so has a political rather than simply a religious basis. However, the view, sometimes expressed, that Jews are collectively responsible for the perceived wrongs of the state of Israel suggests that the animosity goes beyond opposition to the acts or existence of that state.[16]

2 Christian Islamophobia

Several of the anti-Muslim speech cases described in the previous chapters involved Christian clergy asserting that Muslims are seeking to impose Sharia law on Western democracies and are prepared to use violence to achieve this end. In *R. v. Harding*, for example, a Christian pastor distributed flyers in which he claimed that Muslims are hateful towards Christians, Jews, and other "non-believers" and are conspiring to take over Canada.[17] In holding that Mr. Harding had breached the criminal ban on hate speech, the court emphasized that "it is not a crime in Canada to proclaim that a particular religion is the only true religion, and that another religion with conflicting beliefs is false", but noted that the defendant did not limit himself to claims about the "falseness of Islam".[18] Mr. Harding conveyed a message "above and beyond religious opinion", making "alarming and false claims about the adherents of Islam, calculated to arouse fear and hatred of them in all non-Muslim people, particularly Christians."[19] His speech then did not fall within the exception in the *Criminal Code*, s. 319(3) (c), for the expression of an opinion on a religious subject that is made in good faith.

The bulk of the Eurabia writing, described in Chapter 2, frames these concerns about Muslims in more secular terms, presenting the group as a threat to liberal-democratic values.[20] Muslims, it is claimed, are seeking to undermine values such as gender equality, freedom of expression, and religious freedom. In the Eurabia writing, Christianity is assumed to be compatible with these values in a way that

---

[15] *The Protocols of the Elders of Zion* (1903). For a discussion see Stephen Eric Bronner, *A Rumor about the Jews: Reflections on Antisemitism and* The Protocols of the Learned Elders of Zion (St. Martin's Press, 2000).

[16] Criticism of Israel is viewed by some as a new form of anti-Semitism. For a critical discussion see Richard Moon, "Campus demonstrations and the case of Israel Apartheid Week", in James Turk (ed.), *The Limits of Academic Freedom* (Lorimer, 2013).

[17] *R. v. Harding* (1998), O.J. No. 2603, affirmed in Ontario Court of Appeal, 160 CCC (3d) 225; 48 C.R. (5th) 1. The court found that his speech amounted to the wilful promotion of hatred contrary to s. 319(2) of the *Criminal Code*.

[18] *Harding* (n. 17) at para. 15. [19] *Harding* (n. 17) at para. 15.

[20] Leo D. Lefebure, "Violence in the New Testament", in John Renard (ed.), *Fighting Words* (University of California, 2012) at 77: "With the rise of Islam in the 7th Century many Christians came to view the new faith as a threat to their faith – a threat that was foretold in the New Testament's apocalyptic texts."

Islam is not, and indeed is regarded by some as the historical and conceptual foundation for religious freedom and the separation of church and state.[21]

3 Religion and Racism

The justification for racial subordination once drew on biblical text – on the claim that man was created in God's image (and thus had light skin), but also on stories such as that of Ham, who was reported in the book of Genesis to have committed some form of indecent act towards his father Noah, for which he was condemned, along with his descendants, to be "servants of servants".[22] This story was read by some Christians as justification for the enslavement of African peoples, who were understood to be the descendants of Ham. The biblical story of Cain was also used to justify racial subordination and slavery, with some Christians asserting that a dark skin colour was the mark of Cain, placed on him by God after he murdered his brother Abel.[23]

At a time when moral views were generally grounded in a religious tradition, it was hardly surprising that scripture was used both to justify and to oppose racist views and actions.[24] Racism, though, is now seldom justified on religious grounds, and instead finds its rationalization in "scientific" claims or assumptions about racial difference. When racist views are (exceptionally) presented as religious beliefs, they are invariably dismissed by courts and other state actors not just as mistaken but as not truly or properly religious.[25]

The willingness to discount the religious basis for racist views raises the question of why the religious grounding of other forms of discriminatory or hateful speech

---

[21] This is the basis for the decision of the Italian courts in *Lautsi and Others* v. *Italy* (Application No. 30814/06) (2011) that the crucifixes hung in public school classrooms were not specifically religious symbols but instead represented the national and political culture of Italy. In the not so distant past, the conflict between Protestants and Catholics within Christendom generated attacks that today would easily be classified as hate speech. One of the standard tropes on the Protestant side concerned the moral depravity of the Catholic clergy. Indeed, an important contribution to anti-Catholic writing in the United States originated in Canada: *The Awful Disclosures of Maria Monk*, also known as *The Hidden Secrets of a Nun's Life in a Convent Exposed*, was published in 1836 and purported to describe sexual depravity among the Catholic clergy in Montreal and the murder of illegitimate infants born from the unholy sexual relationships between priests and nuns. This book helped to fuel the deep suspicion of Catholicism in Protestant Canada and the United States. More generally, Catholicism was seen as incompatible with the values of Protestant society – such as honesty and sobriety.

[22] Gen. 9:20 (AV).

[23] For a discussion see David M. Goldenberg, *The Curse of Ham: Race and Slavery in Early Judaism, Christianity, and Islam* (Princeton University Press, 2005).

[24] Frederickson (n. 6) at 46: "[s]ince the idiom of this period [pre-nineteenth-century] was primarily religious rather than naturalistic or scientific, it could only be through some special act of God that some people could be consigned to pariah status or slavery". At the same time, this "supernatural racism" was inconsistent with the central idea of Christianity – the salvation of all persons.

[25] This seems to occur despite the courts' adoption in many jurisdictions of a subjective/sincerity test for determining whether a belief/practice should be seen as religious and prima facie protected as a matter of religious freedom.

is not similarly discounted. Religious opposition to homosexuality, for example, is generally viewed as a sincere and serious religious position that, even though mistaken, should sometimes be accommodated. The willingness to give more credence to religious opposition to homosexuality may stem from two things, which I will say more about later in this chapter: first, this opposition focuses on the sinful activity of gays, which is understood by many opponents to be chosen behaviour, rather than on the shared traits of gays as a group, and second, the belief that homosexuality is sinful or immoral was until recently a widely held view and continues even today to be the view of a significant number of religious adherents.

4 Anti-gay Religious Speech

The LGBTQ community is the other significant target of religiously based hate speech. Indeed, religious belief – based on scripture and natural law – appears now to be the formal grounding for most anti-gay speech in the West, although in countries that formally embrace some form of separation between religion and politics, religious adherents sometimes feel compelled to frame their opposition to the legalization of same-sex physical intimacy, or the legal recognition of same-sex relationships, in secular terms, emphasizing the unnaturalness of such relationships, or their role in spreading disease, or the harm they cause to institutions such as the family that are essential to social stability.[26]

Sometimes, although not often today, it is asserted that homosexuality is harmful to others in the community because God may visit his wrath upon (or withdraw his protection from) a nation that tolerates this sinful activity. Religious figures such as Pat Robertson and Jerry Falwell have suggested that America's toleration of homosexuality made possible events such as Hurricane Katrina or the 9/11 attacks.[27]

Religious claims about the sinfulness of homosexuality are seldom sufficiently extreme to be considered hate speech.[28] The simple claim that homosexuality is sinful or immoral or unnatural (grounded in scripture or religious tradition) does not entail that gays are a danger to society and must therefore be excluded or suppressed. Indeed, many Christians believe that they are called upon to love the sinner, while repudiating his or her sin. However, the anti-gay claim that can be regarded as extreme, and contrary to hate speech law, is that homosexuals are – or are more likely to be – pedophiles. While the claim that gays are pedophiles is not obviously

---

[26] Byrne Fone, *Homophobia: The Last Acceptable Prejudice* (Picador, 2000), at 414, describes the way in which homosexuality has often been viewed as a "psychological fault" arising from problems in early childhood rather than simply as sinful behaviour. The Roman Catholic Church, drawing on natural law claims, considers homosexuality to be a natural disorder.

[27] As earlier noted in c. 4: "Falwell: Blame abortionists, feminists and gays", *The Guardian*, Wednesday, Sept 19, 2001, www.theguardian.com/world/2001/sep/19/september11.usa9.

[28] But see *Hammond* v. *DPP* [2004] EWHC 69, which is described below – although the law at the time banned "insults" rather than a narrow category of hate speech.

rooted in religious teaching, it often draws on religious ideas about evil or moral corruption. Religious opponents of homosexuality sometimes accuse gays of spreading corruption in society, leaving it unclear whether their concern is simply that gays are pressing for the legal and public acceptance of same-sex relationships, or more alarmingly that gays are seeking to draw children into sexual relations. Increasingly, in anti-LGBTQ speech, the focus of criticism or attack is not the individual sinner, who is engaging in acts of personal immorality (and who, although flawed, is redeemable), but is instead the "gay lobby" or the "homosexual machine", a depersonalized entity that, in the critics' view, is seeking to corrupt society, and in particular its children. While "loving the sinner" may be an important part of the Christian tradition, the tradition also includes another idea of sin as something that arises from an external source – an evil force in the world that must be fought.

In the discussion that follows, I will focus on anti-gay speech as the most significant form of religiously based hate speech. In a final note, I will also briefly discuss the religious incitement of terrorism. In a number of ways, the promotion of terrorism is similar to hate speech. However, there are also important differences between them that make hate speech regulation a poor model for the restriction of terrorist promotion.

I SOME CASES INVOLVING ANTI-GAY SPEECH

A Owens v. Saskatchewan (HRC)

Mr. Owens placed an advertisement in the Saskatoon *Leader Post* in which he expressed his opposition to same-sex relationships. The ad was simple in its content, although ambiguous in its import. It included the citations for several passages from the *New International* version of the Bible: Rom. 1:26, Lev. 18:22, Lev. 20:13, and 1 Cor. 6:9–10. Beneath these citations was an equals sign, followed by an image of two stick men holding hands within a circle with a diagonal line running through it – what is often described as the "not permitted" symbol.

A complaint was made against Mr. Owens under s. 14 of the *Saskatchewan Human Rights Code*, which prohibits the publication of statements that "expose or tend to expose to hatred" a person or persons on certain grounds, including sexual orientation.[29] The complainants argued that the ad, and in particular its biblical references, would have the effect of stirring up hatred against gays. The provincial human rights tribunal agreed with the complainants and found that the ad breached

---

[29] S. 14(1)(b) of *The Saskatchewan Human Rights Code*, S.S. 1979, c. S-24.1. The provision also precludes speech that ridicules, belittles, or otherwise affronts the dignity of such persons. However, the courts held that this part of the ban is incompatible with the Charter and read these words out of the provision. See *Whatcott v. Saskatchewan HRC* [2013], 1 S.C.R. 467.

the *Code*.[30] In the tribunal's view, the reference in the ad to a passage such as Lev. 20:13 ("If a man lies with a man as one lies with a woman, both of them have done what is detestable. They must be put to death; their blood will be on their own heads"[31]) could reasonably be read as calling for the death of gays, and so amounted to hate speech, or, in the language of the *Code*, "exposed" gays to hatred. However, the tribunal's decision was later overturned by the Saskatchewan Court of Appeal in *Owens v. Sask. (HRC)*.[32] The key question, said the Court, is "whether the advertisement was characterized by 'intense feelings' and a 'strong sense of detestation, calumny and vilification'."[33] In the Court's view, the passages cited by Mr. Owens should not have been read in the same way as "a contemporary poster, notice or publication saying 'Homosexuals should be killed'".[34] The "reasonable" or "objective" reader of the ad would recognize that the Bible carries a variety of messages, including messages of love and forgiveness, and would understand the ad's biblical references in this context.[35] The Court thought that the other elements of the ad also supported a different, less extreme, reading; for example, the ad's use of stickmen "suggests that certain kinds of activity are not allowed rather than suggesting that gay men should be killed".[36] Finally, the Court noted that the ad appeared "in the middle of an ongoing debate" about the legal recognition of same-sex relationships and so could be seen as a contribution to that debate rather than as an appeal to hatred.[37]

---

[30] *Hellquist v. Owens* (2001), 40 C.H.R.R. D/197. On appeal, a judge of the Court of Queen's Bench in *Owens v. Saskatchewan (Human Rights Commission)*, 2002 SKQB 506, agreed with the Tribunal that the ad breached the Code provision.

[31] The other passages are as follows:

> Lev. 18:22: "Do not lie with a man as one lies with a woman; that is detestable."
>
> Rom. 1:26–32: "Because of this, God gave them over to shameful lusts. Even their women exchanged natural relations for unnatural ones. In the same way the men also abandoned natural relations with women and were inflamed with lust for one another. Men committed indecent acts with other men, and received in themselves the due penalty for their perversion.
>
> Furthermore, since they did not think it worthwhile to retain the knowledge of God, he gave them over to a depraved mind, to do what ought not to be done.
>
> They have become filled with every kind of wickedness, evil, greed and depravity.
>
> They are full of envy, murder, strife, deceit and malice. They are gossips, slanderers, God-haters, insolent, arrogant, and boastful; they invent ways of doing evil; they disobey their parents; they are senseless, faithless, heartless, ruthless.
>
> Although they know God's righteous decree that those who do such things deserve death, they not only continue to do these very things but also approve of those who practice them.
>
> 1 *Cor.* 6:9: Do you not know that the wicked will not inherit the kingdom of God? Do not be deceived: Neither the sexually immoral nor idolaters nor adulterers nor male prostitutes nor homosexual offenders . . . will inherit the kingdom of God.

[32] *Owens v. Saskatchewan (Human Rights Commission)* [2006], S.J. N. 221. (CA)

[33] *Owens* (n. 32) at 62. [34] *Owens* (n. 32) at 81. [35] *Owens* (n. 32) at 79.

[36] *Owens* (n. 32) at 85. [37] *Owens* (n. 32) at 66.

B Lund *v.* Boissoin

Mr. Boissoin, a Christian pastor, wrote a letter that was published in the Red Deer newspaper in which he warned readers about the danger homosexuals represent to society.[38] He called homosexuality a "disease" and declared that "[w]here homosexuality flourishes, all manner of wickedness abounds".[39] He claimed that children were being "targeted" and "psychologically abused" by gays. Gays, he said, were "recruiting our young into their camps" and were "just as immoral as pedophiles".[40] He employed war imagery in his call to fellow Christians to fight this wickedness: "My banner has been raised and war has been declared so as to defend the precious sanctity of our innocent children and youth, that you [gays] so eagerly toil, day and night to consume".[41] Boissoin traded on the erroneous belief that gays are more likely than heterosexuals to seek sex with children, warning that "[i]t is only a matter of time before some of these morally bankrupt individuals, such as those involved with NAMBLA, the North American Man/Boy Lovers Association, will achieve their goal to have sexual relations with children".[42] He concluded his letter with a call to action: "It's time to start taking back what the enemy has taken from you. The safety and future of our children is at stake".[43]

Boissoin was found by an Alberta Human Rights Panel to have breached the provincial code's ban on hate speech.[44] In the Panel's judgment, Boissoin's letter was "likely to expose" gays to "hatred and contempt". The tribunal's decision, though, was overturned in the courts.[45] In the Court of Appeal's opinion, the letter was not sufficiently extreme to breach the provincial ban. The Court saw the letter as a contribution to "an ongoing public debate on matters of public interest" and therefore as "distinct from hate propaganda, which serves no useful function and has no redeeming qualities".[46] The Court recognized that Mr. Boissoin's opposition to homosexuality (and more particularly to the school board's plan to teach children that homosexuality is a normal and acceptable "lifestyle") was "expressed in strong, insensitive, and some might say bigoted terms", but accepted that "the aim of the letter was to stir apathetic people, who agreed with him, to his cause" – "to rouse others of like mind

---

[38] The text of the letter can be found at *Lund* v. *Boissoin*, 2012 ABCA 300 para. 4 [*Boissoin*]. The letter sometimes seems to be directed at members of the gay community – as a challenge – but more often is written as an appeal to Christians to resist the "gay lobby".

[39] *Boissoin* (n. 38) at para. 4.   [40] *Boissoin* (n. 38) at para. 4.   [41] *Boissoin* (n. 38) at para. 4.

[42] *Boissoin* (n. 38) at para. 4.   [43] *Boissoin* (n. 38) at para. 4.

[44] Section 3 (1) of the *Human Rights Citizenship and Multiculturalism Act*. *Lund* v. *Boissoin and the Concerned Christian Coalition*, Nov 30, 2007 (Alta. Human Rights Panel).

[45] The Queen's Bench Court judge, who heard the initial appeal, adopted a narrow reading of the Code's hate speech ban: *Boissoin* v. *Lund*, 2009 ABQB 592. In the judge's view the purpose of s. 3(1)(b) of the Act is not "simply to restrain hateful or contemptuous speech *per se*", but rather is to restrict speech that encourages acts of discrimination in employment and other contexts covered by the Act. The CA rejected this narrow reading of the ban – although it agreed with the QB judge that the letter did not breach the Code.

[46] *Boissoin* (n. 38) at 70.

and involve them in the public debate".[47] The Court concluded that "a reasonable person, aware of the relevant context and circumstances" would not view the letter "as likely to expose homosexuals to hatred or contempt".[48] The letter would instead be understood by the reasonable reader "as an overstated and intemperate opinion of a writer whose extreme and insensitive language undermines whatever credibility he might otherwise have hoped to have".[49] This, of course, could be said of all hate speech and so might count as an argument against hate speech regulation generally and not just the restriction of this particular letter.[50]

C Whatcott v. Sask HRC

In *Whatcott v. Sask HRC*, the issue was whether anti-gay flyers that were left in home letter boxes breached the hate speech ban in the Saskatchewan *Human Rights Code*. The provincial Human Rights Tribunal decided that the four flyers distributed by Mr. Whatcott breached the Code because they were likely to expose gays and lesbians to hatred.[51] The Supreme Court of Canada, on appeal, determined that two of Mr. Whatcott's flyers contained text that breached the hate speech ban, while the other two did not.

The Court thought that a "reasonable observer" would conclude that two of the flyers were likely to expose the members of a group to hatred, because they displayed several "hallmarks of hatred". The Court noted that they "portray[] the targeted group as a menace that could threaten the safety and well-being of others"; they draw on authoritative sources, such as the Bible, "to lend credibility to the negative generalizations"; and they create "a tone of hatred" through the use of "vilifying and derogatory representations", describing gays as "filthy" and "degenerated".[52] The Court thought that a reasonable person would take from these two flyers the message that gays are "unclean and possessed with uncontrollable sexual appetites or behaviour".[53] The Court also pointed to the flyers' portrayal of gays as child abusers or predators, in passages such as these: "Our children will pay the price in disease,

---

[47] *Boissoin* (n. 38) at 71.   [48] *Boissoin* (n. 38) at 77.   [49] *Boissoin* (n. 38) at 77.

[50] Unless the definition of the reasonable reader is based on the speaker's intended or actual audience. See discussion below.

[51] The Tribunal's decision was upheld by the Sask. Court of Queen's Bench, *Whatcott v. Saskatchewan (HRC)* (2007), 306 Sask. R. 186, but overturned on appeal to the Saskatchewan Court of Appeal, *Whatcott v. Saskatchewan (HRC)*, 2010 SKCA 26.

[52] *Whatcott v. Saskatchewan (HRC)*, 2013 SCC 11. One of the flyers stated that "The Bible is clear that homosexuality is an abomination" and cited in support of this Cor. 6:9: "neither fornicators, nor idolaters, nor adulterers, nor sodomites will inherit the Kingdom of Heaven". (Note that the King James Version translated this verse from Greek in the following way: "Know ye not that the unrighteous shall not inherit the kingdom of God? Be not deceived: neither fornicators, nor idolaters, nor adulterers, nor effeminate, nor abusers of themselves with mankind".) The flyer also referred to the Biblical story of Sodom and Gomorrah, a city, which in the words of the flyer, "was given over to homosexual perversion and as a result destroyed by God's wrath."

[53] *Whatcott* (n. 52) at para. 188.

death, abuse"; "Sodomites are 430 times more likely to acquire Aids & 3 times more likely to sexually abuse children!"; and "[o]ur acceptance of homosexuality and our toleration [*sic*] of its promotion in our school system will lead to the early death and morbidity of many children."[54] In the Court's view, then, the tribunal was justified in deciding that these flyers would expose homosexuals to hatred, because they "equate[d] homosexuals with carriers of disease, sex addicts, pedophiles and predators who would proselytize vulnerable children and cause their premature death".[55]

The other two flyers, which the Court decided did not breach the Code, reprinted classified ads from "Saskatchewan's largest gay magazine".[56] The flyers asserted that these ads were "for men seeking boys" – although the Court observed that this was not necessarily the intended meaning of the reference in the ads to partners of "any age".[57] In the margins of the reproduced ads, Mr. Whatcott wrote, "The ads with men advertising as bottoms are men who want to get sodomized. This shouldn't be legal in Saskatchewan!" along with the following words from the Bible: "'If you cause one of these little ones to stumble it would be better that a millstone was tied around your neck and you were cast into the sea' Jesus Christ".[58] In the Court's view, the flyers did nothing more than reproduce these ads and claim that they were placed by men who were looking for boys as sexual partners. The flyers may be offensive, said the Court, but they do not "manifest hatred". A reasonable person, "aware of the relevant context and circumstances" would not read these flyers "as exposing or likely to expose persons of same-sex orientation to detestation and vilification".[59] The Court, following the earlier Saskatchewan Court of Appeal judgment in *Owens*, decided that objective observers would interpret the Biblical text in the flyer "with an awareness that [the Bible] contains more than one sort of message, some of which involve themes of love, tolerance and forgiveness" and "that the meaning and relevance of the specific Bible passages cited ... could be assessed in a variety of ways by different people."[60]

D Prosecutor General v. Ake Green

Religious attacks on homosexuality have been the subject of hate speech claims in other jurisdictions. One of the more prominent cases involved a Swedish pastor, Ake Green, who delivered a sermon entitled "Is homosexuality congenital or the powers of evil meddling with people?" to about 50 congregants. He told his audience that homosexuality was a choice, because "[a]nything else would be treachery against humanity".[61] In the sermon, Green described homosexuality as a "cancerous growth on the body of society" and claimed that the legalization of

---

[54] *Whatcott* (n. 52) at para. 183.　　[55] *Whatcott* (n. 52) at para. 190.　　[56] *Whatcott* (n. 52) at para. 195.
[57] *Whatcott* (n. 52) at para. 196.　　[58] *Whatcott* (n. 52) at para. 195.
[59] *Whatcott* (n. 52) at para. 196.　　[60] *Whatcott* (n. 52) at paras. 198–9.
[61] *Prosecutor General* v. *Ake Green*, The Supreme Court of Sweden, Case No. B 1050-05 (29 November 2005), at 3.

same-sex partnerships had led to the spread of AIDS among gays and eventually to "innocent people".[62] While Green "emphasiz[ed] that not all homosexuals are pedophiles", he nevertheless asserted a link between them: "The pedophiles of today do not start out as pedophiles, but begin by changing their social intercourse. That is how it starts."[63] In his sermon, Green also cited Biblical passages such as Lev. 18:22 ("you shall not lie with a man, as a man lies with a woman") and Cor. 6:9, which, he said, teach us "about these abnormalities".[64]

Pastor Green was found at trial to have breached Sweden's hate speech law (which prohibits statements that threaten or express contempt for the members of a racial or other group) but was acquitted on appeal to the Supreme Court of Sweden. The appeal court recognized that his statements were "insulting" about the group in general, "even though he was not completely categorical, and made certain reservations to the effect that not all homosexuals are like those he is criticizing".[65] The Court was unpersuaded by Green's claim that his statements were directed not against homosexuals as a group, but instead against their sinful behaviour. In the Court's view, even though Green's statements referred to "the practice of homosexuality", it is not possible "to draw a sharp distinction between the sexual preference, per se, and such practice of it, which constitutes the focus of that sexual preference".[66] Furthermore, said the Court, Green's statements "overstepped the limits of an objective and responsible discourse regarding homosexuals as a group".[67] However, the Court went on to decide that the scope of the hate speech ban should be narrowly construed. A narrow reading of the ban was necessary, said the Court, to ensure that the law was compatible with the freedom of expression and freedom of religion provisions in the *ECHR*, which had been incorporated into Swedish law. The Court thought it was "likely" that the European Court of Human Rights would find that the restriction of Mr. Green's speech was not proportionate, and would therefore violate the *ECHR*.[68] In the Court's view, even Green's "most extreme statement, describing sexual abnormalities as a cancerous growth", because

---

[62] *Green* (n. 61) at 3.

[63] *Green* (n. 61) at 3: "I would like to emphasize that not all homosexuals are paedophiles. And not all homosexuals are perverted. Nevertheless, the door to forbidden areas has been opened, leading to sinful feelings and thoughts. The paedophiles of today do not start out as paedophiles, but begin by changing their social intercourse. That is how it starts." He seems to view homosexuality as a "gateway" sexual practice that may lead the individual into other, even more objectionable sexual practices, such as paedophilia.

[64] Drawing on these passages, he described (some) gays as "corrupter[s] of boys", "perverted people", and "paedophiles". The Court quotes from a submission made by the Swedish Council of Free Churches: "Merely citing and discussing religious scriptures, for example, does not fall within the purview of criminalized behaviour pursuant to this proposal. However, it should not be permissible to use this kind of material to threaten, or to express contempt for, homosexuals as a group, any more than it would be permissible to use religious texts to threaten, or express contempt for, Muslims or Christians" (*Green*, n. 61, at 3).

[65] *Green* (n. 61) at 8.   [66] *Green* (n. 61) at 8.

[67] *Green* (n. 61) at 8.   [68] *Green* (n. 61) at 16.

it occurred within the context of a sermon, "is not something that can be deemed to encourage or justify hatred of homosexuals".[69]

E Vejdeland and Others *v.* Sweden

In another case from Sweden, *Vejdeland and Others* v. *Sweden*, the ECtHR held that the conviction under Sweden's hate speech law of a group that had distributed anti-gay leaflets in an upper secondary school did not breach the *ECHR*.[70] The leaflets, which were left in or on student lockers, described homosexuality as a "deviant sexual proclivity" that had "a morally destructive effect on the substance of society" and "was one of the main reasons for [the] modern-day plague [of AIDS] gaining a foothold".[71] The leaflets also associated homosexuality with a movement to legalize pedophilia: "homosexual lobby organizations are also trying to play down…paedophilia".[72] The Supreme Court of Sweden thought that, even if the leaflets were intended to initiate debate, they were "formulated in a way that was offensive and disparaging for homosexuals as a group".[73] In the Court's view, the leaflets were "unwarrantably offensive" without contributing to "mutual understanding".[74] In concluding that the speech in this case breached the hate speech ban, the Swedish Court noted that the school was "a relatively sheltered environment as regards the political actions of outsiders" and that the students had received the flyers in their lockers without having any choice in the matter. The subsequent application to the ECtHR was dismissed because, in that court's view, the limit on freedom of expression "could…reasonably be regarded by the national authorities as necessary in a democratic society for the protection and rights of others."[75]

F Hammond *v.* DPP

In *Hammond* v. *DPP*, an English court found that an Evangelical Christian pastor who conducted an anti-gay protest in the city centre of Bournemouth had breached s. 5 of the *Public Order Act 1986*, which prohibited the display of a sign or writing

---

[69] *Green* (n. 61) at 16. Ian Leigh, "Homophobic Speech, Equality Denial and Religious Expression", in Ivan Hare and James Weinstein (eds.), *Extreme Speech and Democracy* (Oxford University Press, 2009), at 391 describes a case from the Netherlands involving an imam who declared on a 2001 television broadcast that homosexuality was "harmful" to society and a "contagious disease". The imam was acquitted in the Dutch courts, which held that the expression of religious belief by a religious authority was protected as a matter of religious freedom.

[70] *Vejdeland and Others* v. *Sweden* (App. No. 1813/07) 9 Feb. 2012. Chapter 61, Article 8 of the Penal Code prohibits communication that threatens or expresses contempt for a group based on race, religious belief, sexual orientation, etc.

[71] *Vejdeland* (n. 70) at para. 8.   [72] *Vejdeland* (n. 70) at para. 8.

[73] *Vejdeland* (n. 70) at para. 15. (Quoting the Supreme Court of Sweden, July 6, 2006.)

[74] *Vejdeland* (n. 70) at para. 15.   [75] *Vejdeland* (n. 70) at para. 59.

that was "threatening, abusive or insulting within the hearing or sight of a person likely to be caused harassment, alarm or distress".[76] Mr. Hammond had expressed his views about homosexuality to passers-by while holding a sign that read "Stop Immorality", "Stop Homosexuality", and "Stop Lesbianism". Members of the public who objected to his views sought to prevent him from speaking. The police then intervened and charged Mr. Hammond with displaying an "insulting" sign causing "alarm and distress". He was convicted at trial and his conviction was upheld on appeal by the Divisional Court, which relied on the trial's judge's finding that Mr. Hammond's communication was "insulting", contrary to the law, because it described homosexuality as immoral. The Court seemed to be not entirely comfortable in reaching this result, acknowledging that Mr. Hammond's assertion that homosexuality was immoral and should be stopped was not expressed in an intemperate manner. The statutory provision under which Mr. Hammond was convicted was subsequently amended to exclude the term "insulting", and so the result in a case such as this might now be different.[77]

G Snyder v. Phelps

In *Snyder* v. *Phelps*, the U.S. Supreme Court held that an anti-gay protest directed at the funeral of a soldier killed in the Iraq war was protected speech under the First Amendment.[78] The protestors from the Westboro Baptist Church were opposed to the acceptance of gays in the military and to the general tolerance of homosexuality in American society. They carried signs with messages such as "God Hates You", "Fag Troops", and "You Are Going to Hell". The father of the deceased soldier brought an action against the church for the "intentional infliction of emotional distress".[79] The focus of the claim was not (or not principally) the protest's anti-gay message, but rather its targeting of a funeral and a grieving family. The Court noted that the protest addressed a public issue in a peaceful way on public property. The Court found that the protestors were far enough from the funeral that there was no disruption of the service.

II THE MEANING OF SCRIPTURE

Even though the biblical passages cited by Mr. Owens, and quoted by Mr. Whatcott, appear to call for violent action against gays, the courts in both cases thought that

---

[76] *Hammond* v. *DPP*, (n. 28). See also *R.* v. *Ali, Javed, and Ahmed* (2012) N. 720110109 (Derby Cr. Ct, Feb 10) involving Muslim anti-gay speech.

[77] For a critical discussion of the *Hammond* case see Leigh (n. 69) at 390. Leigh notes that the Divisional Court upheld the conviction even though under the *Human Rights Act, 1998*, the courts are required to apply British law so that it is compatible with the *ECHR*.

[78] *Snyder* v. *Phelps*, 562 US 443 (2011).

[79] The original action also included a claim for "intrusion upon seclusion".

the passages should not be read in that way. According to the Saskatchewan Court of Appeal in *Owens*, "the Bible passages can be seen in a different light than a plain assertion made in contemporary times to the effect that 'Homosexuality is evil and homosexuals should be killed'."[80] Had Mr. Owens said in his own words that gays should be put to death, the Court almost certainly would have found him to be in breach of the hate speech ban. But these words were not his own, and indeed his ad gave only the citation for the scriptural passages.

The Court of Appeal in *Owens* knew that it must not be "drawn into the business of attempting to authoritatively interpret sacred texts such as the Bible". However, the Court accepted that, in determining whether Mr. Owens's invocation of scripture constituted hate speech under the Code, it could not ignore "the typical characteristics of such texts".[81] It recognized that the Bible is an "ancient and fundamental religious text" that can be read in various ways:

> Many Christians see these passages as rooted in a very different historical period – and believe that they cannot be understood literally, as contemporary assertions. Some, like Mr. Owens himself, might see them as definitive revelations to the effect that God is opposed to certain gay sexual practices. Others might see the passages as meaning the Bible opposes such practices but would consider that same-sex sexual activity is a sin no more heinous than many of the other sins identified in the text such as sexual immorality, idolatry, adultery and male prostitution. Others might contest the very meaning of the passages and suggest they refer to pederasty (a relationship between an older male partner and a youth) rather than same-sex relationships as understood in contemporary terms. Still others might acknowledge that the Bible opposes same-sex relationships but would see its dictates as so dated in time and rooted in ancient culture, or as so foreign to their own beliefs, as to be irrelevant.[82]

One does not have to be a Christian, said the Court, to recognize that the Bible is read by most adherents in a way that does not support violence. The scriptural passages cited in Mr. Owens's ad must be seen "in the context of the other concepts popularly understood as flowing from the Bible" – and in particular Jesus's message "of love, tolerance, and forgiveness".[83]

The Supreme Court of Canada in *Whatcott* adopted the reasoning of the *Owens* Court on the issue of scriptural interpretation. Mr. Whatcott had incorporated

---

[80] *Owens* (n. 32) at para. 83.   [81] *Owens* (n. 32) at para. 78.   [82] *Owens* (n. 32) at para. 80.

[83] The New Testament's message of "Love thine enemy", "Let him who has not sinned, cast the first stone", affects the Christian understanding of these Old Testament passages. The Court continues, noting that the Bible contains many such passages: Mark 12:31, "Love your neighbor as yourself"; Matt. 6:14–15, "For if you forgive men when they sin against you, your heavenly Father will also forgive you. But if you do not forgive men their sins, your Father will not forgive your sins"; Matt. 7:1, "Do not judge, or you too will be judged"; Lev. 19:18, "Do not seek revenge or bear a grudge against one of your people, but love your neighbor as yourself"; Prov. 10:12. "Hatred stirs up dissension, but love covers over all wrongs."

scriptural language directly into the text of two of his flyers, quoting from Luke 17:2 (and Matt. 18:6): "If you cause one of these little ones to stumble it would be better that a millstone was tied around your neck and you were cast into the sea".[84] He did not provide the scriptural reference to the passage, but attributed the words to Jesus. The complainant in the case argued that this language could be understood as calling for the death of those who violate children, which, in the context of the flyer, meant gays. However, the Court thought that the biblical language in Mr. Whatcott's flyers "could be assessed in a variety of ways by different people" and that "objective observers would interpret excerpts of the Bible with an awareness that it contains more than one sort of message".[85] The key question, said the Court, is whether the reasonable audience member would read the ad (and the quoted passages) as extreme – as encouraging hatred. In the Court's view, the quoted passage would not, without more, be read by the reasonable audience member "as inspiring detestation and vilification of homosexuals".[86]

In the *Ake Green* case, the Swedish Supreme Court thought that the pastor's scriptural references should be assessed based "on how a member of the audience listening to [his] sermon must have perceived these statements".[87] And in the Court's view, Pastor Green's congregation would not have understood these passages as encouraging hatred.

But even if it is true that most audience members in these cases will adopt a non-literal reading of the cited passage, some in the audience may consider the Bible to be the revealed word of God that must be read literally, including its call for the earthly punishment of gays. Mr. Owens and Mr. Whatcott believe that homosexuality is immoral because the Bible says it is. Presumably each has his own account of why some parts of the Bible should be read literally and others not, or of how to reconcile the Old Testament's call for the killing of gays with the New Testament's call for love, understanding, and forgiveness. But what about the exceptional reader? If the object of hate speech law is to prevent the spread of hatred across the community, then the focus is appropriately on the reasonable audience member – and the ordinary meaning and effect of the speech. But, if, as earlier argued, the purpose of the hate speech ban is also, or instead, to prevent the encouragement of individual acts of violence – and the risk that some will take the message seriously and act on it – then the impact of the speech on exceptional readers should also matter.

---

[84] *Whatcott* (n. 52) at para. 184.   [85] *Whatcott* (n. 52) at para. 199.

[86] *Whatcott* (n. 52) at para. 199. There is little doubt that the Court's familiarity with the Christian tradition gave it more comfort in reaching this conclusion. In a society in which the dominant religious tradition is Christianity, even non-believers recognize that most Christians do not read these passages literally – as supporting the killing of gays. However, as earlier noted, we seem to be less willing to adopt the same sympathetic view of a minority religion, with which we are less familiar: See the discussion of the Eurabia literature in c. 3.

[87] *Green* (n. 61) at 7–8.

Mr. Owens and others cannot be held responsible for perverse or eccentric read-ings of their words. But even if Mr. Owens's reference to Lev. 20:13 was not intended as a call to other Christians to kill gays, and even if most Christians would not under-stand it in that way, nevertheless it could be read by some as justifying the violent punishment of gays. The cited passages seem to say that homosexuality is immoral and that those who engage in it should be killed. Is it enough for the speaker to believe, or even to know, that most Christians share his belief that punishment for sin comes from God and that the Christian's role is to help the sinner to see the error of his or her ways? It may be that this message of love and forgiveness is so clearly or widely understood that the speaker should bear no responsibility for the influ-ence his words may have on the exceptional reader – who sees the ad or the flyer as calling for violence against gays. If the speech is directed at a general audience, which was the case in both *Whatcott* and *Owens*, then perhaps it should be read as a reasonable audience member would read it. However, when it is directed at a narrower audience of individuals, who are deeply antagonistic towards gays, then the "reasonable" or foreseeable interpretation of the speech, including its scriptural references, may be different.

III HATE THE SIN, LOVE THE SINNER

The courts in Canada and elsewhere have decided that references to scriptural pas-sages such as Lev. 20:13 in speech attacking homosexuals or homosexuality should not be read as calling for violent action – not at least without something more in the communication or context evidencing such a purpose. In eschewing a literal reading of these passages, the courts point to the message of love and forgiveness that is central to the Christian faith and that is expressed in the response adopted by many Christians to the sin of homosexuality, that one should love the person, despite his or her sin, and help him or her to see the error of his or her ways – "to love the sinner, hate the sin".[88] The common Christian view is that we are all sinners, and we can be redeemed if we seek forgiveness. While Christians should not condone behaviour that "violates the Scripture's core values", they should show love and compassion for "those who experience homoerotic desires".[89]

---

[88] Robert A. J. Gagnon, "The Bible and Homosexual Practices", in Dan O. Via and Robert A.J. Gagnon, *Homosexuality and the Bible: Two Views* (Fortress Press, 2003), at 41: "Love mandates that the church resist approval of homosexual behavior while reaching out in humility and gentleness to those afflicted by homoerotic desires". Ted G. Jelen, "Catholicism, Homosexuality, and Same-Sex Marriage in the United States", in D. Rayside and C. Wilcox (eds.), *Faith, Politics and Sexual Diversity* (UBC Press, 2011), at 208 describes the Roman Catholic response to homosexuality as set out by the U.S. Con-ference of Catholic Bishops: Homosexuality is regarded as "an objective moral disorder"; however, Catholics are called upon to show compassion towards those with such inclinations and to refrain from any form of discrimination against them.

[89] Gagnon (n. 88) at 91.

In anti-discrimination cases, the courts have generally rejected the distinction between gay identity and gay behaviour – between the person (the sinner) and his or her actions (the sin). If an employer refuses to hire someone because of his or her homosexual behaviour or "lifestyle", the employer will be found to have engaged in discrimination on the grounds of sexual orientation, even though the employer thinks that homosexuality is a chosen behaviour and would willingly hire the person if he or she refrained from engaging in this behaviour. Because the focus of anti-discrimination law is on the effect of the action and not the intention behind it, a refusal to employ someone because he or she lives a gay "lifestyle" amounts to discrimination on the grounds of sexual identity, whether or not the employer sees it that way. In *Owens* the Court recognized that although "many people do make such a distinction and believe on moral or religious grounds that they can disapprove of the same-sex sexual practices without disapproving of gays and lesbians themselves", "[s]exuality and sexual practices are such intimately central aspects of an individual's identity that it is artificial to suggest that the practices of gays and lesbians in this regard can somehow be separated out from those individuals themselves".[90] Similarly, in the *Ake Green* case, the Swedish Supreme Court rejected Mr. Green's claim that his statements were "not directed against homosexuals as a group", but simply targeted "behaviours that the Bible ... unambiguously characterizes as sin."[91] In the Court's view, a "sharp distinction" could not be drawn between sexual preference and sexual practice.

Yet even if the individual's belief in a distinction between behaviour (sin) and person (sinner), does not excuse him or her from a charge of discrimination, it may nevertheless be relevant in the application of a hate speech prohibition. Because the ban on hate speech is breached only when the speech exposes gays and lesbians to hatred – only when it vilifies the group's members – it matters that the speaker and the audience to which he or she is appealing view the ad as an attack on the individual's behaviour and not on him or her personally or on the members of his or her group. In the view of most Christians, an individual who engages in same-sex relations is not inherently bad or dangerous, even if his or her behaviour is immoral and should be condemned.

---

[90] *Owens* (n. 32) at para. 82. See also the dissenting judgment of L'Heureux-Dube J. in *Trinity Western University* v. *College of Teachers* [2001], 1 S.C.R. 772 at para. 69: "I am dismayed that at various points in the history of this case the argument has been made that one can separate condemnation of the 'sexual sin' of 'homosexual behaviour' from intolerance of those with homosexual or bisexual orientations. This position alleges that one can love the sinner, but condemn the sin ... The status/conduct or identity/practice distinction for homosexuals and bisexuals should be soundly rejected. ... This is not to suggest that engaging in homosexual behaviour automatically defines a person as homosexual or bisexual, but rather is meant to challenge the idea that it is possible to condemn a practice so central to the identity of a protected and vulnerable minority without thereby discriminating against its members and affronting their human dignity and personhood."

[91] *Green* (n. 61) at para. 8.

However, in *Whatcott*, the Supreme Court of Canada accepted that an attack on same-sex behaviour could in some cases be seen as a serious or extreme attack on gays as a group:

> Courts have thus recognized that there is a strong connection between sexual orientation and sexual conduct. Where the conduct that is the target of speech is a crucial aspect of the identity of the vulnerable group, attacks on this conduct stand as a proxy for attacks on the group itself. If expression targeting certain sexual behaviour is framed in such a way as to expose persons of an identifiable sexual orientation to what is objectively viewed as detestation and vilification, it cannot be said that such speech only targets the behaviour. It quite clearly targets the vulnerable group. Therefore, a prohibition is not overbroad for capturing expression of this nature.[92]

The sinner may be redeemable, but he or she is not blameless. In his sermon, Ake Green describes homosexuality as a sickness that can take over the individual and a choice that comes to define him or her.[93] Some religious adherents may believe that an individual who chooses to do wrong, and is determined to persist in that wrong, despite being exposed to the truth, is deeply flawed (if not beyond redemption) and should be personally condemned. A growing number of individuals, including religious believers, have come to accept that homosexuality is a deep-rooted orientation or identity, rather than simply an immoral choice. Different conclusions may follow from the recognition of homosexuality as an identity. A religious opponent of homosexuality may develop greater understanding and sympathy for the "struggle" of gays to suppress their "immoral inclinations". He or she may even come to accept that this "natural" orientation should no longer be seen as contrary to God's law. Or he or she may instead come to view gays as inherently immoral.

Many critics of homosexuality are concerned not just that gays are engaging in sinful acts, but also that they are also seeking to spread their moral corruption to society and, in particular, to its children. Mr. Boissoin's statement that gays are corrupting our children hovers ambiguously between a claim that they are "promoting" or normalizing homosexuality as an acceptable lifestyle (that young people may be encouraged to consider) and an assertion that gays are pedophiles, who are seeking to entice children (groom them) into participating in gay sex.

Boissoin, Whatcott, and Vejdeland, in their writings, focus their attacks not on individual gay men (and their acts of personal immorality), but on the more

---

[92] *Whatcott* (n. 52) at para. 124.

[93] The following is from the sermon given by Ake Green: "Homosexuality is a sickness, i.e. a wholesome and pure thought being replaced by a tainted thought, a wholesome heart being replaced by a sick heart. That is what happened. It is a wholesome body being ruined as a result of a change, according to Paul. Is homosexuality something you choose? The answer is yes. You choose it. You are not born with it. You simply choose it. It is a replacement. Without a doubt, that is how it is. Anything else would be treachery against humanity" (*Green*, n. 61, at 3).

impersonal "gay lobby" or "homosexual machine" – a group of intransigent gay men and women, who want to normalize same-sex relations in society and to encourage others to engage in this sinful activity. Mr. Boissoin states at the opening of his letter that his words are "not intended for those who are suffering from an unwanted sexual identity crisis. For you, I have understanding, care, compassion and tolerance. I sympathize with you and offer you my love and friendship"; however, he goes on to declare "war" against those who support "the homosexual machine".[94] In Mr. Boissoin's view, this machine or lobby represents a threat to society. It is an agent of evil or wickedness that must be battled.

Mr. Whatcott wants to warn his audience about the men and women who have chosen to engage in the immoral, even dangerous, activity of homosexuality, and are working in a coordinated way, as a lobby, to advance their sinful lifestyle and lead the most vulnerable members of society astray. Mr. Whatcott, like Mr. Boissoin, blurs the distinction between educating the general public (including young people) about same-sex relationships, and enticing children to enter same-sex relationships with adults. He warns his audience that "homosexuals want to share their filth and propaganda with Saskatchewan's children" or to "proselytize vulnerable young people" or to have "Saskatchewan's children corrupted by sodomite propaganda".[95] He declares that "Our children will pay the price in disease, death, abuse and ultimately eternal damnation, if we do not say no to the sodomite desire to socialize your children into accepting something that is clearly wrong."[96] In Mr. Whatcott's view, the "gay lobbyist" is not simply a sinner, someone who has simply succumbed to temptation; he or she is an agent of evil and corruption, who is seeking to draw others into his or her wickedness.[97]

Despite the claim of some religious opponents of homosexuality that their position derives from scripture, the passages upon which they rely – that drive them to the conclusion that homosexuality is sinful – are not quite so clear and fixed in their meaning.[98] As the courts in *Whatcott, Owens*, and other cases note, scripture is read in various ways within a tradition. Even those who believe that the Bible is the word of God, which should be read literally, usually accept that some passages must be read in the context of larger scriptural themes or principles. Many of these

---

[94] *Boissoin* (n. 38) at para. 4. Mr. Whatcott's flyers state that if we continue as we have been "our entire culture will be lost and we will incur the wrath of Almighty God if we do not repent", but he believes "there is still hope" and that "[w]e can repent and have our sins forgiven" (*Whatcott*, n. 52, at Appendix B).

[95] *Whatcott* (n. 52) at Appendix B.   [96] *Whatcott* (n. 52) at Appendix B.

[97] As earlier noted, many religious opponents of homosexuality have come to accept that it is a deeply-rooted orientation or identity, rather than simply an immoral choice.

[98] See generally Via and Gagnon (n. 88). Jelen (n. 88) at 210 observes that some have "attempted to turn the 'natural law' argument against homosexual activity on its head by suggesting that sexuality can be animative rather than simply procreative and that same sex relationships can be quite 'natural' in the sense of providing emotional and physical intimacy to couples of the same sex".

literalists simply ignore some of the difficult or awkward passages in the text. If the Biblical passages dealing with homosexuality are contested and do not decisively determine the (im)morality of homosexuality, then it seems that fear of homosexuality or disgust towards acts of same-sex intimacy are to some extent motivating, although not formally justifying, anti-gay words and actions.[99] Behind the "literal" reading of the anti-gay passages in the Bible may lie a deeper, visceral animosity towards homosexuality – stemming from anxiety about the collapse of gender roles and the erosion of patriarchy.[100] Pastor Green, for example, is not content in his sermon simply to describe homosexuality as sinful; he declares that it also "disgust[s] us".[101] Boissoin describes gays as perverse and psychologically diseased.[102] Whatcott in his flyers refers to the "sick desires" of "sodomites" who seek to spread their "filth" and "disease".[103] Adultery may be an equivalent sin, according to scripture, but those who engage in it are not described in these ways. And so even when anti-gay views are formally grounded in scripture, they seem to draw on (and play to) deeper feelings and attitudes that may be less moderate or controlled than the "love the sinner" principle requires. Religiously based anti-gay speech that appeals to disgust, revulsion, and fear may encourage extreme actions towards gays and so may amount to hate speech.[104]

IV EVIL IN THE WORLD

The issue in cases such as *Owens*, *Whatcott*, *Boissoin*, and *Green* was whether a speaker's religion-based claims about homosexuality were sufficiently extreme to constitute hate speech. The court in each of these cases found that the claims did not amount to hate speech (with a few exceptions in *Whatcott*) because the doctrine or scripture invoked by the speakers was part of a religious tradition that emphasized love and forgiveness and so ought not to be read as encouraging hatred or

---

99 Even the New Testament proscriptions such as I Cor. 6:9 can be read in a variety of ways – see Fone (n. 26) and Via and Gagnon (n. 88).

100 Fone (n. 26) at 420–21: "Though homophobes look to ancient doctrines and customs, it often seems that the horror of differences goes deeper than that. It cannot be explained merely by recourse to faith and custom no matter how ancient... For some it seems to have the force of a command of nature, they speak from the deep structures of the inner self, and in these psychological or even pathological dimensions, homophobia emerges as a condition, even a disease of the psyche as well as a disorder of the imagination, the spirit, and the social." Pamela Dickey Young, "It's all about sex: The roots of opposition to gay and lesbian marriages in some Christian churches", in Rayside and Wilcox (n. 88) at 168: "It is not an accident that the churches most opposed to same sex marriage are also those in which women's roles are seen as vastly different from men's."

101 *Green* (n. 61) at 3.   102 *Boissoin* (n. 38) at para. 4.   103 *Whatcott* (n. 52) at Appendix B.

104 Expressions of disgust and comparisons with disease and filth are among the "hallmarks of hatred" set out by the Supreme Court of Canada in *Whatcott* (n. 52).

justifying violence against members of the LGBTQ communities.[105] The common view within Christian and other traditions is that we are all sinners, capable of good and bad; that we must struggle to do good and to support others in doing the same; and that, as children of God, salvation is open to all of us if we seek forgiveness for our wrongs. The division (the struggle) between good and evil, truth and falsity, is something that occurs within each of us. We ought, then, to show compassion and understanding for the struggles of others.

There is also, however, a strain of Christianity (and of other faith traditions) that sees evil as an external threat to the community of (true) Christians.[106] As many have noted, religious faith is "an enormously effective boundary-maker and marker".[107] It connects us with some, but separates us from others – about whom we may sometimes feel suspicion and animosity. We may be convinced that the moral purity of our spiritual community is threatened by outsiders, who are viewed as a source of corruption or contamination.[108] This dualist view of good and evil is visible in eschatological accounts of various religions – including the Christian Bible's Book of Revelation, which describes a future battle in the world between good and evil – between God and the devil. As Steve Clarke notes, "Many fundamentalist Christians believe there is a supernatural power struggle between God and Satan, which spills over into the natural world. Many also believe that their actions here in the natural world can help to shape the precise outcome of this supernatural conflict."[109]

This "dualist" view of the moral world, in which evil is perceived as an external threat to the spiritual community, provides a foundation for hateful speech and

---

[105] In two of the cases discussed, *Hammond* (n. 28) and *Vejdeland* (n. 70), the courts showed a greater willingness to see anti-gay speech as hate speech. The law in *Hammond*, though, banned insults and not simply hate speech.

[106] The appeal of this dualist perspective is obvious. Jonathan Sacks, *Not in God's Name* (Schocken, 2015), describes some of the reasons people are drawn to it: "Good things are failing to happen because someone is preventing them from happening: the devil, Satan ... the infidel, the antichrist" (52). Or "a belief in Satan as an evil force helps [us] feel more positively about God and less likely to blame him for the pain and suffering in the world" (53). "Pathological dualism" "is a form of cognitive breakdown, an inability to face the complexities of the world, the ambivalences of human character, the caprices of history and the ultimate unknowability of God" (54).

[107] James K. Wellman Jr. (ed.), *Belief and Bloodshed* (Rowman Littlefield, 2007), "Introduction" at 5.

[108] Sacks (n. 106) at 39, observes that religious faith creates and sustains "communities of trust and support".

[109] Steve Clarke, *The Justification of Religious Violence* (Wiley, 2014), at 20. See also Mark Juergensmeyer and Margo Kitts (eds.), *Princeton Readings in Religion and Violence* (Princeton University Press, 2011), at 11: "The idea of cosmic war is that of a grand encounter between the forces of good and evil, religious and irreligious, order and chaos and it is played out on an epic scale. Real-world social and political confrontations can be swept up into this grand scenario. Conflicts over territory and political control are lifted into the high proscenium of sacred drama. Such extraordinary images of cosmic war are meta-justifications for religious violence. They not only explain why religious violence happens ... but also provide a large world view, a template of meaning in which religious violence makes sense".

action against outsiders.[110] In Mr. Boissoin's letter and Mr. Green's sermon, the Christian message of love often seems to be eclipsed by fear – of the moral corruption of society by the "gay lobby". Gays (or "sodomites", as Mr. Whatcott calls them) are presented as a source of "wickedness", "evil", and "corruption" that must be resisted. Mr. Boissoin calls on others to recognize and resist this evil: "Come on people, wake up! It's time to stand together and take whatever steps are necessary to reverse the wickedness that our lethargy has authorized to spawn."[111]

We do not need to agree with the claim of the new atheists that religion is the principal source of violence in the world or that religion ultimately directs its followers towards violent action to recognize that religion has sometimes been used to justify hatred and violence. While religious commitment may lead many to do good in the world, it has sometimes been turned (twisted) into a justification for violence in a battle against evil and corruption.[112] The organization and orientation of a religious community may provide fertile ground for prejudiced views and for the incitement of extreme actions against outsiders. A religious community (and in particular a community that sees itself as oppressed and under threat) may be receptive to speech that vilifies outsiders as a corrupting influence or a persecuting force. With the certainty that God is on their side, the members of a spiritual community may feel justified in doing terrible things.[113]

V AN ONGOING DEBATE

The Saskatchewan Court of Appeal noted that Mr. Owens's ad was published in the context of "an active debate and discussion about the place of sexual identity in Canadian society".[114] In this context, said the Court, the ad looks like a "position . . . in a continuing public policy debate rather than . . . a message of hatred or ill will".[115] Similarly, the Alberta Court of Appeal thought that Mr. Boissoin's letter was

---

[110] Sacks (n. 106) at 48: "Radical violence emerges only when we see the Us as all-good and the They as all-evil, heralding a war between the children of light and the forces of darkness. That is when altruistic evil is born."

[111] *Boissoin* (n. 38) at para. 13: "My banner has been raised and war has been declared so as to defend the precious sanctity of our innocent children and youth, that you so eagerly toil, day and night, to consume"; "When homosexuality flourishes, all manner of wickedness abounds".

[112] In various religious traditions, violence is approved of when necessary to defend the spiritual community. John Renard, "Exegesis and Violence", in John Renard, *Fighting Words* (n. 20) at 20, notes that Hinduism, Sikhism, and other traditions include stories of wars and battles, often involving divine powers and sometimes spilling into the natural world, that were central to the emergence and establishment of these spiritual traditions.

[113] Sacks (n. 106) at 180. Sacks further observes at 180 that "Dualism is alive and well in parts of the world today, it has a religious source, or at least speaks a religious language, and it is leading to terror, brutality, civil war and chaos on an ever-widening scale."

[114] *Owens* (n. 32) at para. 67. There was at the time, said the Court, "an ongoing national debate about how Canadian legal and constitutional regimes should or should not accommodate sexual identities" (para. 66).

[115] *Owens* (n. 32) at para. 68.

intended to "rouse others of like mind and involve them in the public debate" about homosexuality and the education of children.[116] The Supreme Court of Canada said much the same thing about Mr. Whatcott's flyers, which could, in the Court's view, be seen as contributing to an ongoing debate about same-sex relationships. According to the ECtHR in the *Ake Green* case, the hate speech ban does not extend "to an objective discussion about, or criticism against, homosexuality" and must not be used "to threaten free public debate".[117]

When harsh anti-gay speech is offered in the context of a public debate about homosexuality (either about the recognition of same sex marriage or the education of children in the schools about sexual diversity), the courts are likely to see it as intended to influence public policy rather than to stir up hatred. Anti-gay speech is different in this respect from racist speech, which cannot now be read (realistically) as calling for political action. Because there is no serious ongoing (uncoded) political debate about the legalization of racial subordination, speech that is overtly racist will more readily be understood as calling for non-state action, including acts of violence.[118]

Yet speech that presses for political action can include extreme claims – which could be described as hateful.[119] The Supreme Court of Canada in the *Whatcott* decision accepted that a call to political action could amount to hate speech, but only when the call was joined with "representations of detestation and vilification delegitimizing those of same-sex orientation."[120] Otherwise, a call for political action will be regarded as a "lawful contribution[] to the public debate on the morality of homosexuality."[121] According to the Swedish Supreme Court, Pastor Green's sermon would only breach the Swedish hate speech ban if it "clearly overstep[ped] the limits of objective and responsible debate regarding the group in question" – if, for example, it had expressed contempt for a group by asserting their inferiority.[122] It might seem then that little turns on whether the speech calls for (or justifies)

---

[116] *Boissoin* (n. 38) at para. 71. [117] *Green* note (n. 61) at para. 5.

[118] This is not to deny that public policy arguments – e.g., in support of the "war on drugs" or the reduction of welfare to single mothers – can sometimes be a proxy for racial bigotry and exclusion. One of Mr. Whatcott's flyers stated that if gays and lesbians "want to remain in their lifestyle and proselytize vulnerable young people, [the] civil law should discriminate against them" (*Whatcott*, n. 52, at para. 19). The Supreme Court of Canada said that when speech seeks to promote discrimination against gays and lesbians or to reduce their rights it may breach the Code, even though it seeks to achieve these ends through a change in the law – through political action. This, though, raises the concern discussed in c. 2 about the breadth of the ban and whether it extends to any speech that might encourage discrimination.

[119] The political treatment of indigenous peoples in Canada provides plenty of examples of oppressive and violent state action.

[120] *Whatcott* (n. 52) at para. 200. In the Court's view, because Mr. Whatcott "combined expression exposing homosexuals to hatred with expression promoting their discriminatory treatment...it was not unreasonable for the Tribunal to conclude that this expression was more likely than not to expose homosexuals to hatred" (*Whatcott*, n. 52, at para. 192).

[121] *Whatcott* (n. 52) at para. 200. [122] *Green* (n. 61) at 4.

political action rather than private violence. Speech falls outside the realm of legitimate political engagement when it involves the vilification of the members of a particular group and so may be read as a justification for extreme action against the group – either by the state or by private actors. However, the importance of protecting political expression may sometimes lead the courts to adopt a benign reading of anti-gay speech as a reasonable contribution to public debate.

In distributing his flyers, Mr. Whatcott's primary purpose may have been to mobilize others to support a particular form of political action; but if his claims are extreme (e.g., accusing gays of corrupting children), they may also justify extralegal violence against gays. State discrimination and private violence are not mutually exclusive responses to the threat that Mr. Whatcott sees coming from the "gay lobby". As well, if those who agree with Mr. Whatcott's claims discover that his "political" campaign against the "pro-gay" school curriculum has failed, or are skeptical about its likely success, they may be drawn to other forms of action. The same may be said about Mr. Boissoin's call to political action. If his claims about the corruption of children do not result in political action, then they may serve to justify private violence.

Because Mr. Owens, Mr. Boissoin, and Mr. Whatcott addressed a general audience rather than a fringe group, the court in each case thought it unlikely that their speech would encourage a "reasonable" audience member to hate gays. Since most readers will not be led by the speech to take extreme action, any violence that follows will be seen as aberrant, the result not of the ad or the flyer but of some defect in the actor.[123] The Court in *Boissoin* thought that "a reasonable person" would view the pastor's letter "as an overstated and intemperate opinion of a writer whose extreme and insensitive language undermines whatever credibility he might otherwise have hoped to have".[124] Surely, though, hate speech is always ignorant and irrational and a reasonable person will see it as such. Hate speech should be regulated not because reasonable people might be induced to hate others, but rather because it might influence the thoughts and actions of the more troubled, suggestible reader – who may be the primary or intended audience of the speech.[125] The focus should be on what the letter says, on the meaning that can "reasonably" be drawn from it, and on the likely or possible impact of the speech on its intended or actual audience.

VI IDENTITY AND INDEPENDENCE

The courts in *Whatcott* and *Owens* acknowledged the possibility that passages from "a foundational religious text" could breach the hate speech ban. Yet, according

---

[123] *Boissoin* (n. 45) (QB), noted the lack in the case of a demonstrated connection between the letter and a particular act of violence.

[124] *Boissoin* (n. 38) at para. 77.

[125] Indeed, the test is meant to be whether a reasonable person would see this speech as likely to generate hatred, and that must depend on the audience to which it is directed.

to the Court in *Whatcott*, "it would only be unusual circumstances and context that could transform a simple reading or publication of a religion's holy text into what could objectively be viewed as hate speech".[126] While religious speech (and, in particular, scriptural text) could exceptionally be viewed as hate speech and subject to restriction, the courts will generally avoid interpreting such speech as carrying a hateful message, unless the speech's hateful character is obvious in the context. Because religious beliefs are often deeply held and because religious membership may be central to an individual's identity, the courts are understandably reluctant to declare that a religious group's doctrine or scripture promotes hatred, even when it is marshalled in support of intolerant political or private action.[127] A determination by a court that a religious group's beliefs or practices are ignorant or bigoted may be experienced by the group's members not simply as a rejection of these beliefs, but as an attack on the identity or dignity of the group's members.[128] The Swedish Supreme Court acknowledged this in the *Ake Green* decision, observing that "the central role that religious conviction plays for an individual" requires "a certain restraint" in the restriction by the state of religious belief or practice.[129]

While the courts may hesitate to view religious speech (and in particular scriptural references) as sufficiently extreme to count as hate speech, the idea of religion as a cultural identity (as a set of practices and beliefs that represents a shared way of understanding and living in the world, and that connects the individual with others in a community) may in another way bolster the argument for the restriction of religiously grounded hate speech.

Hate speech is restricted when it is thought to create a risk of serious harm. The likelihood that an instance of bigoted speech will cause harm depends on its content, but also on its form – on the way it seeks to influence the audience's thought and action. When an individual, a minister or imam, for example, makes hateful statements to an audience of believers, claims to speak with religious authority, and bases his or her speech on the word of God, we might wonder about the capacity of "more speech" to correct these hateful views – or at least "more speech" from outsiders to the religious tradition or community.[130] Individuals who feel strongly

---

[126] *Whatcott* (n. 52) at para. 199.

[127] See, for example, *Trinity Western University* (n. 90). For a discussion see Richard Moon, "The Supreme Court of Canada's Attempt to Reconcile Freedom of Religion and Sexual Orientation Equality in the Public Schools", in D. Rayside and C. Wilcox (n. 88) at 321–27.

[128] A similar view is suggested in Alon Harel, "Hate Speech and Comprehensive Forms of Life", in Michael Herz and Peter Molnar (eds.), *The Content and Context of Hate Speech* (Cambridge University Press, 2012), at 321: "Censoring deeply rooted hate speech is in many cases bound to be understood as a public condemnation of the speaker's form of life and not merely of the expression itself". In other contexts, the courts have been hesitant to make judgments that might be seen as repudiating a particular religious belief or belief system.

[129] *Green* (n. 61) at 12.

[130] Clarke (n. 109) at 19: "What religion offers the justificatory process, which it would otherwise lack, is appeal to narratives about the intentions, needs, desires, and other mental states of supernatural agents. Religion also enables us to appeal to a deeper reality than is apparent to us". Clarke at 108:

connected to a religious community (and for whom that connection is an important part of their identity) may be less critical of claims that are grounded in the
tradition, or are made by religious authorities. References to religious scripture or
doctrine then may add to the persuasive force of religiously based (hate) speech and
the likelihood that it will unduly influence the believer's thoughts and actions. As
earlier noted, the Supreme Court of Canada in *Whatcott* thought that only "unusual
circumstances and context... could transform a simple reading or publication of a
religion's holy text into what could objectively be viewed as hate speech", but at the
same time the Court accepted that the "use of the Bible as a credible authority for
a hateful proposition" is "a hallmark of hatred" – an indicator of hatred.[131] Simply
quoting the Bible will not count as hate speech; but when an individual makes hateful claims and backs these claims up with the Bible, his or her speech is more likely
to stir up hatred in its audience.

In the *Whatcott* and *Owens* cases, the speakers cited Christian scripture and doctrine to support their claims about homosexuality. In *Owens*, the court found that
the ordinary meaning of Mr. Owens's expression was not hateful. Similarly, in *Whatcott* the Supreme Court of Canada found that only some of what was said in the
flyers could be viewed as hate speech. Neither Mr. Whatcott nor Mr. Owens held
any formal role or authority in their religious communities; nor did they direct their
speech exclusively at the members of their communities – although, of course, their
scriptural references would only have had relevance or force for other Christians.[132]
In the *Boissoin* case, however, a pastor invoked Christian teaching and appealed
to fellow believers to take action to prevent the moral corruption of society and its
children. At the beginning of his letter, Pastor Boissoin said that he was addressing
those individuals who "in any way support[] the homosexual machine that has been
mercilessly gaining ground in our society since the 1960's."[133] Yet as his letter proceeds, it becomes clear that he is addressing fellow (heterosexual) Christians. He
concludes his letter in this way:

> If you are reading this and think that this is alarmist, then I simply ask you this: how
> bad do things have to become before you will get involved? It's time to start taking
> back what the enemy has taken from you. The safety and future of our children is
> at stake. (Signed) Rev. Stephen Boissoin, Central Alberta Chairman, Concerned
> Christian Coalition, Red Deer[134]

"The belief that one is fighting for God, or some other supernatural being, in a divinely ordained
struggle, leads the religious to be very confident of the rightness of the orders given them by their
superiors in the context of that struggle".
[131] *Whatcott* (n. 52) at para. 199.
[132] See also *Ali, Javed, and Ahmed* (n. 76), in which three fundamentalist Muslims distributed anti-gay
leaflets in the town of Derby with titles such as "Turn or Burn", "GAY – God Abhors you", and "Death
Penalty?" They were convicted of stirring up hatred based on sexual orientation.
[133] *Boissoin* (n. 38) at para. 4.   [134] *Boissoin* (n. 38) at para. 4.

Mr. Boissoin spoke to a general audience (through a letter in a community news-paper) even if he assumed that his audience was composed primarily of Christians. The situation, though, was different in *Public Prosecutor (Sweden) v. Green*. In that case a Christian minister, Ake Green, delivered his anti-gay views to his church congregation in a sermon. Green spoke from a position of spiritual authority to an audience of believers in a religious setting.[135] In both the *Green* and *Boissoin* cases, the courts found that the speech was not extreme and so did not amount to hate speech, even if presented in spiritual/scriptural terms and delivered by a person who claimed religious authority.

In *R. v. El-Faisal*, the English courts found that a Muslim cleric had used abusive words in his taped sermons in order to stir up racial hatred against Jews, Hindus, and other non-believers.[136] El-Faisal was explicit in his call for the murder of others: for example, "If you see a Hindu walking down the road, you are allowed to kill him and take his money".[137] He was convicted of soliciting murder, as well as using threatening and abusive words in order to stir up hatred. The trial judge found that the offence "was aggravated by the fact that as a cleric [he was] sent to this country to preach and minister to the Muslim community in London, and had a responsibility to the young and impressionable in the community".[138]

This concern about the undue influence that may be exercised by those with religious authority parallels the concern sometimes expressed about the role of reli-gious beliefs or values in public decision making.[139] The familiar argument is that religious beliefs should be excluded from political decision making because they rest on faith or familial and cultural socialization, rather than reasoned judgment, and so are inaccessible to those outside the religious community. It follows then that religious beliefs cannot provide a publicly acceptable basis for lawmaking. Political actors must instead base their actions on nonreligious or secular values or must be able to defend their actions on secular grounds.

This distinction between secular and spiritual beliefs/values (with the latter excluded from politics) has been challenged from two directions. It can be argued that religious values, in either some or all cases, are not beyond reasoned debate, and so are not different from secular values in that respect. At the same time (or in the alternative), it has been claimed that fundamental or abstract secular values, such as respect for human dignity or equality, rest, no less than religious values, on a basic acceptance of their truth and are the premises rather than the conclusions

---

[135] In *Catch the Fire Ministries Inc & Ors v. Islamic Council of Victoria Inc.* [2006], VSCA 284 (14 December 2006) (SCCA, Victoria), anti-Muslim views were presented by a minister to an audience of Christians at a religious meeting.

[136] R. v. *El-Faisal* [2004], EWCA Crim. 456 (CA).   [137] *El-Faisal* (n. 136) at para. 15.

[138] Quoted in Alexander Brown, *Hate Speech Law: A Philosophical Examination* (Routledge, 2015) at 56.

[139] This concern has sometimes led to restrictions on clergy holding elected public office.

of reasoned political debate.[140] In Canada and elsewhere, it is accepted that religious values may play a role in political debate and decision making. For example, in *Chamberlain v. Surrey School District #36*, the Supreme Court of Canada held that it was permissible for elected officials to draw on their religious values (or the religious values of their constituents) when making political decisions.[141] According to McLachlin CJ, "[b]ecause religion plays an important role in the life of many communities, the[] ... views [of parents and communities] will often be motivated by religious concerns. Religion is an integral aspect of people's lives, and cannot be left at the boardroom door."[142]

Even if we reject the argument that religious values or positions should be excluded from political decision making (including the position that homosexuality is immoral and should not be legally permitted or recognized), because we do not accept that religious values, in contrast to secular values, are inaccessible, and immune to reasoned critique, we may still have concerns about the use of religious authority to justify extreme anti-gay positions in public discourse. We may be justifiably concerned that religiously grounded hate speech (hate speech that claims the support of scripture or religious authority) will have an undue influence on an audience of believers – even if we do not go so far as to think that everyone in the audience is unable to think critically or independently about the beliefs and practices of their tradition. It is concern enough that the religious framing of extreme and hateful claims may discourage independent judgment by some adherents, particularly in a world in which individuals and groups increasingly engage only with those who hold views similar to their own.

---

[140] Charles Taylor, *Dilemmas and Connections: Selected Essays* (Harvard University Press, 2011) at 328–29: There is no clear distinction "in rational credibility between religious and non-religious discourse"; "If we take key statements of our contemporary political morality, such as those attributing rights to human beings as such, say the right to life, I cannot see how the fact that we are desiring/enjoying/suffering beings, or the perception that we are rational agents, should be any surer basis for this right than the fact that we are made in the image of God."

[141] *Chamberlain* (n. 4).

[142] McLachlin C.J. in *Chamberlain* (n. 4) at para. 19. While the Canadian courts have said that religious values are not constitutionally excluded from political decision making (that religious belief may be part of the input of law-making), they have, at the same time, held that the state must not support particular religious practices. But this distinction between values and practices is not a simple one. The distinction that the Canadian courts (at least) seem to rely on, if only implicitly, is between, on one hand, beliefs or actions that address civic or worldly matters (values) and, on the other, beliefs or actions that concern the worship or honouring of God (practices). A religious belief should not play a role in political decision making if the action it calls for is spiritual in character (i.e., relates simply to spiritual concerns involving the worshipping or honouring of God). Such an action will be seen as a "private" or personal matter and labelled as a "practice". However, if the belief or "value" relates to a civic matter (e.g., individual rights or collective welfare), then it may play a role in political decision making, and the action it calls for will be viewed as public or civic action rather than religious practice. The line between the "civic" and "private" elements of a religious belief system will be the subject of contest. Where the line is drawn by the courts will reflect the courts' views about the ordinary forms of religious worship, the nature of human welfare, and the proper scope of political action. For a discussion see Moon, *Freedom of Conscience and Religion* (n. 3), c. 2.

VII CONCLUSION

Religious doctrine and scripture are understood by individual adherents in a variety of ways. Scriptural passages that on the surface may appear to call for violence against others are not read by most adherents in that way – and so the courts have not attributed a violent purpose to those who invoke these passages and have accepted that most readers will not understand the author as calling on them to commit violent acts. In a community composed of individuals from various religious traditions, often living side by side, most religious adherents have found a way to reconcile the "hard" passages from their scripture with the practical demands of community life – achieving a peaceful, even respectful and caring, co-existence.

The courts have been understandably reluctant to attach the label "hate speech" to sincerely and deeply held religious beliefs, given society's commitment to protecting religious freedom and respecting religious diversity. Yet, at the same time, the courts have recognized that the rooted and faith-based character of religious commitment means that religion – text, doctrine, and community – can sometimes be an effective vehicle for the spread of hatred. When a religious authority draws on scripture or doctrine to make hateful claims about the members of a group such as gays, those claims may have an undue influence on an audience of believers. Christian opponents of homosexuality have sometimes sought to demonize "the gay lobby" or "the homosexual machine", which they present as a depersonalized enemy of the moral community that is determined to corrupt society's most vulnerable members. This accusation, which is intended to stir fear and animosity, could well be described as hate speech.

VIII NOTE: HATE SPEECH AND TERRORIST INCITEMENT

The Canadian *Criminal Code* prohibits the advocacy or promotion of terrorism:

> Every person who, by communicating statements, knowingly advocates or promotes the commission of terrorism offences in general . . . while knowing that any of those offences will be committed or being reckless as to whether any of those offences may be committed, as a result of such communication, is guilty of an indictable offence and is liable to imprisonment . . . [143]

Similar prohibitions exist in other jurisdictions. In the United Kingdom, the *Terrorism Act 2006* c. 11 (amending the *Terrorism Act 2000*) prohibits expression that encourages acts of terrorism. An individual is forbidden under the Act to publish a "statement that is likely to be understood by some or all of the members of the public

---

[143] *Criminal Code* (Can.) (R.S.C., 1985, c. C-46) s. 83.221(1). For a more thorough critique of the Canadian prohibition, see Kent Roach and Craig Forcese, "Bill C-51 Backgrounder #1: The New Advocating or Promoting Terrorism Offence". One of the principal concerns of Roach and Forcese is that the promotion offence applies to the wide range of actions that are defined as terrorism under the law.

to whom it is published as a direct or indirect encouragement or other inducement" to commit an act of terrorism, if the individual "intends members of the public to be ... encouraged or otherwise induced by the statement" to commit an act of terrorism or is "reckless" as to whether this will occur. The Act goes on to say that a statement will be understood "as indirectly encouraging the commission or preparation of acts of terrorism" if it "glorifies the commission or preparation (whether in the past, in the future or generally) of such acts or offences" and the audience "could reasonably be expected to infer" from the statement "that what is being glorified is being glorified as conduct that should be emulated by them".[144]

Speech that encourages or promotes acts of terrorism will also breach hate speech law if it encourages violence against the members of a particular racial, religious, or other group. More often, though (and necessarily so on some definitions of the term terrorism), terrorist promotion is viewed as the encouragement of violence against members of the general community, or its political representatives, rather than against a specific racial or other identifiable minority group. The audience to which "terrorist promotion" is intended to appeal is often composed of minority group members, who feel marginalized and alienated from the larger community. It calls on them to strike out against their "oppressors", the dominant or mainstream community. Terrorist promotion then can be seen as the inverse of hate speech, which is addressed to members of the "dominant community" and promotes hatred and violence against marginalized groups that have been the historic victims of oppression.

Despite these differences, terrorist advocacy operates in much the same way as hate speech and is dangerous for many of the same reasons. Like hate speech, it takes place at the margins of public discourse, principally on the Internet. Terrorist promotion is removed from general public view and insulated from effective counterspeech. It is directed at "outsiders" to the mainstream, primarily angry, alienated men, who identify as members of a marginalized racial or religious group, and see themselves as victims of private and state discrimination, and it appeals to their feelings of resentment, anger, and injustice. Terrorist incitement is harmful not because its message may spread widely in the community, but instead because it may encourage an alienated individual in the community – a lone wolf – to take violent action against those who he believes are oppressing his group. In this respect, terrorist promotion is similar to most hate speech. In both cases, the speech is effective – creates a risk of harm – when it gives alienated young people – men principally – a focus for their anger and resentment and an illusory sense of purpose and identity that is experienced in the performance of an act of violence. Those who are responsive

---

[144] *Terrorism Act* 2011 (U.K.). The Act further provides that in determining "how a statement is likely to be understood and what members of the public could reasonably be expected to infer from it" a court must have regard "(a) to the contents of the statement as a whole; and (b) to the circumstances and manner of its publication."

to the message of hate speech may formally be part of the dominant community, but often feel left behind and denied the privilege or status they believe is owed to them. The hatemonger and the audience to which he appeals perceive the target of their hatred – a group such as Jews or Muslims – not as marginal and powerless, but instead as wielding power behind the scenes, or as poised to take control of society.

But terrorist promotion is different from hate speech in other, more significant ways that make hate speech law a poor model for its legal regulation. Hate speech attributes dangerous or undesirable traits to the members of a racial or other identifiable group, or it portrays the members of such a group as inherently less worthy or less human than others. These claims are false and are contrary to the commitment to human equality that underpins the social and political order. If such a claim is sufficiently extreme and can reasonably be read as encouraging or justifying radical action against a group, it will amount to hate speech. Such a claim does not have to be attached to an explicit call to violence to be understood as justifying the violent treatment of the members of the target group. The assertion that Muslims are dangerous or subhuman can, without more, be seen as hate speech. It is objectionable because the denial of the equal worth of some in the community, or the "factual" claim that the members of a group are violent or duplicitous, can be seen as justifying their exclusion or suppression.

Terrorist promotion, in contrast, is objectionable not because of the political positions (about foreign policy or domestic discrimination) that are deployed to persuade the audience that violence is justified, but simply and only because it calls on the audience to commit violent acts. The political and religious claims that are sometimes offered to justify terrorist action may be erroneous or overstated, nevertheless they fall within the scope of protected speech – the political speech of the marginalized, criticizing the actions of the powerful. When they are detached from a call to violence, these claims are part of public discourse. Even speech that expresses sympathy for the grievances that motivated Al Qaeda to fly planes into the Twin Towers, or accepts that with 9/11 America got some of its own medicine, must be treated as political and protected, no matter how insensitive or odious it might seem. At issue in the terrorist promotion cases is whether the speech calls for violent action; but such a call cannot be inferred from political claims about the unjust actions of the Western powers. There is a real risk that the community's anger or upset at expressions of sympathy, or understanding, for the motives of terrorists may lead police and prosecutors to view these expressions (and the supporting political positions) as terrorist promotion. Some expressions of outrage about the actions of Western powers may be intended to incite others to take violent action against mainstream society; nevertheless, speech should be suppressed only when it explicitly calls for terrorist action. The risk of error must fall on the side of speech protection.

6

Conclusion

Free Speech, Religious Speech, Hate Speech

I RELIGION AND HATE SPEECH

Religion has come to play an increasingly prominent role in hate speech cases, as either the source or the target of speech that is alleged to be hateful.

Events such as the 9/11 attacks and the Danish Cartoons controversy helped to move religious difference to the forefront of public consciousness. For many in the West, these events seemed to confirm that religion, or at least some religions, represented a threat to liberal-democratic values. They contributed to the idea that different religious world views (or cultural identities) were so fundamentally at odds that co-existence was bound to be difficult if not impossible. Religious differences that may once have been regarded as minor and easily resolved "on the ground" came to be viewed through this lens of intractable conflict, as skirmishes in a broader civilizational struggle. When so much is thought to be at stake in these conflicts, fear and even hatred of the "other" may easily be stirred. Muslims appear now to be the principal target of hate speech in Canada and elsewhere in the West. The focus of this "new racism", at least formally, is on the group's beliefs and practices rather than on its biology. Falsely attributed beliefs are presented as rooted and essential aspects of the group's culture – even if it is also acknowledged that individual members may sometimes reject these beliefs and withdraw from the group.

There is significant disagreement in the community about whether or to what extent the restriction of hate speech can be reconciled with the public commitment to freedom of expression. Hate speech causes injury to others, either directly by intimidating or harassing the members of an identifiable group, or indirectly by persuading a more general audience that the members of such a group are dangerous or undesirable and should be treated accordingly. The regulation of speech that intimidates or harasses the members of a target group can in principle be reconciled with the commitment to freedom of expression, even if there is dispute sometimes about where the line should be drawn between threats and harsh criticism or between harassment and uncivil speech.

The regulation of speech that aims to convince its audience of the dangerousness or undesirability of the members of a particular group represents a more basic challenge to the public commitment to freedom of expression. Governments in Canada and elsewhere have decided that the failure to ban the extreme or radical edge of prejudiced speech – speech that is hateful in its content and visceral or irrational in its appeal – carries too many risks, particularly when it occurs in a context that limits the likelihood of independent judgment by the audience. Hate speech creates a risk of harm when it plays to an audience's fears and resentments and builds on their existing prejudices, and when it circulates within the racist subculture that operates at the margins of public discourse, away from critical scrutiny. The concern is not, or at least not principally, that hate speech will contribute to the spread of hateful or discriminatory attitudes across the general community, leading to more widespread discrimination against minority groups, but is, instead, that individuals, or small groups who are already inclined to bigoted thinking may be encouraged or emboldened to take extreme action against the target group's members.

II RELIGION AS A TARGET OF HATE SPEECH

Hate speech laws ordinarily distinguish between attacks on a group, which may in extreme cases be subject to restriction, and attacks on a group's beliefs, which must be protected as a matter of free speech, regardless of their vitriol. However, our complex conception of religious adherence or membership – as both a personal commitment to a set of truth claims and a cultural identity – complicates this distinction between attacks on the group and attacks on its beliefs in two ways.

Hate speech, when directed at a religious group, often attributes an undesirable belief to the group (sometimes the belief of a fringe element of the group or a belief drawn from a narrow or selective reading of the group's scripture) and represents that belief as an essential and rooted part of the group's belief system or tradition. This speech elides the space for judgment and disagreement within the religious tradition and the distinction between the individual and the religious community with which he or she identifies. The attack focuses on a particular belief, but the implication is that the members of a religious tradition that includes such a belief are dangerous and deserving of contempt or hatred. In this way, the belief serves the same role as a falsely attributed racial characteristic. An attack on a particular (attributed) belief becomes an attack on all the members of the religious group, who are assumed to share this belief. Many recent attacks on the Muslim community rely on a blurring of this distinction between group and individual and between trait and belief. Mark Steyn, for example, at various points in his attack on Muslims, insists that he is simply attacking those in the group who support the use of violence to advance their faith. Nevertheless, throughout his polemic, Steyn assumes or suggests that most in the group are in fact committed to violence against Western institutions. The complex character of religious adherence as cultural identity and personal judgment allows Steyn and others to associate all Muslims with violence – as almost a character trait – while superficially acknowledging that some Muslims may choose to reject violence.

The second difficulty with the distinction between attacks on belief and attacks on believers is that, because religious beliefs are deeply held, and concern sacred matters, an attack on belief may be experienced by believers profoundly and personally and may spark resentment and conflict in the community. This recognition has led some to argue that religious beliefs should be protected from ridicule or intemperate criticism. However, for several related reasons, ridicule and intemperate criticism of religion should not be restricted by law.

Civility requirements in public discourse are difficult to define, particularly when religion is the subject of debate. More significantly, because religion involves truth claims, many of which have public implications, it must be open to the fullest challenge. To take religion seriously is to see its claims about truth and right as important subjects for discussion and debate. It also means that these claims, whether they relate to spiritual or civic questions, must be open to criticism, even that which is harsh or mocking. However, the protection of this speech is not without significant social cost. Attacks on the beliefs and practices of a minority religious group may push the group's members further to the margins of society. A group that is repeatedly subjected to ridicule or harsh criticism of its deepest convictions may become skeptical about the possibility of constructive engagement with others in the society.

III RELIGION AS A SOURCE OF HATE SPEECH

There are at least two ways in which the religious basis for speech that is alleged to be hateful may complicate the application of hate speech law. The first is the difficulty in determining the individual's meaning or purpose when he or she invokes religious text to support opposition to a particular group and its practices. Within every religious tradition there are different approaches to scriptural interpretation and different readings of particular passages of scripture.

The second complication stems from the judicial (and public) commitment to state neutrality in religious matters and the underlying conception of religion as a cultural identity. Because religious beliefs are often deep-rooted, a matter of cultural identity rather than simply personal judgment, the individual adherent may regard state restrictions on the expression of his or her beliefs as an insult to his or her dignity, and a denigration of his or her spiritual community. The courts then may be reluctant to find that religiously based speech is intended by the speaker to stir up hatred – except in the clearest and most extreme cases.

At the same time, the conception of religion as an identity may cut in the other direction and strengthen the argument for the restriction of religiously based speech that is alleged to be hateful. The restriction of hate speech rests on a recognition that the expression of hateful views may encourage audience members to think and act in a hateful way towards certain groups – particularly when the speech occurs in a form or context that discourages informed and independent judgment. When hateful views are expressed by an individual who claims to speak with religious authority, we may be concerned about the undue influence of such speech on an audience of believers. The hateful character and irrational appeal of such speech may be even greater when the religious audience believes that it is engaged in a struggle against the forces of evil.

The courts have accepted that religiously based criticism of homosexuality will not ordinarily breach the ban on hate speech. It appears that the ban will be breached only when the speaker calls for the murder or oppression of gays or when he or she explicitly connects homosexuality with pedophilia. To this point, the courts have not been prepared to treat, as hate speech, claims about the "gay lobby's" attempt to corrupt society and its children – claims that draw on religious narratives about the battle between good and evil. Such claims, though, can easily be read as justifying extreme action against gays and lesbians and so ought to be treated as hate speech.

Index